OF MOBSTERS AND MOVIE STARS

THE BLOODY "GOLDEN AGE" OF HOLLYWOOD

OF MOBSTERS AND MOVIE STARS published by:

WILDBLUE PRESS
P.O. Box 102440
Denver, Colorado 80250

Publisher Disclaimer: Any opinions, statements of fact or fiction, descriptions, dialogue, and citations found in this book were provided by the author and are solely those of the author. The publisher makes no claim as to their veracity or accuracy and assumes no liability for the content.

ISBN 978-1-960332-82-0 Trade Paperback
ISBN 978-1-960332-81-3 eBook
ISBN 978-1-960332-83-7 Hardback

Interior Formatting and Cover Design by Elijah Toten, www.totencreative.com

OF MOBSTERS AND MOVIE STARS

THE BLOODY "GOLDEN AGE" OF HOLLYWOOD

JOAN RENNER

For my brother, Rick Renner, Elizabeth Street, and absent friends.

FOREWORD

It wasn't just the climate that was dry in 1920s Los Angeles. A Constitutional amendment mandated that the once dusty western outpost would have to bustle sans the customary bars and booze-slinging bordellos. Sure, both vices remained viable, and available, but the law and its purveyors peskily complicated the availability of both. The bothersome Volstead act impeded the business-as- usual days that had survived through. The evolution of LA's entertainment district continued unimpeded and largely undeterred by law. All the while, the underworld aspired to control the booze and the studios via means both lawful and otherwise. Mass communication, like it or not, promoted crime. Any publicity is good publicity. Most people would disagree. Nonetheless, crime was problematic in and around Hollywood during an era defined by a national social experiment otherwise known as Prohibition.

Of Mobsters and Movie Stars: The Bloody "Golden Age" of Hollywood slides the crimes of the era through the door slot of the speakeasy that was the City of Angels. Inside await the smugglers and the slayers, the politicos and the predators. Some aim to dismantle the criminal brain trust from points East, others openly commit to criminality or quietly capitulate to an illicit livelihood. It is an odd and unique period for the nation, but nowhere is it stranger than in the semi-arid hills and valleys of California's south end, a region undergoing unprecedented population growth and expansion.

Against the backdrop of the national booze ban lurked some of L.A.'s most notorious crimes. Strewn through the prohibition era were crimes of little significance paired with the notoriously noteworthy. Those that touched the Hollywood crowd were typically writ large. Others garnered a national audience because of their gruesomeness. With the world no longer at war, law enforcement engaged a new enemy, bootleggers.

LAPD, Southern California's largest police force, mobilized vice specialists. The Booze Squad and the Gangster Squad took on mobsters and amateurs in their efforts to simultaneously enforce liquor laws as well as deter and prevent the expansion of the whiskey trade. Some early LAPD pioneers undoubtedly participated. August Vollmer, the chief renowned for his organizational restructuring and recognized as the scientific cop, began his one-year term in 1923. He formed the first municipal police crime lab in the country. Mid-prohibition, the soon-to-be legendary detectives Thad Brown and Harry Hansen signed up, as did Roscoe Washington. Alice Stebbins Wells experienced the onset of Prohibition nearly a decade into her storied career. The future of LA crime fighting was onboard and conscripted to the local battle against booze. Familiar faces, all. Promulgated by books, movies, television, and, of course, LAPD lore, each distinguished by service in the era prowled by mobsters and movie stars.

They begin the shorthand of LAPD history; *Faces, Places and Cases.*

To fully enforce the Volstead act, LA grew west to a locale uncommon to the cops of the day, and into the biggest crime scene ever, the Pacific Ocean. All forms of transportation were eligible for moonshine movement, boats included. Ralph Sears and his gangster squad staked out the seaside. Open air raids on the open sea yielded liquor dumped off-shore for pick up by free-lancers and the southland syndicates. At least briefly, Sears and his subordinates stifled supply chain.

The ocean was an odd place to find LAPD. The city was experiencing a growth spurt, building on terra firma in support of the post-war expansion. The twenties also brought more personnel to the LAPD who would be housed in new LAPD stations in places like Highland Park, Wilshire, Newton, 77th Street, the Valley and, most conspicuously, Hollywood. New places for the dispatch of patrol cars, for the housing of detectives, and the incarceration of bootleggers and bad men. By the end of the ban, police cars would have radios to expedite their responses and facilitate the capture of bootleggers and bad men.

It was this segment of the human race that populated the *Cases*, many of which constitute the erstwhile dark side of LA Especially for the LAPD, an organization completely surrounded by its own legal, moral, and ethical challenges. The Chief was a boomerang, thrown out of office mid-prohibition, only to return before its repeal. As *Of Mobsters and Movie Stars* reveals, a murderous LA cop is sentenced to death for taking a guy "for a ride." Years earlier, California had executed the first LAPD alum sentenced to die. The ex-LAPD officer took advantage of California's penal system and was eventually granted parole.

Social order was upside down.

Veteran homicide detective Jerry Hickey can attest.

His son, LAPD Officer James Hickey murdered his daughter-in-law and grandson.

Responding LAPD officers shot James Hickey prior to taking him into custody. News accounts described Hickey the elder as stoic. The detective parsed the horrific crime, standing by his son while yielding to the law he had long upheld and enforced.

Crime in L.A. was violent and frequent, and LAPD was not immune. More LAPD officers were killed in the 1920s than any other decade. Prohibition was crime's force multiplier. Wylie Smith, who was busily directing traffic was gunned down by a quartet fleeing a robbery Smith earned a sad and unwanted distinction, the first posthumous award of LAPD's medal of valor. The same mobsters shot Smith's colleague, Oscar Bayer, multiple times, but he survived and personally received the medal of valor.

A twice murderous officer, cops shooting the murderous cop who is also a cop's son. Another cop killed in a drive-by and his partner repeatedly wounded. Prohibition brought tough times for the LAPD brand, many were concentrated in that single, awful year, 1925.

Clearly, there was more crime to come. Some of the other stunners are cleverly and concisely covered in these pages. Ample were the crimes that were squeezed into the many years leading up to America's teetotaler Olympic games. Yes, the eyes of the world were on dry-lipped Los Angeles. Fortunately, the Olympic games were prelude to Prohibition's closing ceremony.

Certainly, better days would come, but the damage had been done.

Here in the dark side of paradise where the faces of flappers, fiends and fraudsters could be found in the place called Los Angeles where cases were as plentiful as liquor in an era known as prohibition. An overreaching mandate that was untimely, and ineffective.

Because you can, raise a glass as you read. *Of Mobsters and Movie Stars: The Bloody "Golden Age" of Hollywood.*

Cheers!

Glynn Martin
Author of *Satan's Summer in the City of Angels: The Social Impact of the Night Stalker*
Co-author of *LAPD '53*

Prohibition has made nothing but trouble.

Al Capone

CONTENTS

INTRODUCTION

I have been obsessed with crime since I was a kid. From the time I was 7 years old, I followed each gruesome murder and every lurid love triangle in the newspapers, on radio, and on TV. I didn't always grasp the nuances of the cases, but it didn't matter. I was hooked.

I read autobiographies of prominent trial attorneys like Jerry Giesler, and true crime stories from books like Jack Webb's *The Badge*. Although my interest was primarily in true crime, it was the movie *Chinatown* that set me on my path to explore historic Los Angeles crime. I loved the era depicted in the film, and I wondered if real life Prohibition Los Angeles could measure up to the fictionalized version. I need not have worried. Real life is more interesting than anything a Hollywood screenwriter can imagine.

For years, I have immersed myself in historic Los Angeles crime. I have taken every opportunity to expand my knowledge. I volunteered at the Los Angeles Police Museum under the direction of Glynn Martin for over six years. He gave me dozens of opportunities to learn and grow. I picked up valuable archiving skills and learned a lot about police procedure. In 2012, I worked with the museum on an exhibit about the infamous Black Dahlia case. I was part of the team who developed the material for the book, *LAPD '53*, with Glynn Martin and author James Ellroy in 2015.

After Glynn left the police museum, I followed our mutual friend, Mike Fratantoni, to the Los Angeles County Sheriff's Department. Mike is their museum curator. Mike, like Glynn, has provided me with many opportunities. I've been working with the museum for eight years. I plan to be there for many more.

Each step I've taken has been to further my knowledge and expertise. My work has paid off in unexpected ways. I am a true crime expert and historian, and I have been interviewed for over 60 TV shows since 2009. I've appeared on dozens of podcasts and given lectures to private groups and professional organizations.

In December 2012, inspired by the career of Los Angeles reporter Agness "Aggie" Underwood, I created a blog, *Deranged L.A. Crimes*. I have researched and written hundreds of stories for the blog, and I haven't yet exhausted all the tales the city has to tell.

I am eager to share my passion for Los Angeles' true crime through the stories in this book. I cover the years 1919 to 1939 because they were a time of widespread corruption in the city. Corruption started in the mayor's office and reached down to the lowest level of law enforcement.

Those were also the Golden Years of Hollywood; but there is another, darker side to the glitz and glamour. Studio executives with thugs on their payrolls wielded immense power over actors. They could make or break a career. They could, and did, ruin lives.

Crime in Los Angeles during prohibition was not exclusively political or corporate. A multitude of independent criminals ranged from con artists to murderers. You will meet some of the worst of them in these pages.

It is with pleasure that I bring you *Of Mobsters and Movie Stars: The Bloody "Golden Age" of Hollywood.* I hope you will enjoy the stories and get a better sense of the City of Angels during one of the most turbulent periods in U.S. history.

Fill your hip flask with your favorite libation and buckle up for a trip back in time.

I'll see you there.

Joan Renner

PART I. TWO OF A KIND

Hybristophilia, aka The Bonnie and Clyde Syndrome, is a paraphilia. Commonly, the sufferer is a female who is sexually attracted to a man who commits evil acts. She sees him as the ultimate alpha male. The baddest of bad boys. Not content to stay at home and pen love notes to a guy on death row, some hybristophiliacs want a piece of the action. Whether pulling a bank job or shooting it out with police, when a woman who craves a hands-on thrill makes a love connection, it spells trouble.

The exploits of some law-breaking couples, like Bonnie Parker and Clyde Barrow, became the subject of books and movies. The couples in *Two of a Kind* are as evil as Bonnie and Clyde ever were.

1. The Wages of Sin

In the early 1930s, Bonnie Parker and Clyde Barrow embodied the gangster ethos with swagger and an undisguised contempt for the law. With a cigar in her mouth, pistol in her hand, and her foot on the bumper of a getaway car, Bonnie is immortalized as the quintessential bad-ass gun moll in a famous photo. Bonnie and Clyde are the most infamous criminal couple in U.S. history, but they were still in grammar school when Dale Forbes and Margie Celano embarked on their crime spree. Compared to Margie and Dale, Bonnie and Clyde were posers

Although sources differ on how and when Dale and Margie met, their meeting was inevitable because of Dale's criminal ties to Los Angeles. Raymond Niemeyer belonged to the gang Dale co-lead with fellow crook John Lewis, and he was married to Margie's sister, Elizabeth.

Kindred spirits, Dale, and Margie built their relationship on a mutual love of danger and violence. They were adrenaline junkies, and morphine addicts.

At ten o'clock on the morning of December 8, 1917, a man entered the Culver City Bank and asked teller J. J. Byron to change a five-dollar bill. As Byron turned to get the cash, two masked bandits entered the lobby. One of them commanded the patrons to "Lay down on the floor."

Under threat of a gun, Byron opened the vault, and the bandits looted it. Rushing into the street, they accidentally collided with three movie actors from the nearby Triangle Studio. They shoved revolvers in the actors' faces and robbed them. They escaped in a car with Washington state plates. Receiving information that a fourth man, believed to be the gang's leader, was present at the bank robbery, the police took immediate action. Dale was the fourth man.

The Los Angeles County grand jury, on January 30, 1918, returned indictments against the gang for the Culver City bank job. On April 11, 1918, a jury acquitted them. The Lewis-Jones gang reunited. Dale and Margie traveled back and forth between Kansas City and Southern California. Taking a brief time out from their usual mayhem on May 4th, they got married in San Bernardino, California.

Four miles south of Paola, Kansas, on July 10, 1918, masked bandits held up the Texas Special of the Missouri, Kansas & Texas Railway. After refusing to hand over her money and jewelry, Mrs. L. D. Williams was wounded when they shot several railroad employees and passengers. J. D. Murray, another passenger, told police, "The crew of bandits was well-organized, each man having been given a number by which the leader directed him. I heard numbers called as high as twelve but saw only six men." Margie drove the getaway car.

Two days later, bandits used nitroglycerin to blast open a train safe and stole $50,000 ($922,000 in current USD). To discourage further robberies, U.S. Marines guarded every mail train across the country.

Dale rented a house in a sleepy Kansas City, Missouri neighborhood. He and Margie kept the blinds drawn but hated being housebound. Cheeky as ever, Dale sold a stolen motorcycle to a police officer, and went to the Woodland

Avenue Police Station to collect payment. Nobody recognized him.

Four police officers noticed two bright lights blink off and on in a speeding car during the early morning hours of July 16. They gave chase. The car sped up. From a distance, the police observed four men jump from the vehicle as they continued their pursuit. Running into a nearby field, the men fired at them. Bullets flattened two of the police car tires, but they escaped injury. The shooters escaped.

County Marshal Harvey Hoffman found out, based on a tip, that Dale and his accomplice Frank were hiding in a nearby house on Wyandotte Street. The house belonged to Frank's mother and stepfather. The men were not there, but four women were—one of them was Margie.

Hoffman and his detectives waited in the house all day, hoping for the gang's return. When the phone finally rang, the women were instructed not to answer. Dale and Frank arrived at the house at 9:30 p.m. A detective confronted them. They shot at him before driving away.

In their search of the house, the police found jewelry that matched the description of pieces taken during a recent train robbery. The women played dumb. Dale phoned the police station and said the entire gang was coming for "their women." They never came. The police released the women to set a honey trap for the gang.

Under constant surveillance, the Pinkerton Detective Agency and the local police monitored the house. Chief of Detectives I. B. "Ike" Walston of Kansas City received anonymous telephone calls with false leads to Dale's whereabouts. A Spanish-speaking woman called him on September 6th. He was on the verge of hanging up when the woman spoke in English.

"Hold the line, Ike." A Spanish-speaking man got on the line. Walston's patience wore thin.

"What is this, anyway?"

"Ike, you've been getting a lot of tips on that Dale Jones fellow lately, haven't you? Don't bother to answer, because I'll tell you what the tips were."

Walston signaled one of his officers to trace the call.

"It won't do you any good to trace this call, Ike, for I've got things timed in such a way that Margie and me will be out of this drugstore before anybody can get here. But don't let that bother you, Ike, for I'm ready to give myself up. In case you haven't guessed, this is Dale Jones calling, and I'll be at the Wyandotte house. You know the number; you've been shadowing it long enough."

Following the trace, detectives arrived at the drugstore where the call originated, only to find Dale and Margie gone.

Walston and eight of his detectives drove to the house. As they approached, gunfire erupted from two sides of the structure. Under the streetlamp's glare, the detectives were sitting ducks—yet all escaped injury. Shortly after the shooting ended, a car engine rumbled. As it pulled away, the police heard laughter.

Walston received another call from Dale. "This is Dale Jones again, Ike. What did you think of that little party we just staged? I guess that'll teach you a thing or two! The next thing on the program is that we're going to swipe a car. This Packard we're running around in has got too hot."

Between August 8 and August 12, the Lewis-Jones gang pulled three bank robberies and a payroll robbery. For one of the bank heists, the gang dressed as policemen. The crime spree netted them over $45,000 ($834,000 in current USD). After pulling jobs in Topeka, Kansas City, and in Indiana, the heat was on. The gang prepared to move west.

George T. Cook, president of the Kansas City Bolt & Nut Company, drove his Marmon through Penn Valley Park when a large car with three men pulled alongside him. Two of the men leaped onto the running board, climbed inside, and drew their revolvers. Having been forced to drive two blocks, Cook was then tugged into the rear of the car by the bandits, who then made him lie on the floor. Cook found himself with a revolver against his chest and a bandit's foot on his neck. After driving for an hour, they finally stopped to bind Cook with wire. They tore his shirt off and used it as a gag. The bandits relieved Cook of $60 and his jewelry, then they threw him into a pile of weeds on the side of the road.

Frank and Dale arrived in Denver on September 9, 1918. On the 13th, the gang drove toward Colorado Springs in two cars. As they passed through Castle Rock, they picked up a tail. Dale, Margie, and another gang member set off for Colorado Springs. John Lewis took the rest of the gang back to Denver.

Frank Henderson and Roy Settle, employees at the Vreeland Filling Station in Colorado Springs, were the first to see the gang pull up to a pump. Dale was behind the wheel of the stolen Marmon. Henderson phoned the police and Chief of Detectives John Rowan took the call.

Eight officers in two cars set out for the gas station. Driving through an alley in the station's rear, Detectives Rowan, J.D. Riley, A.E. Berry, James B. Taylor, and Agent Miller planned to surprise the bandits. After the other two vehicles, Chief

Harper's car left the police station within minutes. Executing a classic pincer maneuver, the police plan aimed to trap the Marmon with no possibility of escape.

Dale noticed the cars and saw the men closing in. Reaching into the car, he pulled out a revolver and fired three shots. Berry, Taylor, and Miller took defensive positions in the street. Rowan and Riley stepped from their car. "Put up your hands." Dale fired at them. Crouching low, Rowan moved toward the Marmon.

Dale fired over twenty times with multiple weapons he pulled from the car. As Rowan approached the vehicle, Margie screamed, "Don't shoot my husband!"

Gang member Roscoe "Kansas City Blackie" Lancaster emptied his .38 revolver at the police. After being hit in the right shoulder, Rowan collapsed. The bullet severed his pulmonary artery and right ventricle before exiting his stomach. As another bullet struck Rowan's watch, freezing it at 3:10 p.m., he fired a final round.

Officer Riley jammed shells into his sawed-off shotgun and fired as he ran. Hiding behind a pillar, he leveled his shotgun at Blackie. When he emptied the shotgun, he threw it to the ground and pulled out a revolver. One of Blackie's rounds ripped off one of Riley's fingers. Another bullet tore into his left eye and stopped near his brain. Blackie fired again and hit Riley in the right hand and left foot. Pieces of shrapnel peppered Riley's face. The blood and torn flesh made him unrecognizable.

The police chief and three officers stopped in front of the station. Dale took the wheel of the Marmon. Margie sat next to him. She clutched her side and winced in pain. While preparing to shoot, a passing streetcar interrupted the officers. They held their fire. Dale sped away from the gas station. Margie waved her arms and screamed at the top of her voice, but the Marmon's top was down and the wind carried away her cries.

Although the police gave chase, they could not keep up. Rowan tragically died on the way to the hospital, succumbing to internal bleeding. Riley survived but suffered permanent injury. Frank Lewis and his group got into a shootout in another location. The police apprehended them. The Lewis-Jones gang was finished.

Dale, Margie, and Blackie escaped capture at the gas station. After they reached Kansas City, they hid out in Blackie's family home. Blackie suffered multiple gunshot wounds to his face and legs. Unable to travel, he was a liability. They abandoned him. On his way out of town, Dale tipped off police to Blackie's whereabouts. Over one hundred officers surrounded the home. Blackie died in the shootout. Dale and Margie ditched the Marmon in the Kaw River in two feet of water. Forty-two bullet holes in the left side of the car were evidence of the Colorado gun battle.

In the San Gabriel Valley foothills, Sierra Madre is a city just 20 miles northeast of downtown Los Angeles. A beautiful and serene place to hide out. Using the alias David Moorhead, Dale rented an eight-room home at 90 South Sierra Madre Drive on October 16. He claimed to be a wealthy eastern businessman and carried a wad of cash to prove it. Dale and Margie furnished four of the eight rooms. They bought an expensive Victrola but stole a collie puppy.

Los Angeles County Sheriff's Department got word from the Pinkerton Agency that the couple lived in the hills north of Arcadia. They learned the pair bought gas for their car at the White Oaks filling station owned by R. Krebs, Jr., at the corner of Foothill Blvd. and Double Drive.

On November 19, 1918, police set a trap. Pinkerton operatives hid in an old shed behind the filling station. Deputies George Van Vliet and Edward Anderson hid in the shadows behind the shed.

At 5 p.m., Margie drove one hundred fifty feet past the gas station and stopped the Cadillac roadster near a stand of trees. After stepping out of the car, Dale scanned the area. Margie made a U-turn and pulled into the gas station.

She remained in the car with the engine running, while Dale stopped by the office to buy a chocolate bar and cans of oil for the car. After chatting with the clerk for a moment, he exited the office. The clerk signaled police.

Van Vliet and Anderson stepped out from behind the shed.

"Throw up your hands!"

Dale faced them.

"You've got me!"

He dropped the chocolate bar and cans of oil. He raised his hands, but not in surrender. He gripped a German Luger in one hand and a Smith & Wesson .38 in the other. Van Vliet and Anderson took aim at Dale, perceiving him as the major threat. He dove behind the car and opened fire. Margie fired from the car's rear seat. A bullet struck Van Vliet in the chest. He collapsed. Anderson fired the shotgun, causing half of Dale's head to disintegrate into a mist of blood, brain, and bone. Margie, critically wounded by one of Anderson's shots, continued the fight. As she gasped for her last breath,

Anderson walked up to the wounded killer and fired a round into her chest, putting her down like you would a rabid beast.

Van Vliet died in the hospital four hours later. He left a wife and three children.

Upon being notified of his son's death, Dale's father, Paul, sent a telegram to Los Angeles authorities. "Am the father of Dale Jones, killed by members of your office last Monday. Will have nothing to do with him or his burial. Disowned him years ago."

Margie's mother and her sister, Elizabeth, made burial arrangements for the dead lovers. They lie in unmarked graves in Calvary Cemetery in Whittier, California.

The deaths of Dale and Margie left dozens of unanswered questions. Dale died with twenty-six cents in his pocket. Thousands of dollars in stolen money remained missing. Locals combed the hills for a secret stash for weeks, yet never found a dime.

2. The Not-So-Great Escape

Los Angeles Department Chief James Edgar Davis, in early 1927, implemented a policy of "shoot first and ask questions later" to deal with the annual influx of felons into the city. The unwanted visitors were put on notice by the Chief's mandate, which was short on civil rights and long on rough justice.

On April 17, 1927, LAPD Detective Lieutenants Carl Hull and Harry Gerhardt sat in a barn on a stakeout of the Sheridan Apartments at Valencia and Wilshire. Shortly past midnight, they witnessed a man emerge from the apartment house through a side door. Believing that they recognized the man from the watchlist, they identified him as Paul E. Knapp, a former Seattle cop who had become a violent felon.

Hull stepped out of the darkness, holding a revolver. "Halt! I am a police officer." Knapp whipped a gun from inside his coat and leveled it at Hull. The detective fired and hit Knapp in the shoulder. Knapp dropped his gun. After handcuffing their prisoner, Hull and Gerhardt took him into custody. They treated his shoulder wound at the jail, then transferred him to the General Hospital. They booked him there on suspicion of robbery and as a fugitive.

Detectives suspected Knapp of being a member of a gang responsible for eleven local bank robberies. In Seattle, Washington, the police wanted him for jumping bail. Local law enforcement was aware of Knapp's past. From 1919 to 1923, he was a member of the Seattle police until they fired him for being AWOL, not following orders, and hijacking bootleggers.

Knapp was arrested in 1925 by the Portland, Oregon police for charges related to the Mann Act and impersonation of a Federal Officer. Known as the White-Slave act, the Mann Act made it a federal crime to transport women across state lines "for the purpose of prostitution or debauchery, or for any other immoral purpose." He spent time in the McNeil Island Federal penitentiary.

The Grand Jury indicted Knapp and his associates for robbery. Four women recognized Knapp in a line-up. Actress Paula Drendell alleged Knapp had taken a diamond and emerald ring worth $1000 ($17,000 in current USD) from her.

They charged Knapp with multiple felonies, which included savage attacks on women, robberies, burglaries, and the attempted murder of Detective Hull in May. Knapp loaded his weapon with dum-dum bullets. Dum-Dums, which are also known as armor-piercing rounds, expand upon impact. Their objective is to kill or cause severe harm to a living target. Knapp's choice of ammunition left no doubt about his intention.

Municipal Judge Samuel Black set Knapp's bail at $50,000 ($880,000 in current USD). Describing his unique and frightening M.O., testimony at the preliminary hearing revealed that he would hide in the private garages of wealthy women, waiting to ambush them. He would come out of hiding to rob and assault them. The newspapers dubbed him the "Garage Bandit."

In late July, Judge Hardy approved Knapp's request to visit a dentist whose office was across the street from his mother's home on East Fourth Street. With deputies William Burke and A. R. "Casey" Jones accompanying him, Knapp requested to make a stop at his mother's. Once there, he said he needed to use the bathroom. He dropped through a trapdoor in a closet and ran to a waiting car. They assumed Knapp's wife, Josephine, left with him.

The county grand jury wasted no time investigating Knapp's escape. Allowing bail bondsmen to carry notes to prisoners was one issue, getting prisoners out of jail on court orders was the other. Sheriff William Traeger suspended deputies Burke and Jones. They eventually absolved them of any wrongdoing. Jones, in fact, later became a hero in a deadly shootout in a Hall of Justice elevator.

Detective Hull learned that a friend of Knapp's, not Josephine, drove the getaway car. Renting an apartment on South New Hampshire Avenue was a man who matched the friend's description. Knowing they couldn't show their faces in public, the fugitive couple had groceries delivered by the same friend.

On July 30th, less than two weeks since the escape, Detective Hull caught Knapp and Josephine in the apartment and arrested them. Josephine clung to Paul. She never wavered, even when Hull said, "You know your husband is accused of numerous attacks upon women, as well as fourteen counts of robbery." Josephine replied, "Yes, that is what they say, but he is my husband, and I love him, and I will stand by him to the end." The police booked Josephine and her mother-in-law, L. W. Murray, on various charges connected to Knapp's escape.

At his arraignment on August 5th in Judge Charles Fricke's court, Knapp pleaded not guilty. He faced a sentence of from fifty years to life if convicted.

Attorney Nathan O. Freedman worked out a deal for his client. The D.A. dropped all charges except for three. Knapp, back in Judge Fricke's court on August 25th, entered guilty pleas to the three counts, one of which was the sexual assault of Paula Drendell. Josephine and Knapp's mother were given lenient sentences for conspiracy.

Knapp arrived at Folsom Prison on September 8, 1927. His marital status in the 1940 Federal Census is indicated as M for married but crossed out with a diagonal line and a faint question mark. Perhaps Josephine came to her senses and divorced her sleazy spouse.

At the end of 1943, authorities identified Knapp and a dozen other Folsom inmates in a "con boss" scandal. Con bosses controlled most aspects of other prisoners' lives, including prison work assignments. Prison officials transferred Knapp to San Quentin to break up the hierarchy. In today's world, con bosses are known as "shot callers." Different title, same job description.

The Parole Board released Knapp in 1958. With his lengthy prison record and at sixty-years-old, Paul was unlikely to become a law-abiding citizen. He never made front page news again.

3. Honeymoon from Hell

Burmah Adams met Tom White on a blind date in June 1933. She was smitten. She recalled, "Some strange new feeling stirred in my heart; something that I'd never felt before." At five feet, ten inches tall, Tom towered over his petite companion. Burmah felt secure in Tom's arms. To a young woman with Burmah's lack of experience, Tom's possessiveness seemed romantic. She wanted him to ask her for a second date. Rather than asking her, he dictated the when and where of their next meeting—8:00 p.m. the following night at her parent's home.

June flew by. They spent every night in each other's company. Tom impressed Burmah with his extravagance. They dined at expensive restaurants, out of reach of most Depression era diners. Treating her like a queen, he bought her bouquets of flowers. Tight-lipped about his work, Burmah wondered how he financed his lifestyle.

Burmah finally broached the subject of money. He told her being a stocks and bonds trader paid well. He told her he had received an inheritance that supplemented his income. He did not have a fortune, but enough to live well. Her questions answered, Burmah relaxed.

A schoolteacher from Los Angeles, Cora B. Withington, and a world traveling journalist, Crombie Allen, saw *Tugboat Annie* at Loew's State Theater on August 16th. Cora, who had been friends with Crombie for years, persuaded him to teach her how to drive his new Chevrolet coupe. She got behind the wheel and maneuvered down 3rd Street to Lafayette Place. A car with an attractive blonde at the wheel came near them. The blonde forced Cora to the curb. Crombie recounted the incident. "A man suddenly stepped from the car and waved a revolver at us." Standing next to the running board on the driver's side, the man said, "Shell out, sweetheart." And that goes for you, too, Bo." Crombie thought the man was joking until he yanked off Cora's wristwatch and pulled the rings from her fingers. Cora cautiously reached under the seat in search of her handbag. Tom saw her and believing she was reaching for a weapon, het fired.

Cora screamed and fell forward over the steering wheel. The bullet grazed Crombie's neck. Despite being wounded, he got out of the car and watched the bandit and his blonde driver roar off. He pulled Cora into the passenger seat and drove her to St. Vincent's Hospital. There, she received devastating news. The bullet ripped through her left eye, leaving her blinded for life.

Bandits, thought to be Cora and Crombie's assailants, launched a series of robberies that terrorized the city. Fearful, angry, and frustrated with the recent crime wave, Angelenos demanded police action. Newspaper headlines screamed, "*Crime Runs Rampant in Los Angeles*," which did nothing to put citizens at ease. Although LAPD Chief Davis added officers to patrol units, they failed to find anything. Until September 5th.

Cruising the city, radio Patrolmen Harold Dillard and Clyde Kern spotted a stolen car in a local garage. The officers learned that a man and a blonde woman, matching the descriptions of the bandits, had left the car for repairs. Four detectives assigned to the case staked out the vehicle. Their wait lasted twenty-four hours before the couple came to retrieve it. The detectives followed them to an apartment building on South Coronado.

Detectives Anderson and Bergeron, dressed as auto mechanics, knocked on the door to the blonde's apartment on September 7th. She stood in the doorway talking to them when she saw her male companion creep down the stairs from the floor above. She shouted a warning. "Look out!" The man pulled an automatic pistol from his pocket. He fired, but the detectives dodged in time. They drew their service revolvers and opened fire in the dark corridor. One round knocked the pistol from the bandit's hand. He fell to the hallway floor. The blond screamed. "I don't want to live! He's my husband and now he's gone! We were married only last Friday."

She ran for the window. Only she knew whether she intended to follow her husband in death or escape from the police. Before she could go over the ledge, the detectives apprehended her and took her into custody. She gave her name as Burmah Adams White. Her husband of one week, Tom White, surrounded by police, lay dead in the hallway.

In custody, Burmah spoke to reporter Agness Underwood of the *Los Angeles Post-Record*. Underwood referred to Burmah as Tom's moll. Burmah bristled. "I never took part in any holdups with Tommy." Burmah seemed desperate to get her story out. She told Underwood, "I met Tommy between three and five months ago at a dinner dance, and I went with him steady after that. I never knew of his prison record, either. The cops call me a liar when I say that, but in spite of that, I insist that I didn't know about it."

Burmah started talking to Underwood and would not stop. "Tommy and I were married Friday (September 1, 1933) at my parents' home in Santa Ana with just a few of our friends and relatives there. There was even a story in the Santa Ana paper about our wedding. We planned to travel around a bit and maybe live in San Francisco." Police asked Burmah about where Tom got his money. She told them he had "money in his own right—inherited."

Burmah's denials rang hollow. "How did you happen to be driving the automobile that was used in the Allen-Whittington shooting last August 16?" they asked her. She froze for a moment, then answered, "I never saw that automobile before last Sunday. As far as I knew, we were just trying it out."

Unless Tom committed his recent crimes in the company of another blonde, Burmah was lying. At Central Station, the police put Burmah in the shadow box. In the shadow box, a stage-like box, suspects stood behind a thin screen. Visible behind them were lines showing the height of each person. Because the stage was lit, witnesses could see the suspects, but the suspects could not see the witnesses in the dark room.

Each victim attending the line-up identified Burmah as Tom's accomplice. Leslie Bartel said, "Unquestionably, that is the girl." Gertrude Host told detectives, "I'm positive it is she. There could be no mistake." C. C. Lewis, another holdup victim, identified Burmah, too. Accompanying detectives from Central Station, Bartel and Host went to the morgue and identified Tom as their assailant. Ballistics matched Tom's gun to the weapon that wounded Cora.

According to Underwood, the young widow had a defiant attitude. She behaved just as you would expect from a gangster's moll. Burmah's tough-girl demeanor played a role in the unfolding story of the "Bandit Bride" aka "Blond Rattlesnake," because it made her unsympathetic to potential jurors. Gilbert Brown, a reporter for the *Los Angeles Evening*

Post-Record, likened Burmah to movie gun molls of the day. Brown suggested Burmah imitated blonde-tressed heroines like Joan Blondell and Jean Harlow because of the influence of too many "hot" movies. Brown opined. "For instance, when the cops at police headquarters asked Burmah if she didn't have a mother and sister living in Santa Ana, Burmah snapped. 'So What? I'm in this jam, not them." When questioned about opium and a suspicious bottle found in her purse, Burmah coyly responded by asking, "Does opium come in bottles?" She knew the answer. Before going out on jobs, Burmah and Tom would get high.

Permitted to attend Tom's funeral, Burmah summed up her feelings about the ceremony. "Just a farce, that funeral. There were only a couple of sob sisters for an audience, and what did they care about Tom? Why didn't the county take care of it?"

Faced with eight counts of robbery and two counts of assault, Burmah admitted her guilt. Once again, Burmah met with Underwood for an interview, sharing her side of the story. With the arrogance of youth, Burmah offered a cautionary tale for pretty girls like herself. "Pretty girls stand in so much more danger than a plain girl, and they can't be too careful when they pick their friends—particularly when they pick a man to love."

For several days following Burmah's arrest, Underwood followed the story. After interviewing Burmah, she spoke with Burmah's family, who stood united behind her. Burmah's mother described her daughter as, "A girl who loved her family as much as Burmah did could never have done the terrible things they accuse her of." She continued, "Why, you know, one time we had to kill an old pet cat and Burmah was broken up for three or four days because she couldn't stand to see it suffer, so how could she sit calmly by, as they say she did, and watch human being get shot?"

Burmah confided in Underwood that she feared Tom even before marrying him. "He beat me for the first time just shortly after the Allen hold-up. And, from then on, every time I showed the least trace of defiance, he beat me plenty. And I think you've interviewed me enough to know that I am a pretty defiant young lady."

On September 15, Burmah pleaded not guilty. Judge Fricke set her trial for October 20 in the court of the future mayor, Judge Fletcher Bowron. Donald MacKay, Burmah's attorney, told reporters they would base her defense on the argument that she acted out of "deadly fear." Each time a newspaper reported on her "icy demeanor," Burmah's chances of acquittal diminished.

George Stahlman, a prosecution team member, took the witness stand and read the confession Burmah made to District Attorney Buron Fitts. Evidently, the statement was not interesting enough for one juror, William Linderman, who fell asleep. As his head jerked up, he insisted that he had missed nothing.

On Wednesday, November 1, 1933, at 2:00 p.m., Judge Bowron sent the jury home. He told them to rest and emphasized the importance of being ready to start their deliberations the next day. On November 6th, the jury found Burmah guilty.

Sentenced to thirty years to life at San Quentin, Burmah's sentence set an example. Sadly, she paid a steep price for her youthful hubris. In his remarks to her, Judge Bowron stated, "Burmah White, the penalty I am to impose is not retribution. The law does not wreak vengeance. No amount of punishment can ever wipe out the wrongs you have done or bring back one ray of light in the darkness to the eyes of the unfortunate victim of your criminal enterprise, but it is hoped that your case will serve as an object lesson to others."

To drive the lesson home, one month following her conviction, the radio show, *Calling All Cars,* dramatized the case.

In March and April 1935, Underwood visited Tehachapi Women's Prison and interviewed several inmates. The new women's facility, which opened in 1933, was a far cry from the women's wing at San Quentin. It offered rehabilitation, to a woman who wanted it. Women lived in "cottages," not cells. They had permission to keep a small pet. They could purchase material to make their own dresses, and they could buy shoes. One inmate proudly showed off her bright red sandals. Underwood caught up with Burmah in the visitor's room. Noticing the change in Burmah's demeanor, Underwood reflected on her first interview in 1933. She found Burmah no longer, "Slightly defiant. Cynical. Egotistical," Burmah sat quietly, her hair returned to its natural brunette shade.

As an inmate, Burmah wrote poetry (a hobby she shared with the outlaw, Bonnie Parker), and wrote recipes for the prison's cookbook. She took courses in medical billing and office management.

Denied parole five times between 1935 and 1939, the state granted her release on December 1, 1941, just days before the bombing of Pearl Harbor.

Burmah married for a second time to Alfred Dymond. Because of their excessive drinking, Burmah and Alfred had a miserable marriage. Alfred arrived home from work on September 6, 1962, precisely twenty-nine years after Tom White's death in a police shoot-out, only to find Burmah dead on the floor.

PART II. ALL IN THE FAMILY

You need not worry about being snatched off the street by a sadistic serial killer. If you want to know who may do you harm, turn to the person next to you. The Bureau of Justice statistics reveal that in 2021, an intimate partner killed thirty-four percent of female victims. An intimate partner killed six percent of male victims. If those numbers don't make you want to grab your beloved pet and head for the hills, what are you thinking?

The cast of characters in this section is astounding. The city's first serial killer, a man kept in an attic as a love slave by his mistress, and a hammer-wielding housewife fueled by a jealous rage. Each of the perpetrators had their own reasons for committing a crime.

The people in these chapters are a reminder to us all that behind a loving façade, a killer may lurk.

Sleep with one eye open.

4. Bluebeard Watson

Los Angeles, known as the birthplace of global icons like McDonald's, Barbie, electric guitars, and supermarkets, has made a significant impact on popular culture. Another icon, one the city did not create but produced in sufficient numbers to scare the hell out of the rest of the world, is serial killers. In 1919, the first of them made his way to Los Angeles.

Kathryn Wombacher, an unmarried seamstress, took a chance on love when she answered an ad in a local Spokane, Washington newspaper. As a man in his 30s, the ad's author, Walter Andrew, described himself as sensitive and caring, with a decent income, and a desire to marry. He sounded perfect. Kathryn answered the ad.

A successful meeting led to marriage on November 8, 1919, in Seattle, Washington. Walter told Kathryn they would begin their new life in Hollywood, California. After their marriage, Walter approached Kathryn and asked for her savings, totaling $2200 ($33,653.00 in current USD). As her husband, he assured her he would manage their marital assets. He urged his bride to keep their destination a secret from friends or relatives. He revealed that part of the reason for the subterfuge was his job as a government secret service agent.

Hollywood, in 1919, was fast becoming the film capital of the world. Living in such a glamorous place was something

Kathryn could only imagine. Would she run into Mary Pickford or Douglas Fairbanks? Fatty Arbuckle or Charlie Chaplin? To her, it sounded like a glorious adventure.

After a quick stop in San Francisco, the couple made themselves at home in a bungalow on Rosewood Avenue. Almost immediately, Walter got a call to work. He could not share the details. He made a promise not to be away any longer than necessary.

When he returned, Walter suggested they take a day trip to Catalina Island. Since getting married, they had spent little time together. Located 26 miles from Los Angeles, the small island was an ideal escape for them. The sparkling blue water in Avalon Bay and the rustic, romantic setting charmed Kathryn. Other sightseers, men in straw boaters, women in wide-brimmed hats, topped with a feather plume, crowded the main street. Stopping to buy a souvenir, people flowed in and out of the small shops. Walter and Kathryn discovered a secluded place in the hills above the bay, where they could enjoy the island's majestic views. Just as they were about to relax, a group of picnickers arrived. Annoyed by the disturbance, Walter tugged Kathryn's arm and they left. They were still on their honeymoon, so she assumed he wanted to be alone with her.

As soon as they returned home, Walter was called away again. Surprisingly, he revealed a detail of his mission this time; he was on the trail of diamond smugglers. Proud of her husband's work, Kathryn helped him pack. By April 1920, after only five months of marriage, Walter's absences became more frequent and of longer duration. Living in Hollywood on her own was not what she had dreamed of. She noted the clothing Walter packed always seemed appropriate only for the West Coast. Where did he go? One thing never changed. Whenever

Walter left, he would always take his locked black leather bag with him.

Kathryn grew suspicious. Was Walter a thief? Was he cheating on her? In her quest for answers, she reached out to the Nick Harris Detective Agency. She spoke with Nick Harris himself, and he assigned J. B. Armstrong, one of his best agents, to the case.

Armstrong asked Kathryn about the dates of Walter's absences. Many of them corresponded to big safe robberies in the city. Walter's mysterious black bag would come in handy to conceal tools and weapons.

Three weeks after hiring the agency, Kathryn received a telegram from Walter. He requested she meet him downtown at the Hayward Hotel for dinner. Feeling uneasy, Kathryn reached out to Armstrong. The detective started his surveillance prior to the couple's arrival. After finishing their dinner, Kathryn and Walter took a leisurely stroll around downtown, then boarded a streetcar to go home.

Armstrong, a savvy investigator, had misgivings about Walter. He trusted his gut. He telephoned the Los Angeles County Sheriff's Department. Deputies R. Lee Couts and Harvey W. Bell answered. The men staked out the Andrew home and waited for Walter to make a move.

They followed their quarry downtown to the Hill Street Pacific Electric station, where he picked up his black bag. He retrieved it from the girl at the candy booth. It seemed absurd to the detectives. Why didn't he choose to check the bag in a locker or keep it at home? They boarded the same car as Walter and followed him home. They spent the night outside the bungalow, waiting and watching.

The next morning, after Walter left for a walk, Kathryn let the detectives into the house. They found the black bag and pried off the lock expecting to find burglar's tools, or cash. While searching, they found documents that belonged to a person named Alice Ludvigson. In their search, they came across marriage licenses, letters from women, storage house receipts, and dozens of telegrams.

Walter was not a safe cracker; he was a bigamist.

Deputies Couts and Bell, along with J.B. Anderson, sat with Kathryn and waited for Walter's return. Startled by the unexpected welcoming committee, Walter fought until he was subdued and handcuffed.

Walter insisted he was a government man but refused to show his credentials. If they were to take him to San Diego, he said he could resolve the entire business. The deputies agreed. "Let's go." Placing their handcuffed prisoner in a sheriff's car, they headed south.

Near Oceanside, Walter pulled out the small knife he had concealed in his clothing and slit his throat. Unbelievably, the deputies saw nothing. With his collar pulled up to his chin, Walter bled into his clothing. Finally, when the deputies saw blood seeping through Walter's coat, they rushed him to the San Diego County Hospital. Walter, in a desperate act, slashed his wrists. Carefully, they bundled a weak and pale Walter into their car and drove him back to Los Angeles.

For over a month, deputies Clouts, and Bell, directed by Sheriff Cline and Chief Deputy Al Manning, painstakingly combed through the contents of the bag. Through the process of matching marriage licenses with letters and telegrams, they successfully identified the women.

Walter, known by his aliases James P. Watson and Joseph Gillam, stored trunks in warehouses up and down the Pacific Coast. The dates he stored the trunks corresponded to the dates on the marriage licenses. Watson possessed stacks of blank white paper, each with the signatures of different women on the bottom. He typed lists of the women's relatives and children, if any. The papers, trunks, and jewelry begged the question, what happened to the women?

Investigators established that seven of Watson's wives were missing. The families of the missing individuals received typewritten letters containing the signature of their loved one. Detectives compared verified signatures to those on the documents Watson held. Detectives discovered that the typewritten letters were forgeries.

Evidence led to the identification of a body found near Plum Station, Washington. The deceased was Betty Pryor, one of Watson's wives.

The litany of crimes: bigamy, forgery, misuse of mail and swindles, failed to break Watson—but the discovery of Pryor's body undid him. In a torrent of disturbing details, his confession came tumbling out. Watson made a deal, prepared to do, or say anything to avoid the gallows. He offered to tell all in exchange for his life.

On April 29, 1920, in a three-hour statement to District Attorney Thomas Woolwine, Watson confessed to multiple marriages and murders. He claimed his first victim, Alice Ludvigsen, died in a boating accident. Subsequently, he owned up to killing her. Watson said Elizabeth Pryor died because she attacked him with a hatpin in a house near Olympia, Washington. As he thrust her away from him, she fell and banged her head on the corner of a box. He thought she was dead. Instead of reviving her or calling for help, he bludgeoned her skull in with a hammer. To conceal the gore and destroy any evidence, Watson burned down the deserted house where she died. He disposed of her body in a hole created by an uprooted tree stump.

Nina Lee Deloney, the last of Watson's doomed brides, died at their campsite near Signal Hill, Long Beach, on February 26, 1920. Watson claimed he remembered the details of Nina's murder as it remained vivid in his mind. Once again, Watson placed the blame on the victim. Because Nina badgered him about letters he received from other women, he beat her over the head with a hammer. To ensure she was dead, he beat her again, just like Alice. After wrapping her body with a blanket and canvas, he placed it in his car. Driving to San Diego along the coast road, he turned off towards the Imperial Valley until he discovered a "good place" for a grave near Borrego Valley. With great effort, he dragged the corpse up the mountainside and buried it deep in the sandy soil.

How did the slight Watson manage his wives' dead weight? When the situation demanded it, he claimed to possess superhuman strength. He told detectives he did not kill the women for their money; he married them for it. The wives who died at his hands were only those who displayed an unhealthy curiosity about his business or those he feared might expose him. Next, he planned to murder Kathryn.

His lapse of memory made it difficult for him to put a number to the marriages he made, or the women he killed. Acknowledging that his marriage count might exceed twenty, he confirmed committing seven murders.

The families of the missing women had questions, and the best way to get them answered was to spare Watson's life. Thoms Woolwine and the Sheriff's investigators found the mercy distasteful but necessary. Their top priority was to bring peace to the families.

Watson, weak from his suicide attempt, took Woolwine, deputies, reporters, and a cameraman to Nina's body in the desert, 30 miles from El Centro. Displaying no emotion, he halted and indicated a rocky ledge. "There it is behind that rock." Men dug at the site, throwing shovelfuls of sand and dirt over their shoulders. Watson buried Nina deep. After a long time, they finally reached her remains. Upon uncovering her body, the men paused for a moment and silently sent up prayers.

A mob, eager to dispense justice, gathered at the train station in El Centro. They shouted, "Lynch him! Kill him!" Deputies returned Watson safely to the Los Angeles County Jail. They escorted him to the Shafer & Lemons mortuary to identify Nina's remains. Watson sagged as he entered the doorway and approached the metal coffin.

District attorney Woolwine waited for Watson to come close to where Nina lay. "Mr. Watson, is this the remains of Nina Lee Deloney, who you say you killed in Los Angeles County and then brought to Imperial County to bury?"

Watson, shaken more by his near-death experience at the hands of a lynch mob than by the sight of Nina's body, replied in a hushed voice, "This is Nina Lee Deloney." Gazing into Nina's face, he saw a mass of tissue with a crushed nose and hair matted with sand and blood. Supported by his arms, he collapsed between the two deputies.

Back at the County Jail, Watson faced another hostile crowd—his fellow inmates. Just as the El Centro mob did, they found him execrable. With cries of "Kill him!" they taunted him. Three times that day, Dr. A. C. Saunders injected Watson with a sedative. The prisoner, ironically, received more humane treatment from the authorities than he gave to any of his victims.

In the days following his arrest, Watson penned a lengthy statement printed in the *Los Angeles Times*. The statement, on the surface, was a feeble effort to portray himself as a man who was helpless in the clutches of an uncontrollable desire to kill. Like many future killers, he justified his behavior by blaming it on his "other personality" and his victims. Read between the lines and the subtext is clear; he was desperate to save himself from the gallows. As a narcissist, Watson saw the world only in terms of himself. He wrote, "My every act shows I am to be pitied more than to be blamed for having developed into this strange and uncontrollable condition, for I am anything else by my natural self."

The people of Los Angeles despised Watson and criticized Woolwine's acceptance of the plea deal. The deal resulted in no trial, yet spectators still swarmed the streets around the courthouse on May 10, 1920. An undercurrent of suppressed violence electrified the crowd. If Watson appeared before them, they would rip him to pieces. Through a rarely used door, the guards smuggled Watson, rushing him in secrecy to the county hospital, and then to the courthouse.

Throngs of women awaited Watson's arrival. When they caught their first glimpse of the maniac they came to see, a frisson of excitement sparked through the crowd. An ordinary-looking man, Watson was neither a gargoyle, nor the suave charmer they may have expected. Only his intimate partners and the deputies who took his standing, naked mugshot, knew Watson's deepest secret. He was a hermaphrodite and possessed both male and female characteristics. They did not make his condition public.

Of the several murders he committed, Nina Lee Deloney was the only one for which they held Watson accountable. The judge supported Woolwine's deal. He said, "Your crimes have startled civilization. But to the mysteries of them, you alone held the key. I am convinced that it was with the utmost reluctance that the district attorney agreed to accept from you the confession of your murders upon the terms of recommending life imprisonment. But there was no other course, and it is the opinion of the court that such a decision was just."

In sentencing Watson to life, he said, "The court finds by the evidence that you are physically unsound, mentally deficient and morally depraved." With those words, Watson got life in prison without the possibility of parole. He deserved worse. The "arch-criminal," a model prisoner, died at San Quentin in 1939.

Kathryn Wombacher, the wife responsible for pulling the plug on Watson's life of crime, lived to be 95.

5. The Attic Love Slave

After visiting friends in the Wilshire district, Fred and Walburga Oesterreich arrived home on South Andrews Blvd. around 10:30 p.m. on the evening of August 22, 1922.

Walburga, nicknamed Dolly, went upstairs to her room, switched on the light, and entered the closet. Someone locked the door behind her. Thinking Fred was playing a prank, she called out to him, but got no reply. After a few moments, she heard gunshots. Several of her neighbors heard the shots too, and they rushed to the scene. Near the door, they discovered Fred in a large pool of blood on the floor. He suffered three gunshot wounds. One bullet to his forehead and two to his chest. Upon hearing Dolly shouting, they released her from the closet. After the police arrived, they discovered two cartridges and a .25 caliber automatic pistol on the floor. Apart from the weapon, there was little evidence for them to investigate.

Fred left Dolly a wealthy widow. Having the means and no one to question her, she may have moved on with her life a little faster than most people thought appropriate. In early 1923, she lived in a house she had purchased with Fred's money on North Beachwood, which was near the Wilshire Country Club. Herman Shapiro, an attorney, moved in with her.

Dolly had jilted a previous lover, Roy Klumb, to be with Herman. Eleven months after the murder, in July 1923, Roy sought revenge by running to the police with an intriguing story. According to him, Dolly had asked a favor from him right after Fred's murder when she asked him to dispose of a .25 caliber pistol. He asked no questions and tossed the gun into the La Brea Tar Pits. He pointed out the spot to police, and they located it where Klumb said it would be.

Roy's story was enough to get Dolly arrested for murder. Herman paid her a visit. She broke into sobs. She repeated over and over, "He's there, he's there."

Herman asked her who she was talking about, and she told him her "vagabond half-brother," Walter, hid in a secret room in the house. Dolly instructed Herman to go home, scratch on the wall, and wait for Walter to appear. Despite thinking she had lost her mind, Herman did as she asked. After scratching on the wall a few times, a small, bespectacled man stepped out from behind a secret panel. "Hello, Herman," he said.

Upon hearing from Herman that Dolly was in jail, Walter confessed he killed Fred. While in his attic hidey-hole, he said he overheard a violent quarrel between Dolly and Fred. Fearing for Dolly's life, he emerged from behind the secret panel to his room and pumped three slugs into Fred. Attic hidey-hole? What the hell was Walter talking about? Herman, not believing a word of Walter's fantastic story, sent him packing. Out of concern for Dolly, he kept the incident to himself. The D.A. dropped the charges against Dolly.

In 1930, after living with Herman for seven years, Dolly grew bored with the attorney and ended their relationship. Following in the footsteps of Roy Klumb, Herman rushed to the law to inform on her. He told police all about Dolly's murderous vagabond half-brother and his weird confession.

Detectives found out that Walter was Otto Sanhuber and was Dolly's lover, not her half-brother.

The love affair began years earlier, with Otto working as a 17-year-old sewing machine repairman in Fred's apron factory. Sent by Fred to repair Dolly's home sewing machine, Otto met Dolly when she greeted him at the door. Twenty-six-year-old Dolly stood in the doorway, scantily clad, bored, and randy. She made a powerful impression on the teenager. As soon as they met, they felt a sexual chemistry. They longed to be in each other's arms every minute of the day. To make it possible, Dolly installed Otto in the attic. During daylight hours, Otto emerged from hiding. During the night, in the attic, he sat silently, penning mystery tales. The arrangement, which continued for over a decade, suited them well.

The arrangement ended when Herman ejected Otto from Dolly's home. Dolly felt relieved. Over time, Otto's role shifted from being a lover to being more of a faithful dog. On his own for the first time in years, Otto changed his name, moved to Portland, and got married. He always avoided discussing his past with his wife. He told her he could not remember a thing prior to 1923. Arrested for murder, Otto confessed to reporters that his primary worry was figuring out what to tell his wife.

The district attorney issued a warrant for Dolly's arrest, charging her with conspiracy. Although they charged Otto with murder, the court ended up convicting him of manslaughter. He should have been on his way to San Quentin, but his attorney noticed an important fact the D.A. had missed. The statute of limitations had run out on the manslaughter charge. The conviction was rendered null. Once they released Otto, he vanished. Perhaps he found another closet.

Dolly's trial for conspiracy followed Otto's. Unable to reach a decision, the jury deadlocked. In early December 1930, D.A. Costello stated the evidence was insufficient for a new trial. Reluctantly, they dropped the charges against her.

In the early 1930s, Dolly began an affair with her married business manager, Ray Hedrick. Hedrick's wife filed a $300K ($6.8M in current USD) alienation of affection lawsuit against Dolly, which was eventually dismissed.

Dolly and Ray lived together for years until March 1961, when they filed for a marriage license. The couple married in a civil ceremony. Seventy-five-year-old Dolly was so feeble Ray had to support her while they took their vows.

Dolly died a couple of weeks later, leaving everything to Ray.

6. The Adventures of Tiger Girl

Marie Weitz drove along Montecito Road enroute to her Highland Park bungalow. As she rounded the second bend, she spotted a bundle of crumpled, dirty clothing in the narrow road. She swerved to avoid it and then got out to investigate.

When she stooped to examine the bundle, she saw a woman's face. The features of her face were a distorted mass of blood and bone. Curiously, someone had placed a heavy boulder on the woman's chest. Did her killer fear that she, like Lazarus, might rise from the dead? Driving down the hill, Marie reached a farmhouse and telephoned the Los Angeles Police Department.

The deceased had wounds on her face, head, arms, and breasts. The killer spread her legs apart in a suggestive pose, causing shock and horror. She looked as though an animal attacked her, her dress was pulled up and her silk tap pants were torn to shreds. Her bloody felt hat lay in the dirt nearby. Although she carried no identification, her well-made clothes implied she was a woman of means.

Agony marred her features. Her lips curled away from her teeth in a grimace, and she bit through her tongue. An unsightly purple bruise marred the back of her right hand. A defensive wound. The police suspected a sex crime because of the viciousness of the assault and her shredded clothing.

The scene yielded few clues. Footprints led to the spot where a car was parked, and the car's tire marks indicated it was facing down the hill toward the city. While searching, one person discovered the blood-soaked handle from a hammer in a patch of grass. The killer stuck the woman with such force the hammer broke in two.

LAPD homicide detectives arrived. Carefully, they combed the area for witnesses. They found a little girl who remembered seeing two women and "somebody else" on the hillside. Pointing at the hilltop, she said, "They were up there playing. One of them screamed and laughed."

The grisly slaying dominated the next morning's headlines. More than one thousand people gathered at the morgue to identify Jane Doe. Most of them came for the gruesome spectacle. At day's end, the victim remained unidentified.

Los Angeles County Undersheriff Eugene "Gene" Biscailuz took charge of the investigation. As Biscailuz paced district attorney John Haas's office, a tall, handsome man in his early 30s sat nearby. Haas said, "Gene, I want to introduce you to the man whose wife you are seeking for the murder of the girl out on Two Tree Hill." Surprised, he contained his shock and directed his attention to the stranger who declared, "I am the husband of the woman who killed Alberta Meadows." Alberta is the girl you found on Two Tree Hill." He stopped and added, "My name is Armour L. Phillips."

Armour lit a cigarette and blew out a plume of smoke. He said the night before, his wife came home covered in blood. "I sent her away. And now I am here betraying her—telling you all about it. I walked the streets all night, trying to decide the right thing to do. I felt my duty was to my wife."

Armour accompanied Gene to Sheriff William Traeger's office. He described Clara as twenty-three, five and a half feet tall, one hundred-twenty-two pounds, with blue eyes and dark brown hair. Armour bought her ticket to El Paso and, from there, she intended to cross the border into Juarez, Mexico, where she and Armour would reunite.

Sheriff Traeger questioned Armour, and Gene telephoned the railroad station. They expected Clara's train to pass through Tucson, Arizona, in a few hours. Gene wired Tucson's sheriff, requesting that he hold the fugitive. Subsequently, Gene received a wire that informed him of Clara's arrest.

Sheriff Traeger and his wife, Ruth, left for Tucson to return the wanted woman. It fell to Gene to inform Fred Tremaine, Alberta's father, of her murder. Fred struggled to absorb the news. "Alberta was a wonderful girl," he said. He added, "She had nothing to do with Phillips. She had only seen him once or twice in all her life."

On July 14, 1927, the Golden State Limited stopped ten miles northeast of Los Angeles at the Shorb Station in Alhambra. The sheriff coordinated the unscheduled stop so that Peggy Caffee, a friend of Clara's and the only eyewitness to the murder, could come aboard and identify her.

Two officers supported Peggy between them. Clara held a box of face powder and casually dabbed at her nose with a powder puff. She turned around and locked eyes with Peggy. When asked, "Is this the girl you saw strike Mrs. Meadows on the head with a hammer?" Peggy nodded in affirmation. Peggy made the rest of the trip to Los Angeles in the compartment with Clara and her police escort. As the train passed the big hill where the murder occurred, fat tears rolled down Peggy's cheeks. Clara displayed no emotion.

Peggy met Clara in 1920 when they danced together in the chorus at the Pantages Theatre. They did not see each other again until a couple of days before the murder. While out shopping on Broadway, Peggy bumped into Clara and her mother. After chatting for a while, Clara and Peggy made a shopping date.

On July 11, Peggy and Clara spent the day downtown. Clara bought a skirt, a pair of slippers, and a hammer in the basement of a five and dime store. That evening, Clara unburdened herself to Peggy. Clara intended to confront Alberta regarding the affair. She convinced Peggy to go with her. While waiting in a cab parked outside Alberta's building, Peggy saw Clara go up the back stairs. After a few minutes, she returned. Alberta was out. Instead of facing Armour, Clara spent the night at Peggy's.

The next morning, Clara awoke determined to have it out with her nemesis. In the afternoon, she and Peggy went downtown to the First National Bank, where the young widow worked. Approaching Alberta as she exited the bank, Clara introduced Peggy to her. Clara asked Alberta for a lift home.

They went a short distance before Clara asked Alberta if she would make a detour. She wanted to visit her sick sister. Clara gave turn-by-turn directions to a place on Montecito Road. Instructing Alberta to park, she asked her to step out of the car for a private word. She accused her of having an affair with Armour.

Peggy saw Clara pull a hammer from underneath her cape. Alberta saw it and she ran. The women disappeared over a small hill. They reappeared, and Clara held Alberta's arm. Peggy thought the storm had passed. In horror, Peggy watched as Clara raised the hammer and brought it down on Alberta's head with a sickening thud. Alberta yelled to Peggy, "Lady, help me!" Peggy told the grand jury she tried to intervene, but Clara menaced her with the hammer. After running to a nearby wall, she vomited.

Covered in blood, Clara handed Peggy her a handkerchief, and demanded, "Wipe my face off." After removing the bloody rings from Alberta's fingers, Clara placed them in the dead woman's handbag and dropped it on the rear seat. She took the wheel of Alberta's Ford and said, "Nobody can take my husband away from me."

Clara dropped Peggy at Figueroa and Pico. "If you say anything, I will kill you." The next day, when Peggy's husband noticed she was upset, he pressed her for a reason. She told him everything. He insisted they go to the police. Upon hearing Peggy's testimony, the grand jury indicted for murder Clara.

William Aggeler, of the Public Defender's office, took the case. While preparations for the trial were underway, Armour granted an exclusive interview to the *Los Angeles Evening Express*. Armour claimed he felt "wholly responsible for a tragedy which has brought death to one and a murder charge to another." In the article, Armour described picnicking with Alberta and her sister-in-law, Lillian, on May 30. He said Alberta sent Lillian away to look at the hillside flora and fauna so she and Armour could make love on the blanket. Armour's account was at odds with Alberta's diary. Alberta wrote she spent that day weeping at her husband's graveside in Forest Lawn Cemetery. In an entry from April, Alberta mentioned Armour only once, noting that she met him at the home of a friend. Armour's picnic story, seemed calculated to tarnish Alberta's reputation. Following the bizarre interview, he vanished.

Clara's trial began with jury selection in Judge Houser's courtroom. The state outlined its case on October 25th. After the slaying, Clara earned the nickname, "Tiger Girl," for the ferocity of the murder.

The prosecution called Peggy to the stand. Spectators anxiously held their breath. The only sound was rain drumming against the windows. Asked if she knew the defendant, Peggy glanced over at Clara's glowering face and answered yes. Peggy confirmed Clara's purchases during their shopping trip. "Clara purchased a pair of slippers, a silk shirt, a pair of hose—and a hammer." That was too much for the defendant, who gripped the defense table and jumped-up shouting, "Peggy Caffee—tell the truth! You bought that hammer!" Peggy was still for a moment, then appeared to brace herself. She shouted into the courtroom, "Clara Phillips bought that hammer!"

Clara chewed on her handkerchief. Despite her attorney's efforts, the cross-examination did not go well. He suggested Peggy was too far away to see Alberta's condition. Peggy said she was close enough to see "... blood on her and I knew I could not handle Clara alone." Herrington asked, "Did you know whether Alberta was dead?" Peggy's next statement went off like a bomb. "Yes, sir. Clara was choking her and said, 'Die you____.' Is it necessary for me to use the language she used?"

Clara's account of the day was absurd. She claimed not to recall telling Armour, "I have killed the girl you loved, and I am so awfully happy, and I can cook you the best little supper I ever cooked you in my life."

Peggy had no motive to murder Alberta, but Clara insisted she instigated the deadly encounter and egged her on. Clara insisted that when Peggy saw she was in trouble she stepped in and beat Alberta to death.

District Attorney Burke argued in favor of putting Clara to death. Labeling the defendant a "faker," he concluded with the plea, "All I ask is that justice be done."

The defense countered. They accused Peggy of striking the "mortal blow," they claimed that she alone was responsible for the death of Alberta Meadows. "The mutilation of the body may have been done by the insane fanaticism of this defendant, but the mutilation was done after death."

As Clara waited on the jury, she spoke to the press. "I don't know whether I killed Alberta Meadows or not, but if I did, it was for mother love." She said Armour was her baby, and she fought hard to keep him. "Just as one woman died in the midst of that insane rage, so am I living my death behind steel bars today. Oh, how gladly I would trade places with Alberta."

Following eleven hours of deliberation, the panel of nine men and three women deadlocked. Clara wept with relief.

The jury gave it another go, and on November 16, at 10:35 a.m. they informed the bailiff they had reached a verdict. Judge Houser instructed the spectators to stay in their seats. J. F. McSwain, the foreman, handed the verdict to the court clerk. "We, the members of this jury..." The clerk got no further. With his gavel, Judge Houser brought order to the restless gallery of spectators. The clerk continued, "... find that the defendant, Clara Phillips, is guilty of murder in the second degree."

Clara declared the verdict "an unfair deal." The judge sentenced her to ten years to life. Her lawyer rushed to file an appeal and requested a ten-day stay of execution. After granting the motion, the judge sent Clara back to the County Jail to await the outcome.

On the morning of December 5, inmate Fay Alma Smith called on Clara to report for dishwashing duty but got no answer. Alma observed that there were three sawed-off bars in Clara's cell window. Curtains fluttered through the opening.

Drawings of Clara's supposed escape route appeared in the daily newspapers. They said Clara cut through the bars, then her accomplices lifted her onto the roof of the jail. Lowered by rope to the roof of an adjoining building, they then left the roof via a narrow stairway leading out to Temple Street.

The story was fantasy. She escaped because of corruption in the jail. Clara's was the second breakout in as many months.

In April 1923, after months of false leads, Gene heard a rumor that Clara was in Mexico City using the alias Mrs. R. Young. With a man named Jessie C. Carson, she was on her way to Guatemala. Gene requested that all telegraph companies across the nation inform him of any messages sent to South or Central American countries.

As he waited, Gene sought information about Clara's traveling companion. After Clara's jailbreak, Deputy Norris Stensland discovered that a man named Jesse Carson had abandoned his wife and escaped to Mexico.

On a tip, Gene verified Clara, her younger sister Etta Mae Jackson, and Jesse Carson were in Honduras. They all denied their true identities. Jesse Carson firmly maintained that he was the son-in-law of deceased Mexican general Felipe Angeles. Etta Mae claimed that Jesse Carson was her husband.

After being sworn in as a matron, Gene's wife, Willette, prepared to travel to South America with her husband.

Accompanying them was Deputy Sheriff Walter Hunter, Gene's half-brother. The *Los Angeles Examiner* dispatched reporter Morris Lavine to get the scoop. After leaving on April 27th, he traveled by fruit steamer, special train, automobile, and mule. He beat Gene's party and had ample time to wire exclusives back to Los Angeles. *Examiner* readers were eager to read about the further adventures of Tiger Girl.

Arriving at their destination, Gene went to the office of Colonel Hipolito Reyes, the Chief of Police. As Gene walked to Reyes' office, he noticed a crowd gathered beneath the balcony of a tall building. He saw two women, wrapped in shawls, standing at the railing. Occasionally, the women graced the assemblage with a smile or wave. As he drew closer, he saw Clara's familiar face.

Colonel Reyes escorted Gene to his first meeting with the fugitive. Once they had exchanged pleasantries, she made him an offer of $5,000 ($88,000 in current USD) to leave her alone. Gene was not the first official she tried to bribe.

Gene got a chilly reception from the local press. They deemed Alberta's murder to be an honor killing. Remaining calm, Gene praised the reporters in fluent Spanish for their chivalry. He thoroughly explained to them the homicide laws in California. Though he may not have changed their minds, he still made a favorable impression. The following day, local newspapers referred to him as a "Latin gentleman, muy caballero, eloquent and persuasive."

As they debated Clara's fate, Gene grew more concerned about Willette. She was ill with an amoebic infection. Left with few options, he made a bold decision. He would approach Clara and persuade her to waive extradition. Gene painted a grim picture of her future if she stayed in Tegucigalpa and offered an alternative. "If you return with me," he said, "I'll tell the court that you waived extradition. When the time comes for the board to consider your parole, I give you my word I will not oppose it." Clara said she needed two hours to weigh his proposal. Gene walked to the consulate's office, where he had them prepare the waiver. Upon his return to Clara two hours later, she signed it.

Gene exhausted his funds and asked the American officials at the Cuyamel Fruit Company for aid. They told him they had a ship ready to sail at 3:00 p.m. that afternoon. His party could board at noon.

Three days after leaving Honduras, the ship steamed into New Orleans. Clara and Etta Mae went to the parish jail. With concern for Willette's well-being, Gene took her to a hospital. Until they received funds from District Attorney Asa Keyes, they could not complete the last leg of their journey. Gene received $500 and as a result, everyone boarded a westbound train.

Over 5,000 people waited at the Arcade Station in Los Angeles to witness Tiger Girl's return. They waited in vain. Last minute legal maneuvers cleared the way for her immediate transport to San Quentin. She begged Willette to accompany her. Despite being ill, Willette still agreed.

In 1933, Clara transferred from San Quentin to the new women's prison in Tehachapi. The Parole Board, on May 18, 1934, granted Clara her freedom, which would take effect on June 17, 1935. Gene kept his word and did not oppose her release. District Attorney Buron Fitts called the parole a "public outrage."

Unrepentant, Clara told reporters, "And, boys, in your stories don't say I've paid for my crime, for I didn't commit any crime," she added. "I said long ago, and I say now that I didn't kill Alberta Meadows."

Armour did not meet Clara at the prison gate as he had earlier sworn to do. Hoping he would be there; Los Angeles authorities held a warrant for him on a liquor charge. Armour spent the rest of his life as a petty con man until his death on November 12, 1972, in New York's Lenox Hill Hospital.

Clara moved to San Diego to be near her mother and her sisters. After reclaiming her birth name, Ann Claire Weaver found work in a fish cannery.

At the conclusion of her trial, Clara whined about the verdict, calling it an "unfair deal." That is false. Eugene and Willette Biscailuz were the ones who got the unfair deal. Willette never recovered her health. At 64, she passed away in Santa Monica on August 22, 1950.

Gene never remarried.

7. The Torso Murder

From its source in Canoga Park, the Los Angeles River meanders through San Fernando Valley, Downtown Los Angeles, and other cities before finally reaching the Pacific Ocean at Long Beach. The county, having endured devastating floods in the early years of the 20th century, encased the river in concrete. The river, which was still free flowing in 1929, served as a source of livelihood for many Angelenos.

April 4, 1929, saw such heavy rain it set a record of 1.39 inches. One man's trash is another man's treasure, and the river was the perfect place to find useful discards. While wandering along the riverbank, a man and his son observed a box that the current had swept ashore, just about 100 yards north of Clark Street in Lynwood Gardens. Lying near the box was something pale. He was horrified to realize he had found a female torso. The arms were severed, and the legs torn off. They contacted police.

After Constable Roselle of Compton accompanied the men to the scene, he asked Captain Bright, head of the Sheriff's Homicide Squad, to join him. Smaller communities relied on the Sheriff's Department for homicide investigations. Captain Bright arrived along with Deputy Sheriffs Hutchinson, Gray, and Vejar. By examining the scene, they inferred that the body belonged to a girl aged between 16 and 21, who someone had mutilated elsewhere and then discarded in the water.

Captain Bright asked Los Angeles citizens to report on any missing woman. Bright said, "The help of every citizen is needed to solve this crime, which apparently is the work of a fiend. The woman's torso provides no clew (sic) to her identity. Only by checking the disappearance of every woman reported to the authorities will we probably get a trace of the murderer."

County Autopsy Surgeon Wagner estimated the woman was 25 years old, 5'7" and 135 pounds. From the torso's fair complexion, they surmised her hair was light brown or blond. County Chemist Abernathy, analyzed the woman's vital organs. The victim died because of either being shot or receiving a blow to the head. Regrettably, the head remained missing.

Based on the river flow, detectives determined the killer dumped the torso into the water no further north than the Ninth Street Bridge. The killer(s) threw the limbs in at the same location, but they did not float as the torso had done. Deputies dragged the river, hoping to recover the missing body parts. After examining the evidence, the medical examiner determined the murderer had a background in either surgery or anatomy.

Following his public plea, Captain Bright received dozens of missing persons reports. Besides that, he received reports of several other sinister events. Noticing two men and a young woman in a black touring car drive to the edge of the riverbank at the Florence Avenue Bridge, a female informant reported what she saw. The men, carrying an unidentifiable object to the river, got out of the car while the girl remained at the wheel–then the trio sped off. Authorities asked gas station attendants and car rental agencies to be on the lookout for suspicious characters and any blood stains.

As with any gruesome crime, the scene attracted looky-loos. Deputy sheriffs stayed busy shooing away crowds of morbidly curious sightseers. Afraid that one of them would get caught in the quicksand, as one deputy had, they also worried someone would find a significant piece of evidence and walk off with it.

The Sheriff's Department received dozens of calls with tips and reports, but very few useful clues. If only they could find the missing limbs or, better yet, as horrendous as it would be, the head of the dead woman.

On May 4th, the newspapers reported police had a suspect in the murder. Leland Wesley Abbott, an ex-con, whose estranged wife was missing. He lived near where they found the torso. When Wesley failed to show up for work at a warehouse, co-workers tipped off deputy sheriffs and LAPD. One co-worker, Ray L. Martin, said Abbott told him his wife was "... in love with another man in Lynwood and had gone there to live."

Martin told investigators, "He (Abbott) asked me if I would drive him to Lynwood. When I asked him what for, he said he wanted to go down and get even with his wife. I told him I had a date, and he said he had a job to finish and he had to do it in a day or two, or it would be too late, as he was going back east. The next day, on April 3, it was stormy and raining and Abbott came to me and said that this was an ideal night for him to get even with his wife. I told him he was crazy to think of such a thing and they would catch him. He replied that there was plenty of quicksand in the Los Angeles River that was close by where she lived. I feared he might be in some bootlegging scheme and I told him I was afraid to drive him to Lynwood. He said that it was not connected with bootlegging, but that it was concerned with his wife being in love with another man. He left work and we've never seen him again."

Police issued an all-points-bulletin for Abbott. They described him as, "thirty-three years of age, five feet six inches tall, weighs 145 pounds, with dark hair and dark brown eyes. He had a scar on each wrist and one on his right forearm."

Ray Martin was not the only co-worker Abbott confided in. He told William Spence he planned on "fixing her (his wife) plenty when he got ready." Abbott also said he was aware of the quicksand along the Los Angeles River, and it would be the perfect place to dump a body. With his possession of a surgical knife and an automatic revolver, Abbott became a strong suspect because of threats against his missing wife.

Deputy Sheriff Modie and Detective Allen traced Abbott to a mountain road camp thirty-three miles north of Mt. Wilson. After the discovery of the torso, his sudden appearance at the camp on April 5th raised suspicions.

Abbott denied killing his wife–in fact, he denied ever being married. He admitted he told his warehouse buddies he was married, but he lied. His former co-workers said they never saw Abbott's alleged spouse.

What about the surgical knife? Abbott said that since his stepfather was a surgeon, he considered becoming a doctor himself. The knife was a gift. Somewhere along the way, Abbot took a detour from his medical career path and transitioned into a gun runner, smuggling weapons into Mexico. Tips from his co-workers led police to Abbott's door, but it was his smuggling activities which ultimately led to his arrest by the police. He served a term in Leavenworth Prison for his crimes.

Attorneys for Leland applied for a writ of habeas corpus, but he preferred to stay behind bars until his story checked out. If they freed him before clearing him of any wrongdoing, being a suspect in such a brutal crime could make him a target. Although they had reservations, they released him anyway.

A few days following his release, Abbott walked into Captain Bright's office with the missing surgical knife. He found it in the pocket of an old coat. Even though Abbott cooperated with the investigation, he remained a person of interest.

William Pettibone, Ray Seegar, Floyd Waterstreet, and Glen Druer explored the muddy riverbank for hidden treasures on May 18, 1929. Standing 150 feet from the bridge in the city of Bell, the boys noticed something that resembled a turtle shell or strange prehistoric fish. After picking up a stick, one boy stuck it into an end of the bony structure and lifted it up for the others to gawk at. The boys spent a few minutes before they discovered that their treasure was a human skull.

With the head impaled on a stick, the boy ran up to the roadway. He waved it around until a female motorist stopped. The horrified woman kept it together long enough to drive to a public telephone where she called Bell's Chief of Police. Chief Smith and Motor Officer Steele met the woman and the group of boys near the river. The woman declined to give her name. Smith's officers told Captain Bright about the grisly find. Bright accompanied Deputies Allen, Brewster, and Gompert to the scene. Deputies searched the area, drawing an enormous crowd of curious on-lookers.

The initial autopsy yielded nothing which could identify the deceased. At least the skull still had several extant teeth, which made an identification possible. Local newspapers printed the photos and drawings of the teeth and distributed them to dentists.

With limited remains, the experts needed to perform a miracle. Amazingly, they did just that. They gleaned a remarkable amount of information from a minimum amount of physical evidence. They matched the head to the torso and it was a perfect fit. To move forward, the cause of death had to be determined. The investigators determined that the woman died immediately from blunt force trauma, potentially caused by a hammer blow. Based on the examination, the sheriff's homicide investigators revised the age of the deceased to 60. Investigators postulated that a family squabble led to the woman's death.

Captain Bright reassigned half of his detectives from searching for missing girls under 20 to investigate missing women over 40. The other half helped locate the dentist responsible for the dentition in the found skull.

Captain Bright's detectives rewarded his faith in them when the crime lab produced a partial identification of the victim from her teeth. They tentatively identified her as Laura B. Sutton, 40 years of age. She vanished six days before the discovery of the torso, at the end of March.

Laura's brother, E. J. Groff, spotted the drawings of the teeth in the newspaper and contacted his sister's dentist. Despite being unable to confirm that the teeth were Mrs. Sutton's, the dentist stated that they closely resembled them. To make a positive match, he had to go to the Coroner's Office. Groff disclosed to detectives that prior to her disappearance, his sister behaved strangely. Appearing agitated, she made several peculiar statements. After leaving him, Laura told him about the unrecorded vacant lot. She said, "If anything ever should happen to me, that lot I deeded you is not recorded." Without further explanation, Laura told him that someone stole two Liberty Bonds from her safe deposit box.

Groff provided the name of a man he felt stole the bonds and may have murdered her. Until they investigated further, the detectives declined to name the man.

Sheriff's investigators waited for Laura's dentist to confirm her identity. Eugene Sutton was on their list of people to question, having been divorced by Laura in 1928. Eugene, as an ex-spouse who was behind in his alimony payments, became a person of interest.

Detectives followed leads while the coroner examined knife marks on the torso. Someone who was familiar with human anatomy dismembered the body, and it is possible the killer used a surgical knife. Dr. Wagner, the autopsy surgeon, estimated that it would take the killer roughly three hours to complete the dismemberment.

Dr. Frank William Westlake, retired physician, and a former suitor of Laura's, came forward to make a detailed statement to Captain Bright. Westlake said he saw Laura on March 28th. She came to him saying she planned to travel to Ventura for a few days to see her ex-husband about unpaid alimony. Westlake stated Laura entrusted him with the care of two pet birds.

Detectives and scientists worked around the clock to find Laura and identify the torso. Once again, Captain Bright received a visit from Dr. Westlake. He brought with him several notes signed with the initials L. B. S., which he said were from Sutton. The notes were a mixed bag. While some were typed and others were handwritten, each of the notes referred to the pet canaries in Westlake's care.

Attorney Willard Andrews, the last person to see Laura alive, offered a mind-boggling statement. Laura told him she intended to find her ex-husband and her sister, Mrs. Ida

Kleppe, and "have it out with them." She revealed to Andrews that her sister and her ex were having an affair, which caused their divorce. To make matters worse, her sister and her ex-husband were planning to get married. Talk about awkward family gatherings.

On May 28th, an x-ray of the victim's ears showed piercings, invisible to the naked eye. The x-ray evidence provided a step in the right direction. E. C. Hyde, the dentist, confirmed that the teeth belonged to Laura.

With the victim identified, Captain Bright still had to deal with a growing list of potential suspects. Captain Bright recreated a scene from the movies by summoning everyone connected to the case to the homicide squad's office for questioning. The *Los Angeles Times* listed those who were required to attend. "Eugene Sutton, divorced husband of Mrs. Sutton; Ben King, sweetheart of and roomer at the home of Mrs. Sutton when she disappeared; Dr. Frank Westlake, asserted sweetheart of Mrs. Sutton, said to have frequently aided the woman in financial transactions involving real estate; Mrs. Ida Kleppe, sister of Mrs. Sutton who asserts to Captain Bright that she and her sister had not been friendly for years, and Emerson De Groff, brother of the missing woman."

Her ex-husband, Eugene, may have wanted her dead so he could stop paying alimony. Because of Ida's pending marriage to Eugene, Laura and her sister Ida became estranged. In the letters that they found Laura expressed her desire to start over with Eugene.

Together or individually, Ida and Eugene may have murdered Laura. By courting her, Ben King, who rented a room in Laura's house, became a suspect. What if Ben became so jealous of the doctor that he murdered Laura rather than lose her to another man? Even Laura's brother had a motive. He was supposed to inherit land.

Dr. Frank Westlake was the only suspect with an expertise in human anatomy, and almost certainly the only one suspect who owned a scalpel. Investigators collected a lot of circumstantial evidence, all of which pointed to Dr. Westlake. Westlake possessed deeds for many of Laura's properties, sizeable sums of her cash, and her bank books. Having been named a beneficiary in her will and having a life insurance policy, he stood to gain financially. For six years, Dr. Westlake served as Laura's financial adviser, well before her divorce from Eugene. Westlake took complete charge of Laura's finances after the divorce, convincing her to open a joint bank account with him. She deposited $750. He contributed nothing.

Detectives quizzed Ben King. He proposed marriage to Laura—a union Westlake vehemently opposed. While the three of them were arguing, King claimed Laura grabbed a pistol and held it to her head. After taking the weapon from her, King later gave it to Westlake. After the argument on March 26th, King and Sutton never crossed paths again.

Dr. Westlake's initial statement to detectives was Laura had summoned him to her house several days following the argument because she wanted a ride to the train depot to catch a train for Ventura. The doctor said his car broke down at Pico and Union. After she got out, Laura caught a streetcar. He never saw her again. Westlake's story came apart in crucial ways. The letters Laura allegedly wrote to him turned out to be forgeries. Claiming Laura endorsed it on the 3rd of April and mailed it from a small Arizona town, he presented the note for $200. The experts concluded the signature was a forgery.

Dr. Westlake had a questionable past. Supposedly, he graduated from the Eclectic Medical School in Cincinnati in 1900. Relying on botanical remedies, eclectic medicine stood in opposition to modern Western medicine as it was practiced in the 18th and early 19th centuries. Because California didn't recognize medical degrees from the Eclectic Medical School, Dr. Westlake could not lawfully practice here. Although circumstantial evidence against Dr. Westlake accumulated, what Captain Bright desired most was a crime scene.

During the last week of March, sheriffs discovered a couple who resembled Westlake and Sutton had rented a home. The couple paid for two months in advance. Detectives asked him about it. Westlake admitted he and Laura were "house hunting" for several days before she disappeared. In the Edendale district, they visited at least eight vacant homes, all of which needed to be searched.

Deputies found bloodstains splashed all over the walls and floor in the bathroom of Dr. Westlake's home. To test them, they removed the bathtub and the "gooseneck." The district attorney said the blood in the bathroom "forged the final link in a chain of circumstances." He charged Dr. Westlake with murder. Westlake insisted Laura was alive.

Captain Bright and Assistant District Attorney Jordan spent hours going over the evidence linking Westlake to the murder. His motive, greed. Westlake possessed deeds of trust for several lots, bank books, and cash belonging to Laura. He was the beneficiary of a life insurance policy, and he had given away some of Laura's personal items. Not the action of a man who believed she would return home.

The evidence may have been circumstantial, but when taken together it offered a powerful argument for murder committed for personal gain–especially when her clothing, silverware, and other personal effects were discovered by deputies concealed under the floor and in the attic of his home. Also, there was a typewriter found under a pile of clothing. The same typewriter might have been used to write the letters attributed to Laura.

Coroner Nance conducted an inquest on June 13, 1929. The primary reason was to get on the record the identification of the torso as Mrs. Sutton's.

On August 26th, the trial began. The State claimed Westlake murdered Laura in order to gain control of her assets. To hide the crime, he mutilated her corpse.

Nine women and three men comprised the jury. They would decide the fate of the 57-year-old retired physician. Both the 8-year-old boy who found the torso and the 14-year-old boy who discovered the head were witnesses. The condition of the body, which was still armless and legless, made it necessary for the coroner and the dentist to explain the science behind their conclusions. The scientists provided the jury with a lesson on the rudiments of forensic odontology; and by using the ossification of the victim's bones, Dr. Wagner explained how he estimated her age.

The defense advanced a theory that Ben King committed the murder because he had once worked as a butcher and possessed the skill to dismember a body. Believing the best defense was to deny the torso and head belonged to Laura, they insisted she was still alive but in hiding. When asked by his attorney, William T. Kendrick Jr., if he had killed Laura B. Sutton, Westlake adamantly denied it, saying, "No, I certainly did not."

Thirty-six hours after beginning their deliberation, the jury returned a verdict of guilty. They fixed Dr. Westlake's sentence at life in prison. There would have been a guilty verdict on the first ballot if not for one woman, a juror said. The woman declared she was a psychologist, and from her observations, she deduced Westlake was not the killer.

The District Attorney, Buron Fitts, sent Sheriff Traeger a letter commending the skills of everyone involved in the investigation. "The conviction of Dr. Frank P. Westlake for the murder of Laura Sutton, in the so-called torso murder case, deserves the highest commendation of this office."

Sheriff Traeger praised his deputies, stating that solving the torso murder case was a victory for modern scientific investigation.

Paroled on July 12, 1944, Dr. Westlake served only fourteen years in San Quentin.

8. Enigma Woman

Rarely does a woman receive the death penalty, and even more rarely is she executed. Death Penalty Information Center researchers noted the women who receive the death penalty often go against gender norms, which are societal expectations that define how individuals should behave based on their gender.

It is sad that compared to one hundred years ago, gender norms for women in the 21st Century appear to have changed little. We expect women to be polite, accommodating and nurturing. They should not be too aggressive, outspoken, or smart. Nellie May Madison was determined not to live a life hiding her light under a bushel.

Born in Red Rock, Montana in 1895 to Irish immigrants, Edward, and Catherine Mooney, Nellie lived with her older siblings, Mary, and Daniel on a 1600-acre ranch. Nellie's mother Catherine worked alongside her husband. Irish women in those days grew up with a distinct set of cultural expectations. Despite learning old country ways from her mother, Nellie had a rebellious streak all her own.

Nellie's impulsive nature became evident in 1908 when, at just 13 years old, she eloped with a 23-year-old ex-convict named Ralph Edward Brothers. Appalled, her parents had the marriage annulled.

Ralph was the first in a string of marital mistakes. In December 1911, Nellie married Roy Best. On April 1, 1914, in Boise, Idaho, she married Clarence Kennedy, a firefighter. Each of those marriages ended in divorce. A marriage to Wilbert Trask followed in 1919. The couple moved to Los Angeles in 1920 and divorced soon thereafter.

Nellie's marriage to a local Los Angeles attorney, William Brown, lasted five years before it, too, ended in divorce. Unlike her previous spouses, she and William remained friends. Following their divorce, Nellie moved to Palm Springs.

In spring 1933, Nellie met Eric Madison while they worked at the Village Inn Hotel in Palm Springs. Nellie worked as a manager there, while also holding a position at a sister resort in Lake Arrowhead. Eric worked as a cafeteria manager.

The Village Inn fired Eric for abusive behavior. Nellie ignored the clue to Eric's true nature and moved with him to Riverside. They married in Salt Lake City, Utah, in July. At least Nellie thought they were married. She did not know then that the marriage license was a fake and so was the minister. Knowing that Nellie was about to receive a one-thousand-dollar inheritance in Dillon, Montana, Eric faked the entire ceremony. Although her inheritance was not life-changing money, it equated to more than an average worker's annual salary in 1933. Once the check cleared, Nellie saw the real Eric. The marriage turned into a nightmare.

Eight months after their wedding, Nellie stood over Eric's prone body in their Burbank apartment clutching a still warm Colt revolver. She heard a knock at her door. She stepped into the hallway and joined her neighbors. All of them heard the gunshots and wondered where they originated. Nellie said she thought they came from downstairs. After a thorough discussion, all the tenants agreed the gunshots were most likely coming from the area where Warner Brothers studio was shooting the crime/comedy *Midnight Alibi*, starring Richard Barthelemess and Ann Dvorak.

Satisfied with their conclusion, everyone returned to their apartments—except Nellie. At 8:00 the next morning, Nellie's landlady, Belle Bradley, saw her leave. She had a package under her arm and drove away in Eric's coupe.

At 3:45 p.m. on March 25th, two people carrying a suitcase called on Mrs. Bradley and told her Nellie reserved an apartment for them. Mrs. Bradley knew nothing about a reservation. She went to the Madison's apartment and saw a "please do not disturb" sign on the door. She knocked anyway and, getting no answer, she used her passkey and found Eric.

Police arrived at the Madison apartment. Clad solely in undershorts, Eric's body lay on the floor, a pool of blood around him. All law enforcement agencies in the state were sent a Teletype message to detain Nellie. After an intense 24-hour search, they found Nellie at the ranch of her friend, Bob Cuddy. Sheriff's deputies Rowe and Killion drove 70 miles to the ranch and found Nellie in a clothes closet. They found a note in her purse stating, "If I die, I want all my personal belongings to be given to my sister, Mrs. Mary E. Hennenberry, who resides in Dillon, Montana. There are several items in storage in Palm Springs with Mr. Crandall that I would like to be sent to her." Inside the purse, there was a note and two receipts for two revolvers, one of which was purchased at a hardware store on Hollywood Boulevard. They also found a half-empty box of shells in her car.

Nellie's story hit the front page of every newspaper in Los Angeles, and around the country. Nellie's demeanor captured the attention of the public and the reporters. Calmly, she told investigators she would not make a statement without a lawyer present. People criticized her behavior. She defied expectations for a woman accused of murder. No tears. No hysteria.

Within two days of Eric's slaying, newspapers painted a picture of Nellie as a thrice-divorced cowgirl, handy with a pistol. A homicidal Annie Oakley. Being childless at 39-years-old and having multiple marriages, made her an anomaly. Her stoic attitude resulted in the nicknames, Sphinx Woman, and Enigma Woman.

Nellie declined to discuss Eric, but eagerly shared stories about her early life. Reporters characterized her denial to speak of the murder as defiant. Only Agness Underwood of the *Evening Post-Record* reported Nellie's plight with empathy. She said Nellie made a "broken-hearted" plea to her former husband, attorney William J. Brown, to come to the jail where they held her on suspicion of murder. In an interview, Underwood described Nellie as, "... a pathetic-looking woman. Her blue denim uniform was a poor fit. A while silk underskirt extended eight inches beneath the hem of the uniform. Her tan and white oxford shoes were soiled. Looking like a terror-stricken child who doesn't know which way to turn, Nellie asked Deputy Vada Sullivan, the woman in charge of the jail, if she could get some make-up. Later, a lipstick, rouge, and a box of powder arrived in her cell. Underwood supplied the cosmetics.

On March 29th, the D.A. charged Nellie with first degree murder. Underwood witnessed the proceeding. "Appearing on the verge of a breakdown, and lacking the cold, calm poise which has been hers since her arrest Monday night, Mrs. Nellie Madison, 39-year-old widow, today sat in a coroner's inquest and heard a jury of six men recommend that she be held "for further investigation into the homicidal slaying of Eric Madison."

The press vilified Nellie and beatified Eric. As a long-time friend of Eric's, Mrs. B. E. Cobb informed Deputy Sheriff Rowe that she had known the deceased for eight years prior to his death. Eric, according to Mrs. Cobb, disliked handling guns. "After we had been troubled by an intruder, we bought a gun and when Eric visited, I showed it to him and he said he didn't want to see it or handle it." Not only was Eric gun-averse, but he was also, "... as generous, kindly, and considerate a man as ever lived, and almost as irresponsible, and it was impossible to quarrel with him. I used to wig for him drinking too much and he would just smile at me."

Nellie maintained her innocence. What defense could her attorney conceivably mount? The rumor around the courthouse hinted at self-defense. Captain William Bright of the Sheriff's Department voiced his opinion. "I do not believe that the facts we have unearthed will uphold her in such a plea. It seems logical that this will be the defense."

Reporters and investigators spoke with apartment house resident Wilma Smith, who lived next to the Madison's. She said, "I was lying on my bed about two feet from my door when I first heard shots. I rolled to the floor, almost frightened to death, and looked through the keyhole down the corridor and then I heard four more shots accompanied by the most terrible screams I have ever heard."

Dr. A. F. Wagner, the autopsy surgeon, reported that someone shot Eric four times: once in the back, once in the back of the head, once in the right shoulder, and once in the right arm. He said someone fired two rounds from behind at close range.

On April 27th, in Judge Bowron's court, Nellie pleaded not guilty. As usual, in a case involving a woman, especially one as attractive as Nellie, her outfit drew as much attention as her plea. The *Los Angeles Times* reported, "The defendant appeared in court dressed in deep mourning. She wore a black dress and black hat. A pin set with green brilliants fixed to the left side of her blouse provided the only relief to the costume worn by Mrs. Madison."

Judge Bowron set her trial for May 24. She was expected to appear before Judge Fricke. Judge Fricke deserved his reputation as a hanging judge. A no-nonsense jurist, Fricke never hesitated to mete out the ultimate punishment. Nellie's defense attorney, Joseph Ryan, knew he faced a tough battle.

Following a postponement, Nellie's trial began on June 6. The prosecution sought the death penalty. Nellie could be the first woman hanged by the State of California. The jury heard testimony from various residents of the apartment building. Each witness account more damning than the one before. With a move worthy of a Hollywood crime drama, the State requested Judge Fricke's permission to introduce Eric's blood-soaked underwear and the murder bed as evidence. The defense objected strenuously. Hard-nosed Fricke denied the objection.

Following a short recess, six men brought in the heavy bed and set it up in front of the jury box and a few feet away from the defense table. A *Herald and Express* reporter described the exhibit, "Bullet-scarred, blankets pierced with sinister, powder-burned holes, its sheets stained crimson. The prosecution introduced the bed to support their theory that Madison "was shot while sleeping and that, wounded unto death, he tried to evade his killer, only to fall, lifeless, as more of the bullets found his body."

Deputy Sheriff W. L. Killion testified to the bed's condition when he saw it at the murder scene. He further testified to finding seven lipstick-stained cigarettes and a bottle of whiskey. The testimony helped to cement the perception of Nellie as a cold-blooded, gun-toting killer.

Ryan intended to argue self-defense. Eric's infidelity, and a letter found by investigators stating he married Nellie for her inheritance and planned to abandon her when the money ran out, gave his widow a perfect motive for murder.

Some people who knew Eric spoke of his violent side. Proving self-defense could be possible if Nellie feared him. Ryan dismissed Eric's violent tendencies, and focused instead on the bizarre, but creative, theory that the deceased person was not Eric due to some individuals' inability to recognize the body at the morgue. Ryan argued the shots, indeed, originated from the Warner Brothers lot.

The defense could not compete with Eric's bloody clothes and the bullet-ridden, blood-soaked bed. After deliberating for 30 hours, the jury of eight men and four women delivered a guilty verdict without a recommendation for leniency. The *Los Angeles Evening Post-Record* summed up the verdict, "Iron Woman to Die." The jury foreman, J. W. Grace, said a few of the jurors held out for life imprisonment, however, "There was never any doubt about her guilt."

Guards overheard Nellie in her cell said, "They gave me the works. They gave me the worst they could give me. I'm innocent and I'm confident of the outcome."

On July 5, 1934, Nellie stood in Judge Fricke's court as he pronounced the death sentence. "It is the judgement of this court that on the 24th day of September 1934, you shall be hanged by the neck until dead, and may God have mercy on your soul."

The jury and the public saw Nellie as the Iron Widow, Enigma Woman, and the Sphinx Woman. Her fellow county jail prisoners and the jail matrons saw another side. With tears in their eyes, jail trustees and three matrons watched as Nellie prepared to leave for the women's prison in Tehachapi. One matron said, "She's the sweetest woman who has ever been in this jail." Nellie said, "It's been a terrible ordeal. But I am confident that I'll win a new trial and be exonerated." Toward that end, in August, her attorneys filed an appeal in the state supreme court. The court granted an indefinite delay of her execution.

In May 1935, the state supreme court ruled Nellie's sentence would stand. The twelve jurors who convicted Nellie objected. They signed a petition, affirming that they did not intend for her to receive the death penalty. Despite their efforts, the petition was unsuccessful.

Nellie gained more advocates. Among them, Agness Underwood. Running a story on June 21, 1935, the *Los Angeles Post-Record*, published an article titled *"Nellie Madison Confession Puzzle."* In her confession, Nellie told a horrifying story of Eric's infidelity and violence. Upon returning to their apartment two days prior to the shooting, she discovered Eric in bed with a sixteen-year-old girl. She said, "I was so horrified that I was dazed. The girl screamed and said, 'Don't do anything to me, he forced me to come here!' She grabbed her clothing and ran from the room." Eric turned on Nellie. "Madison's face was livid, and he looked like a wild man—like an animal. He choked me into insensibility and struck me in the face. I was forced to write the following statement. "Dear Eric: I hope you forgive me for what I am going to do. I never loved you, otherwise I would have married you as you begged me to. I have been living with the man I am leaving with all the time I have been with you. Please forgive me for the wrong I have done you."

She said she bought a gun two days later. She and Eric fought. "He threw a knife at me. I remember hearing it whiz past my shoulder. I shut my eyes, shot twice, and screamed. He started to reach for another knife with his left hand, turning his back toward me. I knew he was clever at throwing knives, and again I shot several times blindly. I was shooting wild, with my eyes closed most of the time. I think I shot five times. It all happened in a few seconds. He put his arms over a chair and said, 'My God, don't let anyone in here.' I didn't think at the time he was seriously hurt." The district attorney, sheriff's department investigators, and even her attorney didn't believe Nellie's confession. Ryan said, "Until I hear it from the lips of Mrs. Madison, I will put little credence in the purported confession."

It was Governor Frank F. Merriam's decision to grant Nellie a retrial or sentence her to death. In September 1935, the Governor commuted her sentence to life in prison. Following the commutation, Underwood championed Nellie's case. She learned Eric not only beat Nellie but also beat his ex-wife. He had even forced his ex-wife to make a "confession" like the one he forced Nellie to write.

Domestic violence was not a topic for discussion in the 1930s. What occurred between husband and wife behind closed doors was a private matter. Underwood and others felt differently. Nellie gained public support. A letter-writing campaign to reduce her sentence began.

On March 27, 1943, nine years and three days after Eric's death, Nellie walked out of prison a free woman. Nellie gratefully acknowledged Underwood's role in her release. "I owe it all to you."

A few months after her release, Nellie settled in San Bernardino. She married a house painter, John Wagner.

On July 8, 1953, Nellie died of a stroke.

9. Rattlesnake Romeo

After locking the door to his barbershop at 522 West Eighth Street near Olive Street in downtown Los Angeles, Robert James called it a day in the early evening hours of August 5, 1935.

Bob moved to Los Angeles in the late 1920s, and although he may have glanced over his shoulder a time or two; he had never looked back. The city beckoned to people who sought a fresh start. He had four failed marriages—five if he counted the drunken union in New Orleans he had annulled.

Originally from Minnesota, twenty-seven-year-old Mary Busch came to Los Angeles from Champaign, Illinois in March 1935. She met Bob immediately following her arrival, when she answered an ad he placed in a local newspaper for a manicurist. The handsome red-haired barber and the vivacious blonde clicked. Mary got the job, and within a few months, she married the boss.

After closing his shop for the night, Bob and Mary planned to spend the evening with Jim Pemberton and his fiancée, Viola Lucek. At around two in the afternoon, Bob called Viola and informed her that Mary was not feeling well enough for a night out. She understood. She and Jim knew about Mary's pregnancy. Robert offered to pick up Jim, then swing by the telephone company for Viola so they could ride together.

At eight-fifteen, Bob, Viola, and Jim pulled into the driveway at the back of the house on Verdugo Road in La Canada. The house and yard were dark. Viola turned to the men. "Mary must be sick."

Bob took a few steps into the house and called out to Mary. "Honey, where are you? Are you all right? Your daddy's home."

Viola looked for Mary inside, while Bob and Jim each took a flashlight to scour the grounds. Following a shrub-lined path, Jim reached the edge of the fishpond. He almost stumbled over something. He directed his flashlight toward the ground. Mary, dressed in lounging pajamas, her upper body slumped over the rim of the pond, was face down in the water. Jim called for help. After lifting Mary's body from the pond, Bob and Jim placed her on the grass.

"Oh, I warned her, I warned her to be careful!" Bob sobbed. "She wasn't very well. She was expecting a baby. She had dizzy spells sometimes. But she loved to walk in the garden and stand looking into the pool, watching the goldfish. I was afraid that something would happen—that she would faint just like this."

Jim watched the color drain from Bob's face. Jim supported his friend's weight and walked him to the front porch, where Viola sat. When she heard what had happened, Viola put her arms around Bob to console him. "What will I do without Mary?" He wept, and then vomited on the grass.

Viola stayed with Bob, and Jim drove to the sheriff's La Crescenta substation. Entering the station, he was so agitated that it took a while for the deputy at the front desk to understand what was going on.

"Somebody hurt?" asks the deputy several times.

Finally, Jim choked out a single word – "Dead!"

After calming down, Jim informed the deputy, who was named Fletcher, that he wanted to report Mary's drowning. "We found her in the lily pond in the garden," he said. "We didn't know she was dead, of course, so we pulled her out. But when we saw she had gone, we just left her there at the edge of the pond. That was the right thing to do, wasn't it?"

Deputy Fletcher knew the men should not have disturbed Mary's body. Sending Deputies Jones and Toohey, he directed them to accompany Pemberton back to the James' home. When they found Bob on the front porch, he was weeping and incoherent. They circled around to the backyard.

In the darkness, the officers' flashlights illuminated only thin strips of ground. Still, they saw Mary well enough. She lay face up, with her head resting near the pond. Her pajamas were up past her knees. Deputy Toohey noted that her left leg was "swelled and very blue" and that "ants were walking all over the body."

In cases of a suspicious or unattended death, the sheriff's department protocol was to notify the homicide squad. Deputy A. L. Hutchison, an investigator, drove to the scene. After inspecting Mary's body, Hutchison detected several abrasions on her head, a bruise on her shoulder, and a cut on her left big toe. Just like Toohey, he observed that her left leg was extremely dark, "almost black from the ankle to the knee."

Detectives found a note on the kitchen table, signed by Mary, and addressed to her sister in Las Vegas. It read, "Dear Sis, just a line to let you know I am pretty sick. My leg is all swollen. Something bit me while watering the garden. Am having lots of bad luck. This is ol' blue Monday, but my daddy will be home early tonight, and he takes good care of me."

Dr. A. F. Wagner, a veteran autopsy surgeon, examined Mary's remains. His conclusion—death by drowning. As had Deputy Hutchinson, he found marks on Mary's left foot, which appeared to be insect bites.

They held a coroner's inquest following the autopsy. Bob held a handkerchief to his face and broke down on the witness stand. "What have I done to deserve such misfortune?" At the end of the inquiry, the jury concluded Mary Busch James had drowned, with acute cellulitis of her left leg as a contributing factor to her death. They ruled Mary's death might have been an accident, a suicide, or a homicide.

Bob left the La Canada home and stayed with Jim for a few weeks before moving into a small bungalow on South LaSalle Street with his 21-year-old niece, Lois Wright.

By mid-November, Bob battled Occidental Life Insurance Company, the issuers of Mary's policy. Despite Bob's request, the company declined to pay him $5,000, as well as an additional $5,000, in double indemnity. When they issued the policy, they claimed Bob and Mary were not legally married. The company went to court in to seek a cancellation.

Bob admitted he wanted to bed Mary, not wed her. Positive she would never consent to premarital sex; Bob gave a barroom companion ten dollars to perform a bogus marriage ceremony. Bob claimed he confessed the charade to Mary. They officially married on June 5 in Santa Ana. District Court Judge Leon R. Yankwich denied Bob's claim to Mary's life-insurance policy on April 3.

Following resolution of the insurance claim, police received an anonymous call. A woman claimed that her friend spent a night with Bob in a Hermosa Beach hotel a few days after Mary's death.

Investigators were eager to speak to Bob's playmate. They found Madge Reed, a stunning brunette, whom the Los Angeles Times described as a "spirited young governess." Madge told the investigators she met Bob on July 10, 1935, at the Italian Village, a popular café within walking distance of his shop.

Bob phoned Madge two days before Mary died. He visited her on August 11, less than a week after he appeared inconsolable in the hours following Mary's death. Bob told Madge he thought the police were trying to frame him. He said he would collect the life-insurance money so they could get married and move north.

Bob and Madge checked into a Hermosa Beach hotel, where he offered her $2,000. Not for sex, but for her future perjured testimony. She refused. Bob laughed it off. "Well, let's forget it," he said, "I was only kidding."

Jack Southard of the D.A.'s office, and Scott Littleton, of the sheriff's department, monitored Bob. The widower's frantic social schedule amazed them. Welcoming a new woman to his bungalow almost every night, Bob scarcely had time to shave.

Southard and Littleton got permission from District Attorney Buron Fitts to install hidden microphones. They listened from the bungalow next door. In early April 1936, the detectives and stenographer Dorothy Adams came together with the sole intention of nailing Bob.

One morning, during his turn at the recorder, Southard heard Bob leave his bed and go to Lois' room. As the conversation between the two began, Lois commented on the unkempt condition of their home. Bob said, "Oh, I had Violet here last night," and then recounted his date in graphic detail.

The exchange made Southard uncomfortable. He did not expect to hear that sort of chitchat between an uncle and his niece. It got quiet for a minute, then the wires thrummed with moans. Several times over the next few days, they heard every moment of the couple's lovemaking, often punctuated by a whip's crack. Uncle Bob had a kinky side.

On Sunday, April 19, they heard Bob go into Lois's room. They loosened the window screens and soaped the window frames to facilitate their silent entry. Several detectives gathered at the end of Lois' bed, staring at the writhing couple. Only when Southard declared, "You're under arrest," did Bob and Lois realize they had an audience. Lois, screaming, hastily pulled a sheet up to hide her nakedness. Unfazed, Bob pulled on his bathrobe. "Well, you've got me, but what of it?"

They took Bob to the adjoining apartment, and two teams of detectives questioned him for over forty-eight hours. Later, Bob complained, asserting mistreatment, but there was no tangible evidence supporting his allegation.

Relieved to have Bob in custody, police believed Mary's death was murder, but they needed a break. Charles Hope, a thirty-seven-year-old unemployed short-order cook, gave it to them. He was an ex-sailor with a massive drinking problem and a miniscule conscience. His friends called him Chuck.

One night, after consuming enough booze to loosen his tongue, Chuck wandered into the wine shop of his former boss, Sayles Sands. Sands lent a sympathetic ear while Chuck repeated over and over what an awful fix he was in. "Minna nawful spot," Chuck slurred. "Sawsful, s'terr'ble." He told Sands he helped a guy bump off his wife because she was going to have a baby, and the guy did not want kids.

Chuck related bits and pieces of a murder plot to monstrous to be believed. The man, he claimed, committed murder by using two venomous rattlesnakes named Lightning and Lethal. Sands assumed Chuck suffered from delirium tremens. Although he was skeptical, he read the local papers, seeking confirmation of Charles' story.

In April, Sands saw an interesting news article. Police arrested a man named Robert James for incest with his niece. His pregnant wife had tragically drowned in their fishpond the previous year. The report suggested police suspected unexplained elements in the woman's death. Sands told Chuck's story to an acquaintance, who repeated it to an attaché in the D.A.'s office. Hearing the story, detectives searched for Chuck.

Deputies Virgil Gray and Willard Killion looked for the murder weapons. They recalled a man named Joe Houtenbrink, known by his nickname, "Snake Joe." In his twenties, Snake Joe operated a rattlesnake farm in the Pasadena area. Snake Joe said, "Chuck Hope? Sure, I remember him," Snake Joe told Gray and Killion, "I sold him a couple of diamondback rattlers last August. Said he wanted to prove a bet to a friend of his." "What name?" asked Deputy Killion. "He didn't say. Anyway, this Hope fellow said he'd bet a guy a rattlesnake would kill a rabbit, and he wanted a couple of snakes to prove it. I sold him Lethal and Lightning." Houtenbrink took the deputies over to a pit and pointed at two snakes.

"The next day, I think it was, he brought 'em back and sold 'em to me at half price. He didn't say whether he'd won his bet, and that's all there was to it."

Deputies took Chuck into custody. He told the investigators he and Bob knew each other for about seven years. Whenever he was down on his luck, which was often, he could count on

Bob for a free haircut and a shave. Had Chuck been smarter, he would have known there is no such thing as a free ride. Chuck spilled everything he knew about Mary's death to the police, prompting an exhumation order.

Detectives investigated Bob's early life. Robert S. James was born Major Raymond Lisenba and he had had at least five wives. The detectives found all but one, Winona Wallace, alive. The third Mrs. James died in a bathtub in July 1932, three months after she married Bob in Los Angeles, and one month after she almost died in a suspicious auto accident. Detectives were concerned about the circumstances surrounding Winona's death. It sounded eerily like Mary's death.

On May 25, 1936, Bob sat at the defendant's table and smirked during jury selection. Lois, held in technical custody as a witness for the prosecution, waited nearby. As she waited, Lois sobbed. "I don't want to go through this dreadful ordeal," she cried. "I don't want to face all those people and have them looking at me while I have to tell those awful things to the jury."

The jury listened to Lois' testimony. "Ever since I was a little girl, he promised to take me to California and told me how pretty I was and how he would take me someday to Hollywood and get me in pictures." Bob returned to Birmingham on January 3, 1933, and found his niece had blossomed into a striking eighteen-year-old woman. They began an affair.

Revolted by what they heard; the jury found Bob guilty on all three counts of incest. One week later, he appeared in court for sentencing. The judged handed down consecutive sentences ranging from one to fifty years for each of the three counts. With Bob in jail, people felt safe to talk. Police and sheriff's investigators lifted the rock of his private life, and ugly secrets skittered into the daylight.

They exhumed Mary. Upon reexamination, the coroner ruled a rattlesnake made the bites on her left leg. Further testing of her blood revealed she would have died of the bites had she not drowned before the poison could take effect. Thanks to Chuck, investigators found additional evidence in an incinerator behind a real estate office at Beverly and Vermont. LAPD chemist Ray Pinker examined intact pieces of silk from Mary's nightgown.

Locked up in the Hall of Justice jail, officials tried to keep Bob and Chuck apart because Bob had threatened his co-conspirator. "If you plead guilty, I'll break your neck," he hisses at Chuck.

More terrified of hanging than of Bob's threats, Chuck talked. Operating under the felon's maxim, "first to talk, first to walk," he made a follow-up statement regarding his involvement in the murder. Angry that Chuck had outmaneuvered him, Bob confessed. To the investigator's chagrin, he substituted Chuck's name for his own in his account of Mary's excruciating death. Bob's confession was a tissue-thin pack of lies.

His confession fell on deaf ears, so Bob asked to change his plea to guilty to save himself from the noose. The D.A. refused. He told reporters Mary's murder was "the most cold-blooded in my entire experience." Chuck pleaded not guilty to the murder charge, but changed his plea to guilty days before their joint trial began.

Samuel Silverman, one of Bob's attorneys, devised a plan to save his client's life. He had Bob enter a plea of not guilty by reason of insanity, but the defense backfired. Several psychiatrists examined Bob and agreed he was legally sane. Bob's trial began on June 22 in Judge Charles Fricke's courtroom.

The courtroom filled with female thrill-seekers who wanted to see the red-haired barber and hear the lurid testimony.

Charles Hope took the stand on June 25 and 26. His statements appalled and titillated the spectators. After being sworn in, he explained his participation in the murder. "That fellow James has a hypnotic power over me," he said.

Chuck said on Sunday, August 4, 1935, he took his wife out for a drive to Bob's house. He parked his car a short distance down the road and asked his wife to wait. An intoxicated Bob met Chuck in the driveway. Chuck held the snakes, but Bob said, "You can't have them right now." "They're going to be busy soon."

The two men passed a bottle of false courage back and forth before Chuck noticed several dead chickens lying steps away on the floor of the garage. They looked freshly butchered. The rattlesnakes, Lightning and Lethal, were nearby in boxes custom-built to Bob's specifications.

Bob expected his accomplice to stick around. Chuck walked back to his car and told his wife to go home. For ten minutes, Chuck waited for Bob to return. On his return, Bob seemed agitated. "You're in this whole mess, too," he blurted out. "You're tied up as tight as I am ... People have seen you coming and going from here. Now you do just what I tell you."

Chuck picked up the box containing the two snakes and followed Bob. Once inside, Chuck saw Mary on her back, tied to a table in the breakfast nook. Bob had taped her eyes and mouth shut with wide strips of adhesive. She wore a pink silk nightdress.

Mary was told "Dr. Hope" would perform an abortion, which in those days was euphemistically called an "illegal operation." She could not see or scream, but she could hear. Did the snakes hiss when Bob asked Chuck to hand them over? Did Mary recognize the sound of their rattles? Bob insisted she have a few shots of whiskey to prepare herself for the procedure. Once helpless on the table, did Bob drop the pretense of the supposed abortion and discuss his murder plan with Chuck?

Bob lifted Mary's left leg so Chuck could put the box with the snakes on the breakfast nook seat. Without warning, Bob opened the cover of the snake box and plunged her left foot inside. Lethal and Lightning repeatedly struck Mary's foot and leg. Her body jerked up from the table as far as the restraints would allow. Bob pulled Mary's foot away and handed the box of snakes back to Chuck. "Take that back to the garage."

About twenty minutes later, Bob came out to the garage with a water glass full of whiskey. Chuck shook and paced the floor, careful not to let his eyes rest too long on the snakes or the chicken carcasses. Bob asked him why he was so nervous. "Give me your car keys," said Chuck. "I want to get out of here. I want to take those snakes back." They loaded Lethal and Lightning into Bob's car, then stuffed the dead chickens in a sack.

Chuck drove Bob's car back to Los Angeles to pick up his wife at a friend's home. Together, they returned the rattlers to Snake Joe. Chuck took his wife home later that night and then returned Bob's car to La Canada. He arrived around one thirty on Monday morning. "Where have you been?" asked Bob. "What have you done with the snakes?"

As they shared a bottle of booze, Chuck gave him a rundown of his evening. Bob bitterly complained about the snakes, saying they were no damned good. Mary was not even sick, and Bob had waited hours. "This thing has blown higher than a kite."

Chuck did not move from the garage until 4:00 a.m., when Bob came out to announce that Mary was dead. "You'll have to come in and help carry her out," he said. Chuck saw Mary's body lying in the hallway outside the bathroom door. Bob had changed her into pajamas and slippers. Her hair was still damp. Bob put his hands under his dead wife's arms while Chuck grabbed her by the ankles. Together they carried her to the backyard fishpond.

Chuck said he refused to help Bob stage the accidental drowning tableau. He dropped Mary's feet and went back to the car. Bob returned later with a bucket that held a red sweater, two Turkish towels, rope fragments, adhesive tape, and other evidence of the crime. He stashed the bucket in the trunk and they drove to the city to have breakfast.

Bob still did not understand why Chuck was so nervous. "I'm too smart for those officers," Bob said. He handed Chuck thirty dollars and told him to dispose of the bucket and the sack of dead fowl, then offered him advice. "Get out of town."

Over the fervid objections of defense attorneys, the court allowed Lightning and Lethal to be entered as evidence. They kept them in a large glass box within a few feet of the jury. The confined snakes rattled and struck at their glass cage. Everyone with a clear view watched in horror as a milky venom dripped slowly down the panes of glass.

Everyone who followed the trial witnessed a show more riveting than anything playing in local theaters. The thrills reached a new high when, on July 15, Lethal escaped. The killer snake slid like a streak of mercury under a bookcase and rattled. Pierce Artran, a Laguna Beach snake expert, jammed a wastebasket over the snake's coils, but failed to capture it. Lethal slithered off. Snake Joe Houtenbrink jerked a wire noose over the reptile's head and, with a toothless grin, held it aloft before the courtroom, eliciting screams from the hysterical observers.

On July 24, 1936, after deliberating for nine hours and seventeen minutes, the jury found Bob guilty of murder. Only Lois wept.

The jury sentenced Charles to life in Folsom Prison. They spared him the noose, and he had a chance for parole. "I had it coming," he confessed at his sentencing hearing on July 28. "I never should have let that killing go through."

On September 10, with no recommendation from the jury for leniency, Judge Fricke was bound by law to sentence Bob to death by hanging.

Bob spent the next four years in HOJJ (Hall of Justic Jail) awaiting the results of retrial arguments and appeals filed on his behalf. In March 1939, the California State Supreme Court denied Bob's request for a new trial and affirmed his death sentence. The red-haired barber's face sagged as he received the news that he would die on the gallows. With bravado, he told reporters, "I can take it. Just say Rattlesnake James is not afraid to die, boys."

On February 21, 1942, Robert "Rattlesnake" James came to the end of his fight to escape execution. Judge Fricke, who presided over the grotesque murder trial, fixed the date of execution for May 1, 1942.

Major Raymond Lisenba was arrogant and narcissistic. A compulsive liar who admitted the whole truth only one time in his life. He confessed to one of the Los Angeles missionaries who often visited him in jail he had been "a very wicked man." The gas chamber replaced the gallows in California in 1937; but Bob would hang because his crime occurred before gas chamber executions became legal.

San Quentin warden, Clinton Duffy, wished Bob luck. Bob's luck had abandoned him. Whoever prepared the rope for Bob's execution miscalculated the length. If the drop is incorrect, the condemned can literally lose their head, or they may slowly strangle. It took Bob ten minutes to die. Bob's hanging was the last to be carried out by the State of California.

10. The Death of Love

Born in Kentucky in 1905, Helen Wills learned the value of hard work when her parents, George, and Claudia, divorced in 1920. Claudia reclaimed her maiden name of Durst. She and her children, sixteen-year-old Richard, and fifteen-year-old Helen, lived together in Vanceburg, Kentucky. Each held a job to keep the family afloat. Claudia taught music at home. Richard worked in a button factory, and Helen worked in a cigar factory as a cutter.

Working in a cigar factory is no girl's dream job. Being an actress is a much more glamorous way to make a living. Helen, like most dreamers who came to Hollywood, never landed a movie role. No record of Helen's attempts at stardom exists. Maybe when she arrived in Los Angeles, she realized she needed to alter her expectations or return to Kentucky. While Helen did not leave her mark on Hollywood, she eventually took the lead role in a real life and death drama and made headlines from Los Angeles to New York.

Helen met Harry Love in 1929 or 1930, and they dated for a year before secretly marrying in Ensenada, Mexico, on May 3, 1936. Harry was a successful older man, born in Trinidad, Colorado, in 1890, and was fifteen years Helen's senior. As a young man, Harry worked as a shift boss for Montezuma Copper Company in Narcozari de Garcia, Sonora, Mexico, and as a car salesman in Morenci, Arizona. He was not a millionaire, but he had the means to retire in his early 40s. Newspapers referred to him as a retired capitalist.

Helen understood early in their relationship that Harry was a mamma's boy. At 46, he had never married, and he still lived at home with his mother, Cora. That would be a red flag for most women. Helen unwisely ignored it.

Harry and Cora not only lived together; they took cruises together. One was in the 1920s, years before Harry met Helen. In March 1936, Harry and Cora took a second cruise to Hawaii, aboard the S.S. Chiriqui. What man takes a cruise with his mother right before his marriage?

Harry would never have married Helen if she had not become pregnant. Did Harry wonder how he would explain marriage and child to Cora? After the newlyweds returned home, Helen expected Harry to break the news to Cora. He refused. He kept his new wife in an apartment less than a half mile from his mother's house. Close in proximity, but Helen may as well have been on the dark side of the moon. Harry stayed at Cora's most nights.

While they were dating, Harry threatened to kill Helen if she ever became pregnant. Birth control in the 1930s was unreliable at best, and Helen became pregnant despite Harry's dire warning. Helen may have believed marriage would change Harry's mind about children. When she gave Harry the news of his impending fatherhood, he reacted by pressuring her into having an abortion. Hiding a wife from his mother was doable. Hiding a child was not. Helen agreed to terminate her pregnancy. Many times, a back-alley abortion led to death, or sterilization; Helen was lucky. In September, she was well enough to travel. Harry sent her to New York for a couple of months to recuperate.

Helen acknowledged their problems but remained optimistic about their relationship. She believed the two of them would spend Christmas alone together. Harry had other plans. He thought it would be swell if he and Helen spent Christmas with Cora–who still did not know about the marriage. He always introduced Helen as a friend. Helen gamely went along, hoping Harry would reveal the truth to Cora. Following dinner, Harry and Cora bid adieu to Helen and left together for church to listen to Christmas carols and then go for a drive. Helen had a sink full of dirty dishes to keep her company.

On New Year's Eve, Helen and Harry had lunch in Chinatown. He promised to take her to the Norconian Resort Supreme in Riverside to usher in 1937. Harry reneged on his promise. He told Helen he would spend New Year's Eve with Cora at the Del Mar Club in Santa Monica. The two of them. Alone. Harry picked up Helen that evening but left her in his car in the parking lot of a building Cora owned on South Main Street. He gave explicit instructions to the parking attendants that only he was to take the car out.

Helen sat in the auto for hours, brooding. Finally, an attendant told her she might be more comfortable if she waited inside the building. She agreed, but before she left the car, she took the pistol Harry kept in the glove compartment and stashed it in her handbag.

Frustrated, hurt, and angry, Helen took a cab back to the apartment, where she stewed for a while before she decided on a plan. Fed up with living in the shadows and listening to Harry's empty promises, she grabbed her bag with the pistol, hailed a cab, and headed to the Del Mar Club to confront the Loves.

Helen entered the lobby of the Del Mar. She asked if the Love party had arrived. They told her no. She said she would wait.

A short time later, Harry came from the dining room. He must have instructed the staff to turn Helen away.

Harry walked over to Helen. She looked up at him and said, "Hello, darling." Harry asked her why she was there. She said she intended to spend New Year's Eve with him. Helen turned on her heel and strode into the dining room. She saw Cora, seated at a table for two. Cora turned white and snapped, "This is no place for you. You are not invited! See me tomorrow." Helen said, "Tomorrow will be too late," and went toward the exit. Harry walked next to her. "Have you a gun?" he asked. Helen replied, "You're a big man. Why should you be afraid of a gun?" But he was afraid. He screamed and ran for the door to the street. Helen drew the pistol and fired.

Harry fell on the steps. He got up and ran down the sidewalk screaming for help. Helen ran after him, firing until the weapon clicked on the empty chamber. By-standers carried Harry into the Del Mar and placed him on a couch. Helen sat next to him and watched him die. "I couldn't believe it was true. It seemed like something you see on the screen. I kept thinking of it as a motion picture death." Harry's death was genuine enough to get Helen arrested for murder.

Police arrested her at the Del Mar Club. She said, "His mother is to blame for all this." Cora may well have been a mean spirited, selfish, bitch and Harry may have been a weak, pathetic excuse of a man, but nowhere in the California State Penal Code does it mandate a death sentence for mama's boys or obnoxious mothers-in-law.. Even if it did, it would not have been Helen's job to deliver justice.

After they booked Helen into Santa Monica, they transferred her to the county jail, where they held her without bail. She was so distraught, she attempted to hang herself in her cell with her polka dot scarf. A sharp-eyed matron intervened.

After her failed suicide attempt, Helen spent the next few days crying to anyone who would listen that she wanted to see Harry again. Unbelievably, they gave her permission to view his body at the funeral home. A request made by a killer to view her victim's remains would never fly today.

When Helen arrived at the funeral home, her first question for the undertaker was whether Cora had come in. He said yes. Cora came in earlier and she was in deep shock. Helen stiffened for a moment and then she shouted, "Harry knows whose fault it was. He knows and I know..." Helen walked over to Harry's coffin and lifted the drape that covered it. She kissed him and said, "Darling, you are happier than me. You don't blame me, do you, darling? I love you, my dear. I love you. Your hands don't feel cold to me. You won't be lonely, darling. My heart will always be with you." Helen turned to the undertaker and made him promise to bury a tiny heart-shaped wreath of roses with Harry. "Do this for me. Please say you'll do this for me," she pleaded. Cora buried Harry at the Hollywood Cemetery.

At the inquest, Howard H. Spencer, Cora's brother-in-law, testified Harry was a single man. Helen whispered, "He lies." While the Coroner's jury deliberated, Helen sobbed out the story of her brief marriage to *Evening Herald and Express* reporter Agness Underwood. "We were beautiful in love. But Harry was so afraid of his mother. His affection for his mother and hers for him were strange and frightening. Ten months ago, Harry and I drove down into Mexico and in a little town below Ensenada, we were married. It was a mysterious trip because Harry wouldn't tell me where we were going and when we started, I didn't know he planned to be married."

Because of Cora, Harry refused to announce the marriage, and that stung. "It was agonizing to be so in love with a man and not have him with me," Helen said. "Three months after our wedding, I told Harry I was going to show his mother our marriage certificate. He took it from me and said he had placed it in a safe deposit box and that I would never see it again until we had a home of our own."

Helen entered an insanity plea. She insisted the weapon accidentally discharged. If you have ever handled a weapon, you know it takes about five to eight pounds of pressure to pull the trigger of the average handgun. Helen shot multiple times. Even if we give her the benefit of the doubt for the accidental discharge, it still doesn't explain the multiple shots she fired while chasing Harry. Helen's account was at odds with eyewitness testimony and with her original statement to the detectives in which she confessed to the crime.

The trial lasted several days. Finally, the jury of seven women and five men received instructions from Judge Frank M. Smith. During their deliberations, the foreman, Harry Joannes, reported one juror, Mary Plettner, a 45-year-old housewife, for being drunk. The judge found Plettner in contempt of court. Mary hid a bottle of booze in the women's bathroom, from which she took regular nips. Joannes said that Plettner was in no fit condition to continue. The Plettner issue did not shake Judge Smith's faith in the American jury system. However, he remarked he believed a juror in a case involving a homicide should remain sober during deliberations. Surely not an unrealistic expectation.

An alternate took Plettner's place, and one hour later, the jury found Helen guilty of second-degree murder. Helen stunned the courtroom by asking to waive her not guilty by reason of insanity plea. She said she was not crazy when she shot Harry. Her request delayed sentencing.

Back in county lock-up Helen bragged to her fellow inmates, "I can make myself die whenever I want to." To a jail matron, she said, "I can sit in this chair, or lie down on this bed and kill myself by strength of will power." Three days later, Helen lapsed into a coma, which appeared to be self-induced. Inmates made cracks about Helen, calling her the "sleeping beauty." Maybe they were jealous. If Helen regained consciousness, she would be svelte. She lost 10 lbs. during the first five days of unconsciousness. Nothing gets results like a diet of despair and guilt.

The jail physician, Dr. Benjamin Blank, examined Helen and declared, "She is suffering from a catatonic condition, a form of stupor brought on by extreme mental strain." A *TIME Magazine* article described her condition as, "a fit of sulks so profound that half a dozen solemn psychiatrists could not even agree on a name for it, variously calling it, hysterical fugue, split personality, dementia praecox, triumph of the subconscious, self-imposed hypnosis, voluntary stupor."

As a legal strategy, Helen's coma served her well. Legally, you cannot sentence a person while they are in an insensible state. Her condition put justice for Harry on hold.

Judge Smith expressed skepticism about Helen's coma. He was not alone. Jail matron, Vada Sullivan, said, "Mrs. Love is faking. She has been causing us considerable trouble since the jury returned the verdict that found her guilty of second-degree murder. She has been stubborn and despondent."

After several continuances, Judge Smith ordered the court to be held in the hospital so they could observe Helen's reactions. Doctors stuck her with pins and otherwise abused the comatose woman. She responded only when Dr. Samuel M. Marcus, the fifth psychiatrist to examine her, massaged her head and mentioned Harry's name. Helen muttered, "Please don't go away, Harry!" Helen became known as "the husk woman," and remained unconscious for one hundred fifty-eight hours.

Dr. Marcus was successful in awakening Helen by whispering in her ear. "Here I come—that Dr. Marcus again—I'm knocking, knocking at that door. Let me in now, Helen! Let me in, I say! I am going to get through that door, so open it! Wake up!"

Helen awakened. Film crews recorded everything as her attorney stood by. It took fifty-eight seconds for her to rise. When she did, she was terrified and begged for water. Dr. Marcus asked if she was happy to be back in the land of the living. She sobbed, "No, oh, I haven't done anything wrong! Let me go back!"

She felt better the next day. She said to the assembled newspaper reporters, "Don't I look beautiful this morning?" She awoke ravenously hungry. They fed her intravenously while she was out, but once she was upright, she ate chicken broth with rice, buttered toast and two glasses of milk.

When asked about rumors that she would lapse into another neurotic coma, Helen smiled enigmatically. She did her nails, wrote letters, read her fan mail, and expressed her disappointment at not being able to play golf with Jailer Clem Peoples. She was sure she could beat him because she had once driven a golf ball 240 yards. "Can you imagine that? And me a girl?"

The jury convicted Helen of second-degree murder and sentenced her to serve from seven years to life in prison. Helen left HOJJ (Hall of Justice Jail,) for Tehachapi dressed as though off to a fashionable tea. She wore a black crepe dress embroidered with silver flowers and a black cloth coat.

Around her shoulders she draped a silver fox fur. She wore a black straw hat which she bought in Paris. Black shoes, gloves, and purse completed her off-to-prison ensemble. Women dressed up for everything in those days, and a trip to prison was no exception. It paid to look your best.

Helen did well at Tehachapi. She won first place in a baking contest for her coconut cake. While Helen baked awarding winning cakes, Cora embarked on a scorched earth policy against her former daughter-in-law. She went to court to prove Harry and Helen had never legally married. She got an injunction barring Helen from representing herself as Harry's widow or using the name Love.

In an unrivaled act of optimism, Helen applied for parole in November 1938 under her maiden name but was told she would have to wait two years before applying again. Not unreasonable, given she shot a man to death a year earlier.

In 1940, the litigious Cora sued Rio Grande Oil Co., Richfield Oil Co., KNX and CBS for $1M in a libel suit. Cora claimed they defamed her character in a broadcast of the radio program "Calling All Cars" (an episode entitled The Silver Cord, which aired on January 13, 1939.) Without a record of her suit, we do not know if she won. Listen to the episode and decide for yourself if she had a legitimate complaint. The hyperbolic episode flattered no one.

Cora Love passed away in Riverside, California, on November 17, 1950, ten days following her 85th birthday.

Eventually released, records suggest Helen may have married two or three more times. As far as we know, Helen never killed another husband or lapsed into a self-induced coma.

Helen passed away in San Francisco, California on November 1, 2000, at 95.

11. J'Accuse

James Fagan Culver tramped his way across the country from Henderson, Kentucky, to Los Angeles, arriving on January 2, 1936. He dodged the "Bum Blockade," established by Los Angeles Police Department Chief James E. "Two-Gun" Davis. Supported by most Angelenos, the blockade turned back Dust Bowl refugees at the State border.

James got luckier than most newcomers. He saw an older man outside the Hayward Hotel at Sixth and Spring and "bummed him for a dime," so he could eat breakfast. Grateful, James thanked him and introduced himself as Henry Anderson. The man introduced himself as Sam. He asked James to return the following afternoon.

Each time James and Sam met, Sam gave the twenty-three-year-old drifter money to pay for a room and to eat. Sam treated James to a night on the town. They went to a nightclub and stayed until 6:30 a.m. As the friendship flourished, they visited almost every day until February 16, when police apprehended James for vagrancy. He spent five days in the Lincoln Heights jail. He hurried to see Sam after his release. Sam suggested James move into an apartment in the building next to his. He gave him enough to pay for a week.

Dumbfounded, James now believed everything he had heard about Los Angeles being the land of prosperity was true. When

Sam asked him for a favor, he agreed. He would not deny his benefactor. Sam told him to visit a gunsmith on Western Avenue and purchase a gun. He signed an alias to the register. Sam confided in James he wanted the gun to pull a prank on his wife, Ethel. He said he wanted to "give her a thrill," by having James pretend to rob them in their apartment.

On the evening of March 16, 1936, Sam told James he and Ethel would go out and not return until midnight. He gave James a skeleton key which would open the door to their apartment on Alvarado Street. Sam instructed James to wait in the closet. When they arrived home, James, wearing a mask, was to spring out of the closet, hold them at gunpoint and relieve them of their valuables. Sam handed James a pint of whiskey to get him in the mood.

Sam and Ethel went to the Coconut Grove at the Ambassador Hotel for dinner and cocktails. He suffered a stroke in 1928, which left him partially paralyzed in his legs, which still allowed him to occasionally pursue his career as a church organist. James sat in his apartment and finished the pint of whiskey. At the agreed upon time, James let himself into Sam's apartment. He waited in the closet, pulled the mask down over his face, and held the gun.

James heard Sam and Ethel enter the apartment. He stepped out of the closet wearing a black mask and holding a gun in his gloved hand. He said, "Be quiet and I won't hurt you. How much money have you got?" Ethel screamed.

Sam flipped the script, leaving James perplexed and scared. Sam pointed a gun at James. He fired. Three rounds hit the mark. Stunned, James instinctively pulled the trigger, killing Ethel, then stumbled into the hallway to escape.

Another tenant, a disabled war veteran, Harry E. Failer, heard the gunshots. Failer entered the hallway and bumped into James, who held his side and groaned. James carried his gun, covered with a black cloth. He started up the stairway leading to the roof, then crossed to the roof of the building next door. He went to his apartment. James sat in his room. Why did Sam shoot him? Thirty minutes later, police burst in. They followed James' blood trail to his door. James had two bullet wounds in his shoulder. He gave his name as Jack Lane and, at first, he insisted a pedestrian shot him as he stood on the roof of his building.

A police ballistics expert matched a bullet from James' shoulder to Sam's gun. In James' clothing ,Detective Thad Brown found the passkey that fitted Sam's door. Police Chemist Ray Pinker discovered two small pieces of cloth at the scene that matched James' shirt and necktie.

From his bed at the Receiving Hospital, James declared, "I didn't do it—I won't confess! You can hang a murder rap on me and I won't talk." Police had a lot of evidence against him. Only the murder gun remained missing. As police searched, City Councilman Darwin Tats commended them for their speedy capture of Ethel's killer. Tats said James had "come into the city on a boxcar ahead of the establishment of Los Angeles' border patrol." As far as Tats was concerned, James was the poster boy for the necessity of the blockade.

Early on the morning of March 18th, *Herald* reporter Agness Underwood interviewed Sam. She recalled him in her 1949 autobiography, *Newspaperwoman*. "He was verbose in his declarations of love for his wife, to whom he had been married sixteen years. Maybe I realized that marital affection, though it may persist to a golden wedding anniversary, becomes quieter." As she spoke to Sam, she picked up on inconsistencies in his behavior. She said, "There was something counterfeit in Whittaker's demeanor. I said nothing, for here was a man who made his living in church. Notwithstanding, I began to suspect him as a sanctimonious old scoundrel."

Detectives Ray Giese and Thad Brown escorted Sam to the General Hospital prison ward to identify James as Ethel's killer. Local reporters and photographers came to capture the dramatic moment. Aggie wanted the *Herald's* photo to stand out. She wanted an "I accuse picture of Whittaker pointing at the slayer."

Sam carried a cane, and Underwood believed it would make a dramatic pointer. Her photographer, Perry Fowler, set up the shot. Sam stood too far from James. Underwood tugged on Sam's arm and moved him to a cane's length from James. Satisfied, Underwood backed up.

Something astonishing happened. Underwood said, "As Whittaker raised his cane to the point, and the flashbulb clicked, I saw him deliberately wink—with his right eye, the farthest from the group behind the camera—at Culver." Underwood suspected a nervous tick, yet she told Detective Brown. "Thad," she said, "ask that kid why Whittaker winked at him. Don't let the kid wriggle out of it. Whittaker did wink at him." She said, "There's no mistake about it."

On March 19th, James testified at the coroner's inquest. Rather than maintain the fiction of his original statement, and after Thad Brown confronted him about Sam's wink, James got real. He told the jury he shot Ethel the previous Monday morning in a fake hold-up for which Sam promised to pay him $100. He then discovered Sam's full name was Samuel Whittaker. He was 60 years old and played the organ for churches and theaters. He told the jury Sam shot him in the elbow while he had his gun pointed at Ethel. The shot to his elbow led to an involuntary trigger pull. Sam shot him twice more.

Sam wept in the courtroom as he denied James' accusations. He admitted he knew James and gave him "about $35 or $40," because he "felt sorry for him." The grand jury indicted him and James for Ethel's murder.

Sam insured Ethel's life for $9,000 ($197,000 in current USD). With a double indemnity clause, his payout would be twice that amount. He set James up as the killer. Had his plan succeeded, he would not have wounded James, he would have killed him, leaving no one to refute his account of the crime.

James pleaded guilty to second-degree murder. The judge sentenced him to San Quentin. He served three years. Released in June 1939, he returned to Kentucky.

Sam got life in prison. Defiant at the news of his fate, Sam addressed the courtroom. "God may strike me dead before I get to my cell if I am guilty of this horrible crime."

On March 7, 1937, while standing in line waiting to be assigned a cell, Sam collapsed. He died in the prison hospital three days later.

12. Death by Dermatology

Eugene Hollander performed the first facelift in 1901 in Berlin, Germany on an elderly Polish aristocrat who wanted her cheeks and the corners of her mouth lifted. The surgery succeeded, and the patient was thrilled with the outcome. In 1907, Charles Miller of Chicago wrote the first textbook on facial cosmetic surgery, *The Correction of Featural Imperfections.*

The horrific injuries suffered by many soldiers in WWI led to improved cosmetic surgical procedures. Legitimate medical professionals and their patients benefitted from scientific advancements, but criminals also profited. The pressure to be young, vibrant, and beautiful is nothing new in Los Angeles.

As the movie industry grew, so did the demand for cosmetic enhancements. Movie stars were not the only ones who sought physical perfection. Average citizens wanted to look their best, and if that meant visiting a doctor for a nose job or chin implant, they were game.

Medical quacks have flocked to the city for over one hundred years. Some practitioners were sincere but deluded. Others were conniving and cynical, seeking only to separate gullible Angelenos from their cash.

Personal ads in local newspapers hyperbolized the wonders of modern medical science. The ads promised the successful removal of pimples, wrinkles, crow's feet, double chins, thin necks, and superfluous hair. One ad exclaimed, "*Premature Ugliness is a Crime which has its effect on coming generations.*"

Among the earliest practitioners of cosmetic procedures in Los Angeles were Professor David and Mme. Gertrude Steele. An advertisement for their services appeared in the *Los Angeles Times* on April 21, 1907.

According to the hype, the Steele's could perform a multitude of dermatological miracles, but in March 1908, Gertrude permanently disfigured a woman. Mrs. Du Bois read the Steele's advertisement, and it sounded wonderful. They guaranteed the harmless removal of wrinkles and spots from her face. They also claimed they could fill in hollows with a unique chemical substance—returning the full bloom of youth. The doctors promised a refund if their work was unsatisfactory. What did she have to lose?

A few days following her treatment, lumps formed on either side of Mrs. Du Bois' nose, on top of it, and on the left side of her neck. She struggled to lie down at night and suffered excruciating pain. The doctors told her they could not remove the lumps without risk. Arsenic, prescribed to cure the facial spots, scorched out the roots of her eyebrows.

The injured woman sued. She requested $1000 [$26,000 in current USD] in damages and the refund of her original payment of $100.

At the one-day hearing in Judge Hutton's court, Mrs. Du Bois, and the Steele's each presented their side of the case. Mrs. Du Bois spoke of the pain and suffering she endured. Mrs. Steele insisted Du Bois went home and "manipulated" her face to extort money from her. Judge Hutton ruled against the Steele's and they were required to pay Mrs. Du Bois the full amount of her suit. Mrs. Du Bois went home to her life of constant pain and deformation. The Steele's remained in business. Mrs. Steele continued to deliver lectures on "*How to Remain Young Forever.*"

In December 1919, Gertrude Steele killed her son-in-law George Blaha with an accidental overdose of chloroform. The faux physician used an anesthetic to numb the pain caused by removing freckles on his face with a mixture of chloroform and carbolic acid. The authorities revoked Gertrude's naturopath license because of the botched operation. Gertrude's lawyer won the case by arguing she had the right to perform the procedure because her license did not state what she could not do. Her license restored; she was back in business. The LAPD, the State Board of Medical Examiners, and the District Attorney were dissatisfied with the outcome in George's case. The death of another of Steele's patients prompted a more thorough investigation.

Mrs. Christina Leslie was sixty-seven-years-old and sought to restore a "youthful bloom" to her face. Instead of having her youth restored, Mrs. Leslie died of blood poisoning. For many weeks, only a few of Mrs. Leslie's closest friends knew the cause of her death. No one performed an autopsy. The circumstances of her demise reached the ears of Chief of Detectives George Home, who ordered an immediate investigation.

Scores of Gertrude Steele's patients stated that her lotions and scalpel had left them disfigured for life. They filed complaints with the State Board of Medical Examiners. She caused deformities and deaths because she was untrained in surgery. Her daughter, Mrs. Solomon, acted as her mother's assistant in all her operations. Mr. Steele was no longer part of the practice, although it is not clear what happened to him.

Solomon had no medical training either, although she had compassion for the victims of her mother's ineptness. She described the post-surgery horror Mrs. Leslie endured. "A few days after the operation, Mrs. Leslie came back. Infection had begun in the incisions. She remained at my mother's house for ten days and all that time I begged my mother to call in a physician. But she would not. She would take the top of my head off for butting in and all the time she was trying to treat Mrs. Leslie, who appealed more to the divine powers to help her rather that her own common sense."

Mrs. Emma Graham, a close friend of Christina's, arrived at the clinic. Aghast at her friend's condition, she removed her. Rather than take her to a hospital, they transferred Christina to Emma's home where, at least, she was under the care of a certified physician. Emma told investigators, "I learned that Mrs. Leslie was in a bad condition and that she was being kept at Mrs. Steele's house. I went to see her, I found her reclining on a window seat. Her face was in a terrible condition and her clothing was all bloody. I had her removed to my home." Emma said, "At my home, Mrs. Leslie grew worse each day. She told me Dr. Steele had performed the operation. Terrible abscesses appeared all over her and she complained of pains in her swollen hands."

Dr. James Reeve Dean, the physician who attended Mrs. Leslie for the last few weeks of her life, said, "I found two incisions had been made upon Mrs. Leslie's head. These incisions began at the hairline on the forehead and each extended downward and along the side of the face, in front of the ears and then curved back behind the ears. Upon Mrs. Leslie's neck, I found an ugly abscess, filled with infected matter, with a drain at the top of the abscess instead of at the bottom where it should have been. The incisions on the forehead had left ugly wounds. Pyemia had set in and had centered on one of the patient's hips and upon one of her hands, which was swollen to twice its normal size."

After three weeks of unbearable pain, Mrs. Leslie succumbed to blood poisoning. In Dr. Dean's opinion, the cause of Mrs. Leslie's death was infection because of the dirty conditions in the surgery in which Steele performed the facelift.

Investigators found the names of other people who had suffered at Steele's hands. Michael Goane, 19, died in the doctor's office while undergoing treatment for the removal of a scar from his cheek; Martin J. Colbert, from San Francisco, died from shock caused by a carbolic acid application and anesthetic treatment; Miss Pauline Hall, motion picture actress, won a judgement of $2500 against Steele for the mutilation of her face. Miss Hall testified in court that her lower lip was "frozen" and during the procedure, the doctor communed with the Universe and prayed for success.

Arthur Carew had an operation for a hump nose. Steele cut a piece from Carew's nose, cut strips of flesh from each temple, and severed an artery. She attempted to close the wound with her fingers and attempted to stop the flow of blood with prayer. Carew had a stroke of luck when someone took him to a hospital, and he survived his ordeal.

A former employee of Ambassador Beauty Parlors, Miss I. Vogel, claimed Steele botched her nose surgery and left her face disfigured.

The list of people maimed or killed by Steele seemed endless. One patient said the doctor requested all her patients sign a form absolving her from the after-effects of her operations. "I hereby certify that the operation and subsequent treatment to be performed upon me is at my own request and I hereby absolve Dr. G.D. Steele and Company from all responsibility from any results therefrom."

In her advertisements, Steele insisted, "The work is done conscientiously, with perfect technical skill in feature correcting under Divine Guidance. God does the healing."

In October 1924, they indicted Gertrude Steele for manslaughter in Christina Leslie's death. Detectives arrived to arrest Steele, but all they found was a For Rent sign on her property and her daughter, Mrs. Solomon, whom she had abandoned without a thought. Solomon said, "She left me penniless and ill and with all her own troubles to contend with; bill collectors, complaints from her patients and such. I am glad the investigation was made. It has taken a great burden of worry and sorrow from my mind. I feel so much better now." Solomon continues. "She is my mother, but I believe, as the authorities believe, that she should be stopped from continuing with this work, of which she has no scientific knowledge."

California revoked Steele's license to practice naturopathy. It no longer mattered. She had vanished.

In January 1925, someone reported seeing Steele in Oberhausen, Germany. California requested extradition, but it appears she never returned to the U.S. to face justice.

Gertrude Steele must have found herself at home in Germany during the mid-1920s.

By 1925, Adolf Hitler had begun his ascendancy to power.

PART III. TARNISHED TINSELTOWN

Perhaps the most shocking thing about Tarnished Tinseltown is the power wielded by studio bosses. It may surprise you to learn MGM had its own police force. Not rent-a-cops but sworn officers with powers identical to those of the Los Angeles Police Department, or the Los Angeles County Sheriff's Department. A private police force invites corruption.

The studios had fixers on their payroll. Fixers were shady characters, thugs, who dealt with situations the bought-and-paid-for cops could not handle. A suspicious death might demand a sanitized cover story. A boss had only to contact his fixers. Deployed with pockets stuffed with studio money for pay-offs, or weapons to break arms and legs, the fixers worked at the boss' pleasure.

13. The Prince of Whales

If you visited a local movie theater in September 1921 to see a comedy, Roscoe "Fatty" Arbuckle's films would be at the top of your list.

Making nine feature films over twenty-one months is exhausting. Arbuckle needed a break. He planned a road trip to San Francisco for Labor Day weekend. Traveling with him in his eye-catching $34,000.00 ($603,000 in current USD) Pierce-Arrow, were Lowell Sherman and Fred Fishman. Sherman, a dramatic actor, played the villain in films like *Way Down East*. Fishback, cast in minor roles, became Arbuckle's assistant director. The men left their wives at home. This trip was an extended boy's night out. The trio checked into rooms on the twelfth floor of the luxurious St. Francis Hotel. Actress Virginia Rappe, publicist Alfred Semancher, and actress Maude Delmont, who was a friend of Rappe's, stayed at the nearby Palace Hotel.

At the St. Francis, Fishman ran into a friend of his, Ira Fortlouis, who suggested they invite Rappe to Arbuckle's suite. Rappe received an invitation, and told Semancher and Delmont, "I'll go up there, and if the party is a bloomer, I'll be back in twenty minutes." Rappe arrived at the party suite around noon on September 5th. She dressed in an outfit of her own design, in jade and white, topped by a Panama hat.

The party had not begun, but alcohol already flowed. The Volstead Act became the law of the land on January 17, 1920. Prohibition failed to stop people from drinking, especially famous and wealthy people like Arbuckle.

Rappe thought Arbuckle's party had potential. Maybe she could make important Hollywood connections. Rappe phoned her friends and told them to come by. She spent the afternoon drinking gin blossoms, made with gin and orange juice, also Arbuckle's favorite cocktail. She chatted with the other guests and danced. At 3:00 p.m., she tried to get into the bathroom in room 1221, but Delmont and Sherman were there. She went to use the bathroom in room 1219. Arbuckle entered the room after her to change his clothes. He locked the door behind him.

Who were Arbuckle and Rappe before they met in San Francisco?

Arbuckle's life before stardom was hard. In 1888, his parents sold the family farm in Kansas and headed west, settling in Santa Ana, California. Before the family established themselves, Arbuckle's father, William, left for San Francisco and did not return. William's departure made his wife, Mary, the sole breadwinner. At five-years-old, Arbuckle picked up odd jobs running errands for local shopkeepers.

His older siblings left home when he was just a child. He spent a lot of his time alone, working, or running errands for his mother. He had no interest in school and did not attend beyond the second grade. His lack of interest may have had something to do with his size. A chubby kid, he earned the nickname "Fatty," further isolating him.

Arbuckle found joy in sneaking into local vaudeville shows. He loved to watch the actors, and he longed to escape into a character. He later said, "My stage career was thrust upon me in the twinkling of any eye."

The Bacon Stock Company arrived in Santa Ana in 1895. Bacon staged comedies and musical revues like, *Turned Up*. The revue had a minor role for a child, but the kid they cast was a no-show. Frank Bacon noticed eight-year-old Arbuckle. The part was for an African American. In those days, Caucasians filled such roles in blackface. Other actors applied the black makeup to Arbuckle's face. He wore short pants. They told him to go home and retrieve a pair of black stockings. Arbuckle did not want his mother to see him. They improvised and smeared black greasepaint on his legs and feet. He took the stage.

Beneath the lights, staring into the audience, Arbuckle was hooked. Bacon paid him fifty cents for three weeks' work. He told his mother he earned the money sweeping floors. Mary discovered what he actually did. Deeply religious, she objected at first. A young boy, working among degenerate actors—not her son. Arbuckle persuaded her he had found an honest way to make money. She relented. Arbuckle played children's roles for the traveling stock companies that stopped in Santa Ana for the next four years. Not only did he act, but he was also a hypnotist's assistant, a psychic, and performed in drag.

His lack of a formal education did not hinder him. He learned the skills he needed to make him a rich man in show business. On stage, Arbuckle blossomed. Off stage, he remained an introvert. He did not play sports, but he learned to swim and loved it. Despite his girth, Arbuckle had a physical grace about him. He moved like a dancer.

His life settled into a routine. Church on Sunday with Mary, where they sang in the choir, and acted whenever he got the opportunity. Life as he knew it ended with Mary's death at age 50 in 1899. Arbuckle stayed with a sister for a while before she sent him north to Watsonville to live with his father, who owned a hotel. Arbuckle had not seen his father in a long time.

He arrived in Watsonville and went to the hotel only to find William had sold it and moved away. He felt devastated. A desk clerk at the hotel took pity on him and let him stay. He earned his room and board by doing odd jobs. A singer at the hotel encouraged Arbuckle to perform. He had a lovely voice. He sang for tips, and he entered a talent contest at the local theater. The audience loved him and called for an encore. Not knowing what to do, he improvised. He danced, sang, and got his first laughs. Making an audience laugh was intoxicating.

Virginia Rappe's childhood was as difficult as Arbuckle's. Virginia Caroline Rapp grew up believing her mother was her sister. Such arrangements were common when a woman bore a child out-of-wedlock—especially in 1891. Her mother, Mabel, worked as a chorus girl and as a model. Police arrested her for passing bad checks in 1898. Mother and daughter moved to New York, where they stayed from 1900 to 1905. Mabel died before turning thirty. Virginia returned to Chicago.

Virginia, now an orphan, lived with an "aunt" and a "grandmother." Neither woman was likely a blood relation. At sixteen, Virginia changed her name to the more exotic-sounding Rappe (Rap-pay). She worked in department stores modeling and as a salesclerk. The ambitious girl and her friends, Gladys, and Ethel Sykes, pinky-swore never to accept a marriage proposal. They moved from Chicago to New York. She embarked on a career as a full-time model.

In 1913, an interview with the sought-after young model appeared in syndicated newspapers. She advised other young women, "Be original—every girl can be that." Virginia took her own advice. She traveled to Europe, and she made front page news on the return trip. A photo of Rappe and a friend accompanied the headline, *"Girls in Pink Bloomers Mystify Ship's Passengers."*

Rappe designed her own line of clothing, which took her to San Francisco. There, she made friends with millionaires. Her originality expressed itself in her designs. She considered herself an artist who worked in fashion. In 1915, when she designed a woman's tuxedo, newspapers featured the daring creation of the "*Tuxedo Girl.*" By her early twenties, she was a successful entrepreneur and a feminist.

Beginning with "*Paradise Garden*" in 1917, Rappe appeared in a total of four silent film productions. Despite the films, she did not meet Arbuckle until the San Francisco party, when something tragic happened. Only they knew the truth. The rest of us have speculated about it for over one hundred years and created a plausible scenario.

As far as we know, Rappe and Arbuckle entered room 1219 separately. About ten minutes elapsed before Arbuckle opened the door and announced to his guests Rappe was ill. A few of them entered the room and saw Rappe on a bed, writhing in agony and tearing at her clothes. Everyone assumed she was drunk.

The female guests undressed Rappe. A few male guests lifted her into a cold-water bath, an old-fashioned remedy for drunkenness and pain relief. Fishback carried her back to the bed, where she vomited. Arbuckle and Delmont then rubbed ice on Rappe's private parts. It was not a sexual act. Ice was another old-school remedy.

Arbuckle arranged for Rappe to have a private room. They transferred her to 1227 and phoned the hotel doctor. Just as the guests had done, the doctor assumed Rappe was drunk. He left, and a second hotel doctor arrived. A "Doctor Feel Good," he injected Rappe with morphine and gave her an enema. None of the guests wanted to take her to the hospital. Selfishly, they worried their reputations would suffer if the story went public.

The next day, September 6th, Arbuckle, Fishback, and Sherman took a steamship down the coast to Los Angeles. Arbuckle's Pierce-Arrow made the trip with them.

Rappe stayed in the hotel room, her condition worsened. They moved her six blocks to the Wakefield sanitarium. At 1:30 p.m. on the 9th, thirty-year-old Virginia Rappe died. The next day, at Rappe's autopsy, the surgeon discovered she died of a ruptured bladder and peritonitis. She may also have been pregnant. Two days after Rappe's death, Arbuckle was back in San Francisco accused of murder, facing a potential death sentence. Virginia once pinky-swore never to marry, but her oath did not include getting engaged. Her fiancé, movie promoter Henry Lehrman, with whom she had worked on one of her films, called Arbuckle a "Beast from the gutter, I would kill him." Following his arraignment for murder, the rumor mill churned out one vile accusation after another. Rappe fared no better. Newspapers ignored her accomplishments and defamed her daily. The dead cannot sue.

In a frenzy of tabloid journalism, newspapers claimed Arbuckle pushed Rappe onto a bed and threw himself on her, rupturing her bladder. They painted Rappe as a depraved starlet who died because of a botched abortion. When you sling as much mud as the newspapers did, some of it sticks. To this day, most of what people believe about Arbuckle and Rappe is untrue. Rappe was not a prostitute, and Arbuckle was not a killer.

The D.A. reduced the charges against Arbuckle from murder to manslaughter. After two hung juries, the third panel took six minutes to acquit him. They fined him for unlawful possession of alcohol and he paid a fine of $500. Not only did they find him not guilty, but they also issued a written apology. "Acquittal is not enough for Roscoe Arbuckle. We feel that a great injustice has been done to him ... there was not the slightest proof adduced to connect him in any way with the commission of a crime. He was manly throughout the case and told a straightforward story, which we all believe. We wish him success and hope that the American people will take the judgment of fourteen men and women that Roscoe Arbuckle is entirely innocent and free from all blame."

Still in its infancy, Hollywood moguls understood changes had to be made. Perception is everything, and members of the public saw the town as Sodom and Gomorrah West. The irony is, to some extent, the public was right. Arbuckle was Hollywood's first scapegoat. His was the first major scandal. Yet, two days after his second mistrial, another larger Hollywood scandal unfolded. The February 1, 1922, murder of director William Desmond Taylor. Taylor's murder added to people's impression of Hollywood as a den of iniquity.

The third jury acquitted him, but Arbuckle's career still suffered. Theaters banned his movies, his popularity waned. Fellow comedian Buston Keaton stood by him. Arbuckle found support among his fans, too.

On December 29, 1922, the *Los Angeles Times* printed a letter to the editor written by Robert Knox of San Louis Obispo. He wrote, "Confound it! Here, some idiots want to place a ban on films made by 'Fatty' Arbuckle." Knox made a case for understanding, not exile. He closed with, "The placing of the badge of public disapproval upon every effort of one we have damned is far from a Christ-like spirit and gains the world nothing but that damnable practice of the cad—to kick the chap you've just knocked down."

On the same day as Robert Knox's letter appeared, Reverend John Wood weighed in with a contrary point of view. He wrote, "If it be true that 'Mr. Arbuckle is not any worse than anyone else in motion pictures today,' all the more reason to forbid Arbuckle's return." He concluded, "Arbuckle must not come back. If necessary, every city in the land must be asked to prohibit the showing of films featuring Arbuckle."

Over the next decade, Arbuckle struggled. He and his wife, actress Minta Durfee, divorced. He married a second time in 1925 to Doris Deane. The marriage ended in divorce in 1929. His friends, Buster Keaton foremost among them, gave him work writing screenplays under a pseudonym, William Goodrich—sometimes, humorously, Will. B. Goode. He drank too much and worked too little.

In 1932, Arbuckle's life came together. He signed a contract with Warner Bros. to star in a film series under his own name; and on June 21, he married for a third time to Addie Oakley Dukes McPhail. At a celebratory dinner with friends on June 28, 1932, Arbuckle said, "This is the best day of my life."

Later that night, he suffered a heart attack and died in his sleep. Addie honored his wish to be cremated and have his ashes scattered in the Pacific Ocean.

They buried Virginia Rappe at the Hollywood Forever Cemetery. Her last love, Harold Lehrman, rests in a grave near hers.

14. Cut and Print!

Hollywood suffered a blow to its reputation when, in February 1922, two scandals vied for headlines. The first was Roscoe "Fatty" Arbuckle's second trial for manslaughter in the death of actress Virginia Rappe. Second, the mysterious murder of director William Desmond Taylor. Taken together, the two cases came close to destroying Hollywood.

Rumors of sex orgies, drugs, and deadly love triangles disgusted the legion of fans who idolized movie stars. People around the country devoured movie magazines, which put the stars on pedestals—American royalty. The stories coming out of Hollywood shook their faith. A wave of anti-Hollywood sentiment followed. People clamored to "Destroy Hollywood." Editorials expressed the sentiment that Taylor deserved what he got.

The fresh scandal began on February 1st, when Taylor's valet, Henry Peavy, arrived at the bungalow at 7:30 a.m., as he did every morning, to prepare breakfast for the director. He carried with him a bottle of milk of magnesia from a local drugstore. He picked up the newspaper from the front stoop and, using his own key, pushed on the door. What he saw stunned him. He shrieked so loud; the neighbors came running. Taylor's clothed body lay sprawled on the living room floor.

Lieutenant Ziegler, of the LAPD, arrived to find a doctor, whose name he never got, examining the body. In the doctor's opinion, Taylor died of natural causes. Perhaps heart failure. Police informed the coroner of the death. As they waited for the coroner, Charles Eyton, a friend of Taylor's, arrived. He went up to Taylor's bedroom and collected some of the dead man's private correspondence and many of his belongings.

Failure by police to secure the scene was a mistake. Lieutenant Ziegler said he did not stop Eyton because he knew him as a friend of Taylor's. According to Eyton, to avoid a scandal, he wanted to retrieve letters between Taylor and some of his married lovers.

Unconvinced his friend died of natural causes, Eyton went to the body and turned it over. Taylor had a bullet hole in his back. The bullet entered his left side and traveled upward, lodging near the base of the right side of his neck. Lieutenant Ziegler contacted headquarters. They dispatched the Flying Squad, so-called because of the speed of their response.

Rampant speculation about the murder began. Detectives brain-stormed theories. Maybe the killer was an intruder who came to rob Taylor. Taylor surprised him, so he panicked and pulled the trigger. Evidence supporting the robbery theory was the bullet hole in Taylor's coat did not correspond with the hole in his vest. That they did not match suggested he had raised his hands over his head. They dismissed the robbery theory when they found $78.00 cash ($1400.00 in current USD) in Taylor's pockets. He also wore a two-carat diamond ring and a platinum watch. Expensive items no robber would ignore.

Searching for clues to the motive and identity of the killer, detectives found an open checkbook and a half-completed income tax form on his desk. Taylor had $6,000.00 ($108k in current USD) in the bank. His combined assets amounted to $25,000.00 ($500k in current USD). Not much for a man with a reported annual income of $40,000.00 ($720k in current USD). In Taylor's bankbook, they found a check for $2500.00 ($45k in current USD) made out to cash, with the same amount deposited in his bank a few hours before his murder. Detectives suspected blackmail.

News of Taylor's death spread fast, and his friends came running. Nineteen-year-old actress Mary Miles Minter arrived in a state of hysteria. She said she had not seen him or visited with him lately. "He was one of my best friends. His death is a great shock to me. I cannot conceive of the character of a person who would voluntarily wrong him or cause his death. There is no personal or financial sacrifice that I would not make to bring the slayer to justice. In the toe of a riding boot, they found dozens of letters, written in code, and unsigned. They examined the letters and attributed them to Mary. She lied about her relationship with Taylor.

By modern standards, Mary's love letters are tame. "I'd go to my room and put on something scant and flowing; then I would lie on the couch and wait for you. I might fall asleep, for a fire makes me drowsy. Then I would awake and find two strong arms around me and two dear lips pressed to mine in a long, sweet kiss..."

Rejection may have driven her to murder. They were three decades apart in age. Maybe her attention flattered the older, sophisticated Taylor at first, but he often declined to see her, and he told friends he was too old for her. Detectives gathered the letters as evidence.

Mabel Normand, a famous comedic actress, was more of a match for Taylor, and he may have been in love with her, but she did not reciprocate. Other than his killer, she was the last person to see him alive. She said, "There was no affair of the heart between Taylor and myself. His feeling for me was that of an older man for a girl who admired him, and who was not afraid to show it." She and Taylor often swapped books and got together for conversations covering a myriad of topics. Mabel explains, "I was eager to glean a little knowledge from the vast storehouse which he possessed. He was a man who knew everything. Besides having the education and instinct of an artist, he was a deep student of science and philosophy as well." Detectives had only Mabel's word that she and Taylor were not romantically involved.

District Attorney Thomas Woolwine received an anonymous letter on the morning of February 3rd. He suspected a woman wrote it. It said if detectives went to Normand's apartment at Seventh and Vermont, they would find a .38 caliber revolver in the basement. The same caliber weapon used to murder Taylor. A search of Normand's basement turned up two .25 caliber revolvers. Neither of which was the murder weapon.

Her chauffeur, William Davis, supported Normand's account of her day. He drove her around town in the afternoon to do some shopping. They stopped at her bank, where she phoned home and found out Taylor had tried to reach her. He left a message that he had a good book for her and wanted her to stop by that evening. Normand went to Taylor's, but she had an early morning studio call the next day, so she did not stay long. Taylor walked her to her limo. She got in and, holding the book he loaned her on her lap, blew him a kiss.

Delving into Taylor's life, detectives discovered his name was William Cunningham Deane-Tanner. In Hollywood, nobody expected you to use your birth name; and if you played loose with the facts of your life before stardom, you were not alone. Taylor arrived in San Francisco in 1912, where he reinvented himself as William Desmond Taylor. The handsome Irishman appeared in his first film in 1913. He transitioned from acting to directing and made a name for himself in Hollywood. Later, in July 1918, he joined the Canadian Expeditionary Force Canteen Service. After leaving the military, he returned to Hollywood, and the Motion Picture Directors Association honored him at the Los Angeles Athletic Club on May 14, 1919.

Taylor directed famous actors like Wallace Reid, Mary Miles Minter, and Mary Pickford, known as America's Sweetheart.

Edward Sands, Taylor's former valet and cook, affected a cockney accent, worked under many aliases and, in 1921, he forged Taylor's names on checks and wrecked his boss' car. Sands even burglarized Taylor's home. Taylor was out of town when Sands committed the crimes. Did Sands find incriminating documents? Could he prove rumors about Taylor's suspected affairs with men? Did he confront Taylor and attempt to extort money from him? No one ever interviewed Sands. He vanished without a trace.

Taylor's valet and cook, Henry Peavey, discovered the body. Police are always suspicious of the first on the scene. The biggest red flags were Peavy's arrests for "social vagrancy" and being "lewd and dissolute." Interpret those charges to mean Peavy engaged in same-sex hook-ups. In the 1920s, homosexuality was illegal. Did he and Taylor have an illicit relationship?

Peavy discovered the body, but Normand was the last person to see Taylor alive. Some people thought Taylor dealt drugs to his Hollywood cronies, and he delivered them in hollowed out books. If the allegation was true, people wondered if Normand came for cocaine. Many thought she was addicted. Did she fight with Taylor, then kill him?

Charlotte Shelby, Minter's mother, reported to be the stage mother from hell, may have vied with her daughter for Taylor's affections. An alcoholic, Shelby suffered from clinical depression and was unstable.

One of the many lurid theories is a drug-dealing Taylor kept an unnamed young woman as a virtual sex-slave by rationing her supply of morphine. If Taylor dealt drugs, it seems likely he would have had more money in his bank account, on his person, or hidden in his home than the amount that was found. The sex-slave story has no merit and was typical of the sensational coverage spawned by the murder.

The police had a dizzying array of suspects, most of them with a viable motive. How would they ever make sense of it? They did not have to. Some investigators said higher ups advised them to "lay-off." Homicide detectives do no lay-off by choice.

George Cryer was mayor in name only. His former campaign manager, Kent Kane Parrot, pulled the strings. Parrot was a member of the "Combination," the city's shadow government, a group of gamblers and crooks who controlled brothels, speakeasies, bootlegging, bookmaking, and underground casinos. Parrot controlled the crooks.

Studio executives wielded power over politicians. Savvy politicians courted studio heads for campaign contributions. Every mayor who ran for office, and won, in the 1920s and 1930s had reform on his lips, but rarely in his heart. City Hall corruption festered. Pay-offs and dirty deals were the norm.

LAPD, going through a period of instability, had several chiefs in the early 1920s. None of them dared oppose the Combination.

The Arbuckle scandal, and then Taylor's murder, cost Hollywood millions of dollars in lost revenue because of the nation-wide backlash against the rumored depravity. The studios had to stop hemorrhaging cash, which they may have done by leveraging politicians to abandon the investigation.

In the decades since Taylor's murder, many people have claimed to have solved the case. Some theories are plausible—most are nonsense. Taylor's murder remains unsolved. All the people involved are long dead. What remains is an enduring Hollywood mystery, with an extraordinary cast of characters.

15. Ladies They Talk About

In April 1889, twenty-four-year-old John Mackaye departed Glasgow, Scotland, and arrived in Philadelphia, Pennsylvania. As did many immigrants, John made his way west, settling in Denver, Colorado. He met a local girl, Lella, eleven years his junior. The couple married on November 1, 1894. John and Lella welcomed their firstborn, Dorothy, on May 9, 1898. Eight years later, they had another girl they named Melba.

Dorothy yearned to act from an early age, and Lella supported her efforts. Dorothy's ambition meant frequent travelling to establish her career. In those days, actors were nomads. In 1910, Lella and Dorothy went to Vancouver so Dorothy could play the lead in *Mary Jane's Pa.* A local columnist F. Lewis, interviewed her. He had no experience interviewing children, so, in a condescending tone, he inquired, "Have you been on the stage long, Miss Dorothy?" In all seriousness, Dorothy responded, "Yes, indeed, ever and ever so long—oh, since I was five years old, indeed!" Lewis then asked, "You intend, then, to be a great star?" In a practiced move, the auburn tressed charmer tossed her long curls and answered with conviction, "Indeed. I am to be a great star! I will be! I *will* be! I work so hard—you have no idea! I think of it all the time, all the time!"

Dorothy had earlier expressed no interest in vaudeville, but by her early teens she was a regular on the circuit. In December 1920, she accepted the lead role in *Blue Eyes*, which required her to move to Los Angeles. Stage veteran, Ray Raymond, co-starred in the production. Never a classic stage beauty, Dorothy's auburn hair and her dark eyes made her unique, and reviewers felt her charisma. Handsome and in his early thirties, Ray and Dorothy connected. Ray dumped his wife, Flossie, who was also the partner in his act. He married Dorothy in 1923.

The *Los Angeles Times* interviewed Ray in November 1926. "Isn't Hollywood the great city? This place gets a person. In New York, I was the hard-boiled baby. I just received a settlement for Dorothy's and my services in a play which didn't even open. I went to court for that money and loved getting it. But since I've been here, I can't get excited fighting for my rights. Just give me enough money to keep going and I'll be happy."

Ray was equally effusive about his wife. "Dorothy ought to film well. She has a lot of little mannerisms, which are like no one else. She can steal almost any show." Movie work was not on the couple's radar. Dorothy had a lisp, which could have affected her career when talking films became popular in the late 1920s.

From the end of 1926 to April 1927, Dorothy appeared on stage at the Belasco Theater and took Los Angeles by storm. In November 1926, she accepted the lead in *The Son-Daughter*. The play opened on December 20th, and the capacity crowd honored Dorothy and the cast with a standing ovation.

In November 1926, Ray took a lead role in a production of *Castles in the Air* at the El Capitan. In a sweet moment during the play, his daughter with Dorothy, 4-year-old Valerie, made her stage debut. At the end of her performance, she blew her dad a kiss and charmed the audience out of their seats.

While Dorothy and Ray established themselves in the local theater, former child star Paul Kelly arrived in Hollywood to appear in a film. On October 12, 1926, the *Los Angeles Evening Post-Record* reported, "Paul Kelly, remembered for his role in *The New Klondike*, is spending a few days at the beach prior to starting his next production." The paper also lauded his performance as the "boob baseball player" in *Klondike*, said he "received compliments from all over the world." Dorothy and Paul met years earlier when they were child performers working in New York. Their experiences as child actors forged a bond between them. They resumed their friendship when Paul arrived in Hollywood. Ray expressed disapproval of Dorothy's time with Paul. She dismissed his concerns as petty jealousy.

Keeping secrets is challenging in Hollywood. Most of Dorothy's cast witnessed the couple's inappropriate behavior.

Paul's career was not on fire, as were Dorothy's and Ray's, but he got noticed and appeared to be on the cusp of success. Ray preferred to see their names in lights, not in print over a messy love triangle. Motivated as much by personal pride as fear of scandal, Ray finally demanded that Dorothy stop seeing Paul. She refused. To ease Ray's suspicions, Dorothy told him she never saw Paul on her own. She always brought a chaperone. Ray knew Dorothy's dubious chaperones, like her pal Helen Wilkinson, would lie for her.

On April 16, 1927, Dorothy and Helen, sat with Paul in his apartment drinking bootleg gin. After several cocktails, and with encouragement from Dorothy, Paul picked up the phone and called Ray.

Their conversation was acrimonious and conducted at high volume. Paul said, "I told him (Ray) that I had heard he was talking about me, and I wanted him to cut it out." Then, according to Paul, Ray responded, "You're damned right I have. I wish you were here now so I could give you what you deserve." Paul made a beeline for the Hollywood hills.

Ray opened the door to Paul and said, "I haven't eaten. I'm a wreck and I can't fight." Blinded by rage and fueled by booze, Paul punched Ray to the floor. Each time Ray got back on his feet, Paul knocked him down. The cuts on Ray's face were raw and bloody. Ray hit the floor and stayed down. Paul slammed the door on his way out.

Dorothy returned home at 9 p.m. She told Ray she spent the day running errands. He knew better. His condition worsened overnight.

Dorothy phoned the nearest physician, Dr. Walter Sullivan. He arrived to find Ray in excruciating pain, with bruises covering his body. He called an ambulance. Instead of accompanying Ray to the hospital, Dorothy went to Paul's apartment. She stopped by the hospital later but left again for Paul's. Alone, Ray succumbed to his injuries. Ray's death certificate, prepared by Dr. Sullivan, attributed his death to natural causes. With money Paul gave her, Dorothy paid Dr. Sullivan $500 for his services.

Local newshounds got wind of the fight and Ray's death. They called on the county coroner, Dr. Frank Nance and pestered him for details. Because Ray was obviously beaten to death, Dr. Sullivan or the hospital should have reported his demise to the coroner's office. Nance called the hospital demanding answers. They verified Ray's death and told him an undertaker had removed the body. Furious, Dr. Nance located Ray's body at a Hollywood mortuary. He claimed the corpse to perform an autopsy.

In a joint statement to the press, Dr. Nance and Chief Deputy Coroner MacDonald said, "It is horrible. It appears doctors and hospitals are deliberately 'neglecting' to report the cause of many deaths. God knows how many people have been murdered and buried already. Raymond's death has opened our eyes and we are going after doctors and hospitals from now on."

Dr. Nance disputed Dr. Sullivan's conclusion using the graphic and unemotional language of an autopsy. He summed up his findings for the press. "The cause of death was hypostatic pneumonia, following extensive subdural hemorrhage on right side of brain. Contributory, acute alcoholism."

The autopsy was damning. Not finished with Dorothy and Paul, Dr. Nance castigated them to reporters. "Fortifying himself with four or five drinks—probably to brace up his bully courage — Kelly deliberately went into Raymond's home to beat him. I am also informed that Mrs. Raymond was in Kelly's apartment when he left his home to go to her home to beat up Raymond and it is my belief that it was because of her influence that Kelly went to Raymond's for the sole purpose of attacking him." Dr. Nance's outrage prompted a police investigation and a grand jury inquiry into Ray's death.

On April 20th, Dorothy spoke to reporters. Sobbing, she said, "This will make a pauper of me and my baby. My career is already ruined. I will be looking for a job in the 5 and 10-cent store soon." She collapsed in hysterics in the courtroom as the grand jury probed the alleged "bare knuckle murder." Dorothy faced reporters, her thoughts only for herself. "It has been a terrible ordeal. Why, oh, why, do they have to do all this to me? I would be all right, but my nerves are shot to pieces. I hope I won't have to go through all this again very soon."

Dorothy's self-pity, and Paul's lack of remorse, was galling. Paul said he called Ray to demand an apology for bad-mouthing his relationship with Dorothy. He went to Ray's home "to give him the threshing that was coming to him." Then Paul shut up, except to profess his undying love for Dorothy.

The D.A. took Dr. Sullivan to task for his role in the suspected cover-up. In the District Attorney's office, Dorothy came to the doctor's defense. "I have absolute faith in Dr. Sullivan's statement that Ray's death was due to natural causes. He (Raymond) hadn't been well for some time and we had been afraid of a nervous breakdown." She continues, "Mr. Kelly, I have known for years. I knew him as a youngster in New York when he was first starting out. My feeling for him has always been, and is, I suppose, a sort of sisterly love." She dismissed any talk of a future marriage to Paul as a private joke. Nobody found it funny.

The grand jury indicted Paul for murder, and Dorothy and Dr. Sullivan as accomplices for concealing facts in the case. In anticipation of the enormous crowds expected to turn up, police erected a barricade. Crowds of colorful flappers filled the courtroom hoping to hear lurid details of an adulterous affair and the violence of the murder. One reporter observed, "The new type of audience has brought out the mirrors, powder puffs and lipsticks, and face dabbing is a popular courtroom occupation."

W. I. Gilbert, Paul's attorney, prepared his defense. His argument was simple. Ray did not die because of Paul's beating, rather he was in poor physical condition made worse by alcoholism.

District Attorney Asa Keyes sought the death penalty. Some observers thought it was a stretch for a case where a voluntary manslaughter or second-degree murder charge might be more appropriate.

Paul's trial was a hot ticket. Judge Charles Burnell tried to accommodate as many of the curiosity-seekers as possible. He said, "All spectators now in the courtroom must leave at the recess in the morning to make room for the hundreds of people awaiting in the corridors." Several women fainted in the mob that stormed the courtroom. The welfare of the crowd concerned the judge. "The health of members of that mob was impaired, and I intend to make the spectators alternate twice a day so that at least four sets of new faces will be in the spectators' chairs daily."

Dorothy's testimony made it clear her affair with Paul was of longer duration than anyone, especially Ray, suspected. Establishing the illicit relationship between Paul and Dorothy was essential for the prosecution. To the delight of the courtroom flappers, several of Paul's love notes to Dorothy were in evidence and read aloud in the packed courtroom.

W. I. Gibson went easy on Dorothy during questioning. He guided the brush as she painted an unflattering portrait of Ray. She spoke at length about his drinking. She claimed that on New Year's Eve 1926, Ray smacked her around and dragged her into a closet.

Ethel Lee, the family's housekeeper, who testified against Dorothy earlier in the trial, asked to be returned to the witness stand to rebut Dorothy's allegations against her. Dorothy said Ethel was drunk. Ethel said, "I haven't told half of it. I was not intoxicated that night and Dorothy knows it. She is trying to save Kelly at the cost of my reputation, and she can't get away with it."

Helen Wilkinson attempted to save her friends by professing her love for Paul. "I love Paul with all my heart; there is no man I have ever loved or ever will love as much. It would be more like it to say that I am the one who accepted and desired his attentions." With overwhelming evidence of the affair between Paul and Dorothy, they dismissed Helen's declaration as ludicrous.

The daily drama in Paul's trial shamed any screenwriter's scenario. Dorothy, clad head-to-toe in black with a heavy black veil covering her face, was a portrait of domestic despair.

W. I. Gilbert's 90-minute closing statement aimed to discredit the prosecution witnesses and propose that Ray's death resulted from medical problems and alcoholism.

Forest Murray, Deputy District Attorney, launched an attack on Dorothy, who he referred to as "a miserable little soul." He faced the jury and said, "They (Dorothy and Paul) were not satisfied with breaking up his home and his heart, but they had to dash his brains out."

The jury deliberated for two days. Eight jurors agreed Ray died from a subdural hemorrhage caused by violence. Two jurors favored acquittal. They debated a second-degree murder verdict but settled on manslaughter. Paul, his face ashen and his body trembling, stood before Judge Burnell to learn his fate. One to ten years in San Quentin.

The indictment against Dr. Sullivan and Dorothy charged, "Walter Sullivan and Dorothy Mackaye Raymond, well knowing Paul Kelly to have done the crime of murder, did willfully conceal from the magistrate and coroner the fact that the murder had been committed." They indicted Dorothy and Dr. Sullivan together, but attorney Thomas White believed a separate trial would better serve his client. The judge agreed.

Eight women and four men heard the case against Dorothy. Ethel Lee took the stand. She recalled for the jury a telephone call from Dr. Sullivan. She said the doctor told her to tell Dorothy to hurry to his office because he could not wait. "Newspaper reporters are after me," he said. "It was a police case and I will have to report it."

Paul's testimony surprised no one. He attempted to shield Dorothy. He admitted she "bawled me out" for the fight but did not say a word about her divorcing Ray.

The defense and the prosecution delivered closing arguments on June 28. George Kemp, the deputy district attorney, compared Dorothy to Cleopatra. He said she "wrecked the lives of three men," Ray, Paul, and Dr. Sullivan. In his closing, Dorothy's attorney, Jerry Giesler, appealed to the jury not to be swayed by her adultery. He emphasized the defense theory that Ray died from a subdural hemorrhage suffered in a fall from bed. If he did not die from Paul's beating, then there could be no cover-up.

The jurors spent three hours and fifteen minutes before arriving at a guilty verdict. On hearing the verdict, Dorothy fell into the arms of her friend Helen and cried.

As Paul started his trip to San Quentin to begin his sentence of one to ten years, Judge Burnell sentenced Dorothy to from one to three years. She stayed in the county jail, awaiting the outcome of her appeals.

Paul arrived at San Quentin and they assigned him to work in the jute mill for what he referred to as a "ten-year engagement."

Dr. Sullivan's luck held. On October 29th, Deputy District Attorney McKay notified the court that the evidence was insufficient to guarantee a conviction. Sullivan walked.

By the end of February 1928, Dorothy had exhausted her appeals. Wearing a dark blue dress, carrying a red coat, and wearing a black hat trimmed in red, she and a matron from the Sheriff's Department boarded a northbound train for the women's wing at San Quentin.

Dorothy addressed the reporters at the train station. "No more pictures. I've had enough of publicity and I'd like to take this last journey without advertising the fact of my destination." Dorothy, accompanied by law enforcement officials and newspaper reporters, took the ferry from Richmond to her destination. She smiled and waved to the small crowd who saw her off, Dorothy called out, "Leave 'em smiling." She was in character as a plucky gal, determined to smile through her undeserved fate.

As prisoner number 44960, Dorothy arrived on March 1st in a group of women about to begin sentences for everything from forgery to manslaughter and murder.

Dorothy adapted well to her new role. On December 27, 1929, the *Los Angeles Times* caught up with her in what they called a "vaudeville show originated and presented by women inmates of San Quentin prison." The article reported, "a flapper bandit provided the music; Clara Phillips, hammer slayer, danced and tooted a saxophone; and a forger in a pink dress attempted a recitation." Dorothy acted as the schoolmistress in a country-school act.

After serving ten months, Dorothy left prison for Los Angeles. From the office of her attorney, Roger Marchetti, she revealed her plan to resume her theatrical career. "There will be no motion pictures included in my plans. I have had many offers, but most of them have had to do with exploiting my misfortune. These I never will consider. I have studied hard and now feel better equipped to pursue my career. All offers, however, will have to be on a legitimate basis of my talent and the role in which I am cast must be conventional."

Dorothy reflected on her prison experience for reporters. "No, prison didn't give me a cynical outlook upon life. Indeed, on the contrary, it really opened my eyes." She said, "I had considerable leisure while in prison and devoted my time to the study of my work. I organized the play for the annual prison High Jinks last December and found that I can still carry on my work, even better than I did before my trouble." According to her, Paul was in her past.

Picked up by a private chauffeured car, Paul left San Quentin after serving twenty-five months. He won parole for "excellent behavior" and said he intended to resume his acting career. "I'm headed straight for the comeback trail. I've got a job with the New Century Play Company in New York and I'm going to hit it hard."

Paul traveled to New York, where he found the pay for ex-con actors to be subpar. His talent was not in question; rather, it was a condition of his California parole. He could not accept a salary of over thirty dollars per week. Dorothy appeared on stage in Los Angeles in a production of *A Cup of Sugar.*

Rarely do lovers who commit a crime together make it past the courtroom. They turn on each other, hurl epithets and whatever love they shared burns to ashes.

By early January 1931, rumors circulated that not only had the pair reunited, but they also planned to wed. In the *New York Daily News,* a photo of Dorothy appeared with the caption, "Love Conquers All." The article romanticized the couple's lurid history. "Dorothy Mackaye, actress, will marry Paul Kelly, actor. Simple statement, that. But back of it lies the story of an amazing love. For Paul Kelly killed the husband of

Dot. Both Dot and Paul served prison terms. Now free, they'll marry when Kelly's parole expires." Paul and Dorothy married on February 11th in a friend's New York City apartment.

Dorothy quit acting but continued to write. She wrote a play *Women in Prison,* aka "*Gangstress,*" with co-author, Carleton Miles. The play, inspired by her time in prison, became the screenplay for the 1933 pre-code film "*Ladies They Talk About,*" starring Barbara Stanwyck.

Dorothy and Paul bought a ranch in the San Fernando Valley and named it KellyMac. Paul adopted Dorothy and Ray's daughter, Valerie. They retrieved her from the home of her maternal grandparents in Denver, Colorado where she lived while Dorothy was in prison. They renamed her Mimi. It is surreal that the individual she once denounced to the press as a "bad man" for fatally attacking her father became her step-father.

On January 4, 1940, as she returned to the ranch after making funeral arrangements for her father, Dorothy was in a car accident. She said encountered a fog bank and slowed down. She saw headlights of an approaching car. As she swerved to avoid it, she hit a soft shoulder. Her car overturned. Witnesses said she climbed out of the car and insisted on going to the ranch.

The day following the accident; she complained of abdominal pain. Her doctor, Edward Ehret, ordered her removed to the Monte Sano Hospital and Sanitarium for x-rays and observation.

On January 5th, Dorothy appeared well, but then she collapsed and died. Dr. Ehret reported the case to the coroner's office, and they removed her body to the County Morgue for autopsy.

Dorothy died of a ruptured bladder. The Christian Science funeral services were closed to all but family and a few intimate friends. They buried her cremains in an unmarked grave in Oakwood Memorial Park in Chatsworth.

Despite the life they built together after prison, neither Dorothy nor Paul ever escaped the shadow of Ray's death.

Dorothy is forever a lady they talk about.

16. Hooray for Hollywood

Founded in 1921, Christie-Nestor Motion Picture Company, at the corner of Sunset Boulevard and Gower Street, was Hollywood's first movie studio. David Horsley, the studio's producer, cranked out three complete motion pictures each week. The hectic schedule scarcely kept up with the public's demand for the new medium.

Over the next several years, movie makers from the east coast recognized the advantages of setting up shop in Hollywood. The Los Angeles Chamber of Commerce praised the region's natural beauty, enhanced by year-round sunshine. Sunshine made a difference before indoor studios and artificial lighting. Locals provided cheap labor and extras for crowd scenes. A decade later, the sleepy burg of 5,000 residents became a thriving city of 35,000—most of them in the movie business.

With the studios, and the busloads of dreamers, came the first fan magazines. Magazines such as *Motion Picture World* and *Photoplay* played a part in creating the culture of celebrity by showcasing the lives of famous people. People bought movie magazines for the gossip, fashion, and lifestyle—harmless fun. The magazines fueled the dreams of those who longed to be famous. Few made the cut. Filled with photographs showing stars decked-out in diamond jewelry, standing on the grounds of their Beverly Hills mansion, or seated behind the wheel of an exotic car, the magazines gave would-be extortionists, blackmailers, kidnappers, and robbers ideas of their own.

On January 20, 1929, while making the rounds of local studios, Fern Setril met world renowned director D. W. Griffith. She was thrilled when he tells her she was a "girl of unusual type of beauty, unspoiled," and that she had "remarkable features that would film well in motion pictures." Despite Griffith's apparent interest, Fern's movie career did not take off. Not until 1931 did her name become associated with his.

On February 24, 1931, newspapers broke the story that Fern sued Griffith for $601,000 (equivalent to $12.3M in current USD). The suit specified $500,000 for actual damages, $100,000 for punitive damages and $1,000 for medical treatment. Fern claimed on June 25, 1930, she met with Griffith in his apartment to discuss her role as Ann Rutledge in his upcoming film, *Abraham Lincoln*. According to Fern, they did not run lines. Griffith plied her with champagne and raped her.

From his room in the Astor Hotel in New York, Griffith responded to the charges. He called them absurd, and without foundation. He said, "I am astounded at the charges made against me. The whole story is untrue. The name Fern Setril means nothing to me. I don't know anyone by that name." Griffith vowed to "fight these charges to the limit."

Fern's attorneys, Josef Widoff, and J. B. Mandel, denied requests from reporters for an interview with their client. Even without her cooperation, reporters dug up enough information from the lawsuit filing to keep the story above the fold on the front page. They learned that before she moved to Hollywood to pursue an acting career, Fern lived in Wasco, California. Most of the time, she worked as an extra, acting in only a few minor bit parts under the surnames Barry or Darry.

Although Fern filed a civil lawsuit, District Attorney Buron Fitts had no choice but to begin a criminal investigation into the alleged rape. He assigned his chief investigator, Blayney Matthews, to the case. Matthews found out for two weeks following the alleged attack, Mrs. C. E. Taylor and her son, Earl W. Taylor, nursed Fern back to health in their Pasadena home. Mrs. Taylor told reporters, "It was another Arbuckle case. The girl nearly died here in my apartment." Mrs. Taylor said she first met Fern when Earl brought her home. "The girl was penniless," she commented. "If my son hadn't brought her in, she would have been left on the street." Mrs. Taylor refused to name the Pasadena physicians who attended Fern. According to Mrs. Taylor, she and Earl took Fern to a hospital where doctors operated on her for an unspecified condition.

As often happens in breaking news, the rapid twists and turns had reporters struggling to stay on top of the story. This led to conflicting reports. Newspapers usually hit the street once a day unless they printed a special edition, which meant the news cycle was not in real time. Within a few days of the first report, Griffith suggested to reporters he might be the victim of an extortion plot cooked up by Fern and Earl. D. A. Buron Fitts declared, "If the facts develop sufficiently to justify a prosecution on the charge of a conspiracy to commit the crime of extortion or attempted extortion, this office will prosecute."

While Griffith remained in New York, Matthews delved further into Fern's background. So did reporters. As they did, their coverage shifted in tone. They did not find enough to pillory Fern, but they could build the framework.

Marguerite and Verona Shearer, Fern's former Hollywood roommates, told Matthews Fern filed for a divorce from someone named Frank in August 1930. Fern was married during the time she visited Griffith's apartment. Fern made it sound like she visited Griffith only twice before he pounced, but that conflicted with what the Shearer sisters told Matthews. Verona heard Fern talk about a friend named Lou, which was Fern's name for Griffith.

Marguerite and Verona were a wealth of information. They tell Matthews that several times over the summer of 1930, they heard Earl say he, "was going to see to it that Fern sued D. W. Griffith to the limit." Fern's story unraveled with each new report. One of the most egregious holes in her account was her contention Griffith offered her the role of Ann Rutledge in *Abraham Lincoln.* Griffith finished shooting the film in May, with Una Merkel in the role, a month before the alleged attack. The film debuted in New York on August 24.

The discrepancy in her account shocked Fern's attorneys. They rushed to file an amended complaint, deleting all references to the movie. Another problem for Fern was Earl's involvement. He contacted local newspapers to "buy this little girl's story." Over the telephone, he told reporters, "... this little girl is just out of the convent."

Earl struggled to convince jaded reporters of Fern's story. It would have been tougher still if anyone had thought to check newspapers from a few years back. If they had, they would have found out a love triangle, in which Fern played a pivotal role, was front-page news for a nanosecond in 1926.

In early May 1926, Setril's photo appeared in the *Los Angeles Times* and the *Illustrated Daily News.* Lillian Schmid said her husband, Frank, betrayed her with her best friend, Fern. Lillian told the judge in her divorce case that Fern had lived with her and Frank for five months. After Fern left, Lilian found a letter from her in Frank's pocket. She confronted him with it. At first, he played dumb. Later, he admitted he loved

Fern and was going away with her. Lillian said, "He left me that day."

Lillian's attorney, Frank C. Dunham, read aloud a portion of Fern's letter to the court. "By the time this reaches you, I shall be gone. As I know in my heart, it is the only fair thing to do. I just can't go on living the way I am. There is no use hiding the fact any longer—I love you dearly. I fought hard to hide my love because it is not fair to Lillian. She has been a good wife to you, Frank, and she loves you. I am not the kind of a woman who would come between you and Lil, so I am going to leave."

Lillian got her divorce, and Fern and Frank married in Pasadena on May 15, 1927. Fern got lucky. Reporters never picked up on her earlier peccadillo, but she was not out of the woods. Reporters located the divorce records in the county clerk's office.

Fern left Frank in August 1929 and returned to her mother's home in Wasco. Frank followed her there and, at gunpoint, forced her to return to Los Angeles with him. In the divorce, she charged Frank with cruelty and won an interlocutory degree on October 16, 1930. That was not the end of her marital woes. Frank appeared in court to have the decree set aside. He accused Fern of misconduct with one "John Doe." Frank said Doe gave Fern money and expensive gifts. He also said she bragged to her friends about being in love with Doe. Frank failed to appear on January 7, 1931. Fern won her decree by default.

Fern replaced her troublesome husband with a problematic boyfriend, Earl Taylor. In August 1928, Judge Fletcher Bowron (future mayor of Los Angeles) sentenced Taylor to San Quentin for embezzlement. Taylor embezzled two $5,000 promissory notes belonging to Lynn. C. Booze. Besides swindling Booze, he stole from several Compton and Long Beach businessmen. Taylor applied for probation, but the judge denied him. After a year in San Quentin, they paroled him on October 29, 1929—Black Tuesday, the day the stock market crashed and plunged the U.S. into a decade-long depression.

Fern and Taylor likely met when he worked at one of the local movie studios following his parole. Did Fern meet Griffith in 1929? Maybe, but there is an equal chance that she and Taylor fabricated the story. Blayney Matthews began his investigation, and the couple's scheme unraveled. At the end of February, he questioned Fern and Taylor separately. On the advice of her attorney, Jerry Giesler, Fern declined to make a statement. Taylor should have followed Fern's lead. Instead, he spoke at length and dug himself a deep hole. Matthews determined Taylor was the "mastermind" behind the extortion plot.

A movie technical assistant, Frank Leyva, told Matthews that Fern and Taylor tried to extort him, too. In October 1930, Fern threated to charge him with rape if he didn't pay. He went to the police instead.

While Matthews questioned Taylor, James Lewis, assistant State parole officer, positively identified Taylor as the man sentenced to San Quentin in August 1928. Lewis said, "Taylor has been on the border line of trouble several times since he was paroled. I warned him once before not to be too friendly with Mrs. Setril. That was before she was divorced from her husband, who complained to me of Taylor's attentions to his wife."

Lewis had news for Taylor. His parole would not expire until August 18, 1931. A violation would return him to prison. Fitts held Taylor in technical custody until they could settle the

Griffith case. Fern sued Griffith, but never had him served. The case fizzled. So, too, did the criminal investigation into the alleged sexual assault.

In custody, the strain got to Taylor, who threatened to commit suicide. "If they don't do something to break this strain pretty soon, I'll jump out of a window." Fern pleaded with him to hang on, "for my sake." Taylor fought in vain. They returned him to prison. Fern broke her vow to wait. In the summer of 1932, she announced her imminent marriage to a man she did not name. No record of the marriage appeared in local newspapers. Fern disappeared.

Following his parole, Earl Taylor re-invented himself as a Hollywood writer's agent. In 1935, two women accused him of fraud. A jury acquitted him.

In June 1939, under the sensational headline, *L.A. Gunman Runs Amok in Hotel*, the *Daily News* reported a retired furrier, Frank Setril, took potshots at lights and windows at the Vanderbilt Hotel. Frank locked himself in his third-floor room. Police flushed him out with tear gas. No one could explain his behavior.

D. W. Griffith's first full talking film, *Abraham Lincoln*, fizzled at the box-office. He followed it up in 1931 with *The Struggle*, which also failed. He never made another movie.

17. The It Girl and the Secretary

A natural talent, Clara Bow appeared in forty films by the time she made *WINGS* (winner of Best Film at the first Academy Awards ceremony), and *IT* in 1927. Critics praised her as "a joy to behold." Moviegoers rooted for Clara as she schemed to marry her boss in *IT*. Her performance earned her the nickname she would have for life: IT GIRL.

In February 1927, *Cosmopolitan* magazine published a two-part serial where Elinor Glyn described 'IT' as, "That quality possessed by some, which draws all others with its magnetic force. With IT you win all men if you are a woman and all women if you are a man. It can be a quality of the mind as well as a physical attraction." Everything about Clara personified IT. The public adored her. She had sex appeal infused with enough sweetness to make her approachable, not saccharin.

Until 1928, Bogart Rogers, son of famed attorney, Earl Rogers, and brother of writer Adela Rogers St. Johns, managed Clara's wealth. That changed in 1930 when she placed her money and her personal affairs in the hands of Daisy De Voe, her hairstylist turned personal assistant.

On November 10, 1930, local newspapers reported a story which illuminated both Clara's fortune and Daisy's management skills. The story claimed Clara and Daisy had parted ways. They denied it. De Voe said, "As far as I know,

I am still her secretary. Miss Bow has not served notice on me. I guess I'll have to find out all about it." Clara refused to comment.

A few days later, a follow-up report revealed Clara fired Daisy. On her way out, Daisy took some of Clara's valuables: diamond jewelry, a sapphire ring, and the actress' insurance papers. Daisy took a $20,000 cashier's check, and a mass of personal papers, canceled checks, paid and unpaid bills, and personal correspondence. Loyal to a fault, Clara may have turned a blind eye to Daisy's mismanagement of her finances indefinitely, but Rex Bell, her cowboy actor fiancé, stepped in and fired Daisy. He contacted the district attorney's office to ask them to investigate.

District Attorney, Buron Fitts and his investigator, Blayney Matthews detained Daisy in a local hotel room while they got a warrant to search her home and her safe deposit box. One of the found items, a cashier's check, was in dispute.

Daisy said, "Clara was going to use this (the cashier's check) in a business deal I had advised her against going into, so that is the reason I kept it from her. She knows as well as everybody else that I could never have cashed it. I intended giving it back the same as everything I had that belonged to her. They (the D.A. and cops) treated me terribly and I think it is absolutely unjust the way they treated me and kept me at the hotel. I believe, as does my attorney, we have justifiable cause of action against them."

Daisy's lawyer, Nathan O. Freedman, prepared to sue Buron Fitts, and Blayney Matthews. Daisy claimed the two held her incommunicado for several days in a hotel room while they cleaned out her safe deposit box. Most of the items found belonged to Clara.

Fitts, who doubted Daisy's case, informed reporters he made a formal request to charge Daisy De Voe with embezzlement against Clara Bow. He had chief investigator Blayney Matthews investigate. "After several days of investigation, Mr. Matthews reported back that Miss De Voe had made a thirty-page confession of the theft of some $35,000 of Miss Bow's money, a great deal of which was found in her possession."

Daisy refuted the confession and boasted she had nothing to fear from the grand jury. Her confidence was premature. The grand jury indicted her on thirty-seven counts of grand theft. Daisy posted a $1000 bond.

Freedman filed a complaint against Clara, Rex, and the District Attorney's office. The complaint asked for $7200 (equivalent to $100,095.52 in 2023 USD) damages based on a claim of unlawful detention.

The trial began on January 13, 1931. Freedman shifted the jury's focus away from Daisy's questionable behavior to Clara's raucous Hollywood lifestyle. Clara spent a whopping $350,000 (equivalent to $4.8 million in 2023 USD) between February 1929 and October 1930 on clothing, automobiles, and nights on the town. Freedman asked Clara about whiskey payments (illegal because of Prohibition). Under cross-examination, he asked her if she authorized one check for $143.50 for whisky and another on March 10, 1930, for $117.50 or whiskey. Clara replied, "I authorized Miss De Voe to spend whatever was necessary to maintain the household. I trusted her. If she wanted to buy whiskey, why, I suppose, she made out the checks and signed them."

Deputy District Attorney David Clark, who, in 1931, would be involved in a double murder, showed Clara a canceled check in the amount of $850. He asked her if she allowed the purchase of a fur coat with the money. "That is my check. I signed it myself. But Miss De Voe brought it to me and said it was to go on my income tax and I signed it because I trusted her." Clara broke down in tears when questioned about an engraved silver dresser set. She felt betrayed. Daisy presented the set to her as a birthday gift. The D.A. asked, "Did you authorize Miss De Voe to draw a check upon your special account to pay for this set?" She said, "I never did. I thought she was just being sweet and kind to me, that's all."

Clara reiterated she permitted Daisy only to draw checks for her own salary and for household expenses. Clara leaned forward in the witness box and looked straight at Daisy. "Go ahead and sneer, Daisy, that's all right."

Daisy's worst betrayal was taking Clara's personal papers. A telegram dated September 8, 1930, from Rex to Clara while she stayed at Tahoe, read, "Dearest sweetheart, darling baby, I do miss you, and this is only the beginning. Rex."

Daisy took every opportunity to defame Clara. She described her duties. "Well, I did plenty. Her house was terribly dirty. I had the whole place renovated, the drapes taken down, and the rugs taken out and cleaned; floors polished; furniture gone over, and everything and, well, I don't know what I did."

She continued, "... Miss Bow was drunk and if I had gotten into any argument with her, she would have tried to kill me because she had tried to once before... I think it would be better to walk out and later on straighten out her affairs. I wanted to get her things settled as quietly as possible, and keep Clara out of the papers, because one more slam in the papers and Clara is through in pictures."

It sounded like Daisy planned to extort Clara by threatening to make her private papers public. Daisy said, "I think it would be to her advantage to keep my mouth shut." She admitted to withdrawing $35,000 above her salary from Clara's account. In her mind, it was all Clara's fault. "It was her fault. If she had paid attention to business, I wouldn't have taken a dime from her because she would have known about everything."

During the court proceedings, Freedman interrogated the actress, tormenting her with questions about her relationship with Rex. Seething with anger and exasperation, Clara expressed her frustration. She responded to a question regarding Daisy's firing. "As a matter of fact, he (Rex Bell) discharged Miss De Voe from her position as your secretary?"

Clara snapped. "He didn't!"

But Freedman continued. "Well, he's your secretary now, isn't he?"

"He is not; I know it has been printed that he is, but it is not the truth."

At last, the D.A. questioned her about Daisy's extortion attempt. Several days after Daisy's dismissal, Clara's attorney, W. I. Gilbert, relayed to her that Daisy had visited him. She wanted $125,000 for her silence, then she audaciously demanded Clara rehire her.

A turning point came when a forensic accountant testified to his findings. While double-checking his way through 1,558 of the special account's canceled checks, he discovered a shortfall of $48,000 in the account. The account which Daisy had access to.

The defense again shifted to Clara's lifestyle. Feeling emboldened by her attorney's questions, Daisy declared to the packed courtroom, "Clara would prefer to stay home and play poker instead of going to the theater or any other place." We played all the time; six nights a week, at least. She never carried any money with her and I had to pay off her debts. Sometimes it was only $4 or $5 and sometimes it was $200."

The strain of having her private life exposed to public scrutiny and ridicule caused Clara to stay away from the trial. Her physician, Dr. Wesley Hommel, said, "Miss Bow is suffering from a severe cold and from a nervous strain attendant on the trial. She is running a temperature, and I ordered her to bed. Her condition is not serious and she should be up and around in a few days."

Rex attended every day while Clara was absent.

Three weeks into the trial, Judge Doran halted the rampant mudslinging coming from Daisy's corner. Due to the notoriety given to the actress, the Riverside County Board of Censorship banned one of Clara's films.

Daisy's jury deadlocked. Despite substantial evidence against her, the jury convicted Daisy on only one of the thirty-plus counts of grand theft. They recommended leniency.

The judge sentenced her to five years' probation and eighteen months in the County Jail. Daisy requested bail while she waited on her appeal. After denying her twice, they finally released her on March 28, 1931, on a $5000 bond.

Overwhelmed, Clara admitted herself to the Glendale Sanatorium in May 1931. Her contract with Paramount was "terminated by mutual consent." She moved to Rex's Nevada ranch.

Daisy used her insider knowledge of Clara's private life to attempt extortion. She knew little worth reporting. Clara liked to party—not big news in Hollywood during the 1920s and 1930s.

Fred Girnau, publisher of the scurrilous rag, *The Coast Reporter*, saw an opportunity to make money by exploiting Daisy's anger at her former employer. When he approached her about getting even with Clara and Rex, Daisy became his willing partner. After putting their malicious heads together, Fred and Daisy authored a repugnant 60-page document titled "*Clara's Secret Love-Life as told by Daisy.*" Out of spite, Fred sent copies to Will Hays, Hollywood's censorship czar. He sent copies to Superior Court Judges, and local PTA officials.

Over the years, many outrageous stories circulated about Clara. The worst of them trace back to Girnau. *The Coast Reporter* accused Clara of engaging in everything from drug addiction and drunken sex sprees to bestiality.

Clara's fragile emotional state made no difference to Paramount producer B. P. Schulberg. Relentlessly bullying her, he finally convinced her to return to the studio for "The Secret Call."

She got through the costume fitting and a private rehearsal with director Stuart Walker. On the day of the shoot, she awoke before her 6 a.m. call sobbing hysterically. Unable to calm Clara, her housekeeper phoned Rex for help. He found her repeating, "I can't do it, I can't do it." Rex carried her to his car and drove her to the Glendale Sanitarium, where doctors diagnosed her with nervous exhaustion.

Schulberg used Clara's emotional fragility to his advantage. He said her well-being was the studio's primary concern and they would not hold her to her contract if she wanted out. Though it sounded friendly, the intention was to trick Clara into admitting her inability to fulfill her contractual obligations.

In an interview, she told Hollywood gossip columnist Louella Parsons, "I don't wanna hold Paramount to no contract."

Schulberg found the perfect escape hatch, and he was despicable enough to crawl through it. He had a release form drafted, relieving the studio of any financial obligation to Clara. She saved Paramount $60,000, which is equivalent to $900,000 in current USD, by signing it.

Ironically, B. P. Schulberg's Hollywood career did not last long after Clara's departure. Paramount ousted Schulberg. He worked as an independent film producer and made a few films for Columbia. Washed up by 1950, he tried to offer his services to the trade papers. They rejected him. His son, successful screenwriter Budd Schulberg, supported B. P. for the last five years of his life. B. P. Schulberg died in Biscayne, Florida in 1957.

Clara and Rex married after the trial ended. They had two boys together and remained married until Rex's death in 1962. Clara suffered from emotional problems throughout the years and her issues resulted in an estrangement from her family. Living in Culver City, she spent the last years of her life under the constant care of a nurse.

What happened to Daisy De Voe and Frederic Girnau—the people who caused her so much heartache?

Fred spent forty-two months in a federal prison for his poison pen attacks on Clara. After being released in September 1934, Fred violated his parole by driving drunk. They returned him to Leavenworth Prison to finish out his 8-year term. He died in 1955.

Daisy, whose real surname was De Boe, served eighteen months in the Los Angeles County Jail for stealing one of Clara's fur coats. Years later, she looked back with remorse for her treatment of Clara. The harm she and Fred caused Clara is incalculable. But Clara won the game, set, and match.

Although Daisy and Fred enjoyed fleeting notoriety, Clara left a legacy of brilliant performances.

Clara said it best. “My life in Hollywood contained plenty of uproar. I’m sorry for a lot of it, but not awfully sorry. I never did anything to hurt anyone else. I made a place for myself on the screen and you can’t do that by being Mrs. Louisa May Alcott.”

18. Only a Comedy

Knowing their stars' personal lives could be messy, studio moguls hired fixers to handle damaging press. Eddie Mannix, who hung out with mobsters, and Howard Strickling, a former journalist, were the busiest fixers in Hollywood. Using bribes, fixers could bury stories about drunkenness, affairs, sexual assaults, or an out-of-wedlock pregnancy. Occasionally, they turned to harsher tactics. They may even have covered up a murder.

In 1932, producer Paul Bern arranged with millionaire Howard Hughes to borrow Jean Harlow for MGM's *The Beast of the City,* co-starring Walter Huston. Critics were unimpressed with Harlow's acting, but the public and the critics often disagree. Harlow gained a following. Women all over the country envied her because of her striking blonde hair and slinky shape. Platinum blondes popped up in big cities and small towns. Bern booked a 10-week personal appearance tour for her on the East Coast. She dazzled the crowds, so Bern extended her tour for six weeks.

Harlow and Bern grew close. Just as he had done for others in the past, Bern promoted her career. She was not an easy sell. Mayer felt she was not classy enough for MGM. Bern circumvented him and went to the studio's legendary producer, and his best friend, Irving Thalberg. Thalberg, the

"Boy Wonder," agreed with Bern. MGM bought Harlow's contract from Hughes for $30k ($697,000 in 2023 USD). On April 20, 1932, she became a part of MGM.

On the evening of July 2, 1932, forty-two-year-old Bern, wed twenty-two-year-old Harlow in a private ceremony at her mother's home in West Los Angeles. Among the guests were Irving Thalberg and his wife, actress Norma Shearer, along with Louis B. Mayer, David O. Selznick, and several other close friends of the couple.

Their marriage, Harlow's second and Bern's first, came as a surprise to Hollywood. The couple seemed mismatched, the drop-dead gorgeous platinum blonde, and the short, dark-haired man with a receding hairline.

Within days of the wedding, snarky references to the age difference between bride and groom appeared in newspapers. One Hollywood columnist wrote, "The new husband is Paul Bern, a mild voiced man of middle age. Of course, Hollywood already is speculating the ultimate outcome of the Harlow-Bern union. Marriage wouldn't be marriage out here unless everyone was allowed to guess how long the knot will last. For some vague reason, many of the experts are willing to bet that Bern and Miss Harlow are playing for keeps." The naysayers were right about the Harlow-Bern marriage. It ended, but not as predicted.

On Monday, September 5, 1932, at 11:45 a.m., Winifred Carmichael, Bern's butler, found him dead in a second-floor dressing room. Naked in front of a mirror, Bern had a gunshot wound to his head. Unable to reach Harlow at home, Carmichael called "Mamma Jean," Harlow's mother, who contacted Harold Strickling at the studio.

Minutes after the call, the house on Easton Drive swarmed with MGM studio executives. The men took in the scene. Near the pool they found a half-empty bottle of champagne and a glass with lipstick traces on the rim. Pieces of a shattered champagne glass dotted the flagstone patio. Lying across a chair was a bathing suit, too large to fit Harlow. The suit was still wet.

Among the men called to the scene was studio photographer Virgil Apger. After snapping photos of everything, he handed the film to Strickling. MGM police chief Whitey Hendry arrived. Four hours passed before anyone called the Los Angeles Police Department.

Strickling thought he knew what happened. Bern entertained a woman on Sunday night. They quarreled. Bern entered the house and went to the upstairs bathroom. Leaving his still damp bathing suit on the bathroom floor, he showered. The unknown woman followed him into the house and found him as he was drying off. She pointed a .38 caliber pistol at Bern and fired, striking him in the head.

Everyone there felt they knew the identity of Bern's killer—his common-law wife, Dorothy Millette. Depending on Millette's connection to Bern at the time of his death, she could destroy Harlow's career. Did the couple formally terminate the relationship? Would Bern be outed as a bigamist? This was a nightmare of gargantuan proportions for Mayer and MGM. If Harlow went down, the studio would crumble into ashes around her. Mayer relied on Strickling for a way out.

Strickling assumed control as if he were directing one of Mayer's films. The stakes were higher than just ratings. With Hendry's assistance, Strickling rearranged the scene to make it appear as if Bern had committed suicide. Knowing people's curiosity, he understood they would want to know why a man, who was married to one of the most desirable women on the planet, would take his own life.

Mayer, thumbing through a Moroccan leather-bound guest book near the front door, found an odd note on page thirteen.

"Dearest Dear, Unfortunately, this is the only way to make good the frightful wrong I have done you and to wipe out my abject humiliation,

I love you
Paul

You understand that last night was only a comedy"

Mayer, wondering what the police would make of the note, stuffed it into his pocket. He showed the note to Strickling. The fixer recognized its potential. The undated note could be Bern's last message to Harlow. Bern might be distraught enough to commit suicide if he failed to perform sexually.

The false story of Bern's impotence was cruel. Strickling, with Mayer's blessing, pressured people to spread the rumor that Bern, frustrated by his failure to perform in bed, beat his wife. It did not matter that Bern's friends knew he was not a violent man, or that nobody saw bruises on Harlow. Besides being a well-respected producer, Bern was also a writer. His friends knew he would never write a note with misspellings and no punctuation.

Police arrived, and they had no reason to be suspicious. With pressure from District Attorney Buron Fitts, Strickling and Hendry pitched the suicide story. Strickling fed newspapers the false narrative and they devoured it. So did the public.

On September 6, 1932, the *Daily News* published Strickling's version of Bern's death scene. "With a bullet hole in the temple, Bern's unclad body was found in a dressing room on the second floor of his hillside home at 9820 Easton Drive. He clutched a .38-caliber revolver in his lifeless hand, with one bullet fired from it. Ten feet away, on a dressing table in his bedroom, the police found a farewell note addressed to Miss Harlow.

The day after Bern's death, Millette jumped off the deck of the Delta King into the Sacramento River and drowned. The Captain of the Delta King, W. J. Atthoe, said he found a pair of shoes and a pair of silk stockings along the stairway leading from her cabin to the main deck. He believed she jumped overboard nude. Millette's death eliminated a damaging loose end. Within a few days of his death, reporters discovered her connection to Bern, but now they would never have the chance to speak with her. Headlines called her Bern's "Mystery Wife."

Bern met Millette in the early 1910s. They lived together for several years until she suffered a nervous breakdown. Following her hospital discharge, she made her home at the Algonquin Hotel in New York. All expenses paid by Bern. He felt a responsibility to her, and he honored it.

On May 4, 1932, Millette registered at the Plaza Hotel in San Francisco. The manager of the hotel, Ray Maxwell, described her to reporters. "She was reserved and secretive. I can't understand stories told of her 'derangement.' She seemed perfectly normal."

Thalberg refused to go along with the ruination of Bern's reputation. Mayer leaned on him, and he folded. Everyone knew their paycheck depended on supporting the party line. The Great Depression had begun only a few years earlier, and millions of Americans were out of work. Nobody at MGM wanted to stand in a bread line. Privately, Bern had friends and supporters who either knew the truth or guessed it. They were among those who attended his service.

At the end of the funeral, the priest intended to use a pulley system he invented to hoist Bern's coffin aloft. The priest arranged it in such a way that the lid would slide down to mid-chest, allowing the bereaved to have one final opportunity to see their loved one. The priest kept his plans a secret from everyone. As the lid slowly slipped down, the horrified mourners saw Bern staring back at them. Harlow and Thalberg burst into tears. Clark Gable ran for the door. Actor John Gilbert vomited.

Mayer and his fixer destroyed Bern's reputation; it has never recovered. If either man ever looked back with regret or shame, they never said.

To her credit, Harlow refused to defame Bern. Two weeks after his death, she returned to work and dealt with her grief privately.

In every photo of the crime scene since 1932, Bern is holding a gun in his hand. In 1990, another photograph of the crime scene surfaced. Taken at the scene by studio photographer Apger, the photo showed Bern in his death pose, without a gun.

Paul's reputation has suffered for over ninety years. The time has come to restore it.

PHOTOS

Burmah White in jail. 1933. Herald Examiner Collection, Los Angeles Public Library.

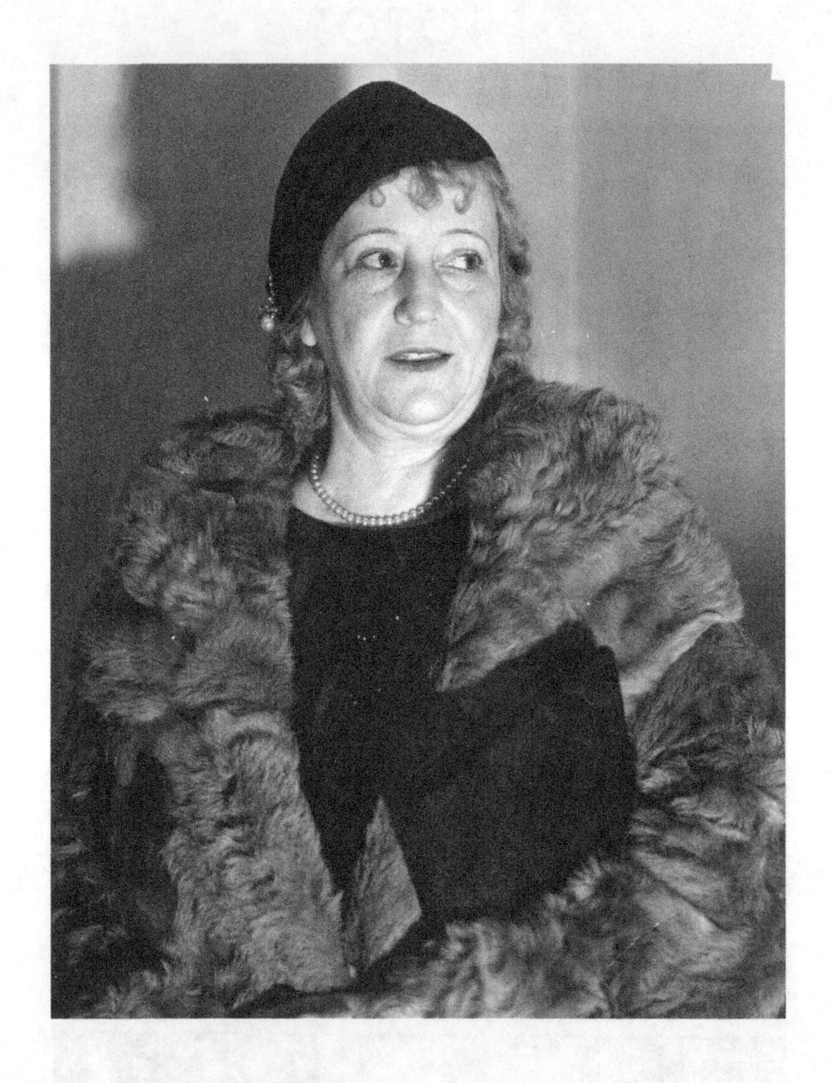

Dolly Oesterreich, 1930. Herald Examiner Collection, Los Angeles Public Library.

Otto Sanhuber, 1930. Herald Examiner Collection, Los Angeles Public Library.

Clara Phillips in maid's costume. Author's personal collection.

Clara Phillips arrives in New Orleans.
Author's personal collection.

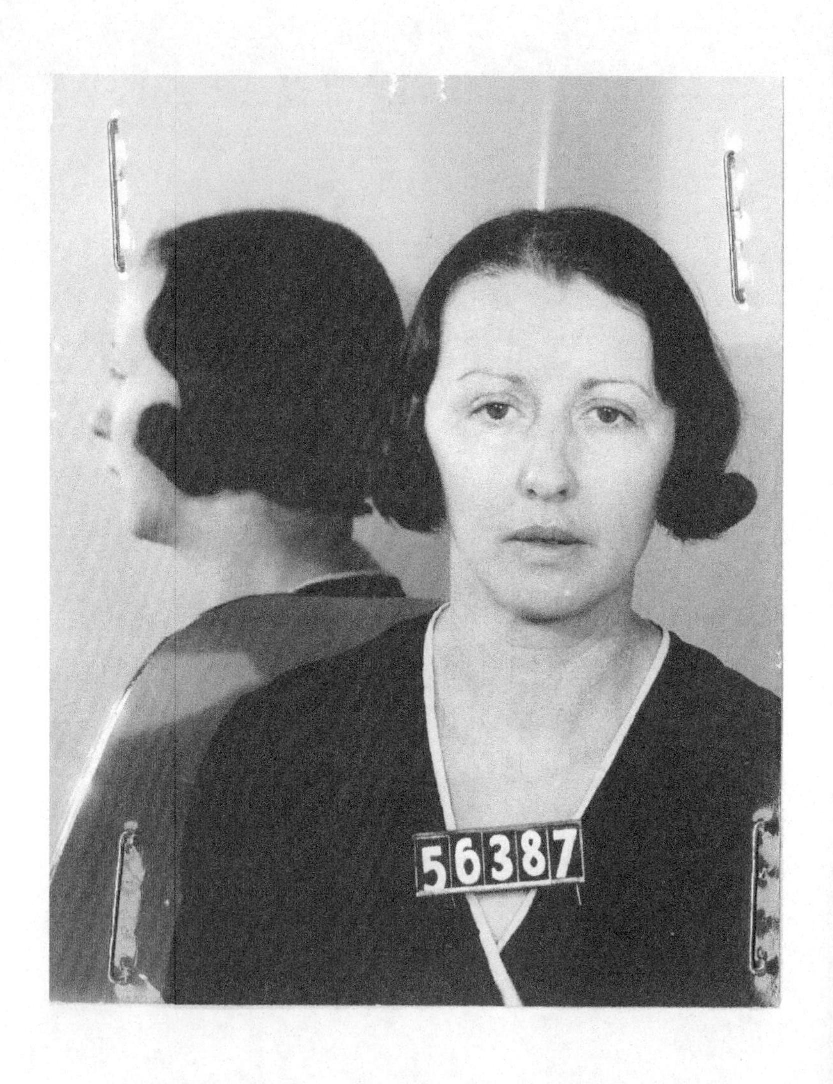

Nellie Madison, San Quentin Prison, #56387, California State Archives, Office of the Secretary of State, Sacramento, California

Robert James at fish pond, 1935. Herald Examiner Collection, Los Angeles Public Library

Ethel & Lois Wright, 1936. Author's personal collection..

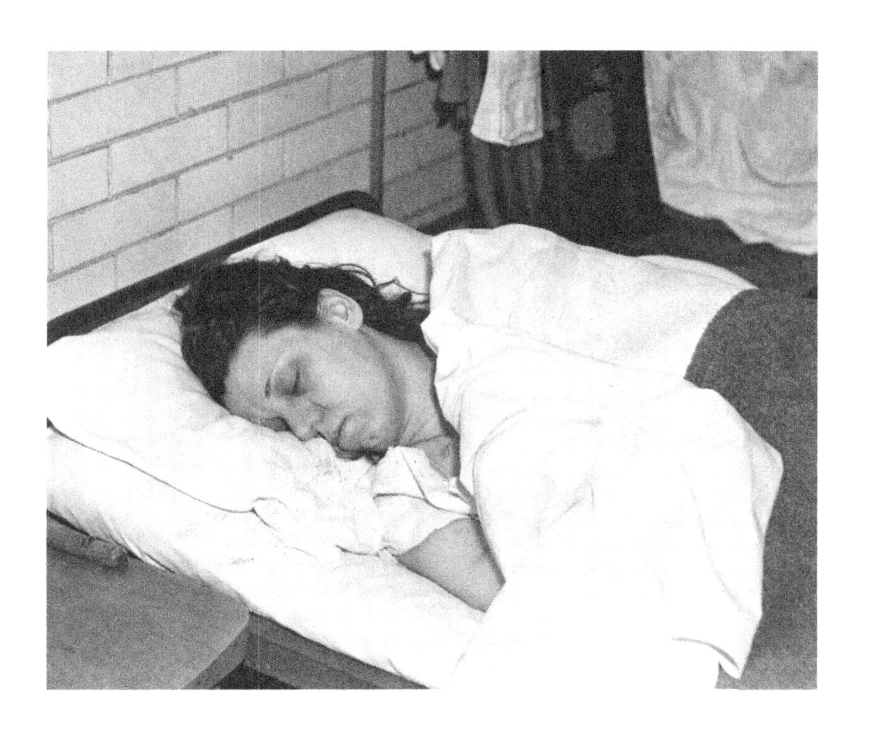

Helen Love in coma, 1937. Herald Examiner Collection, Los Angeles Public Library

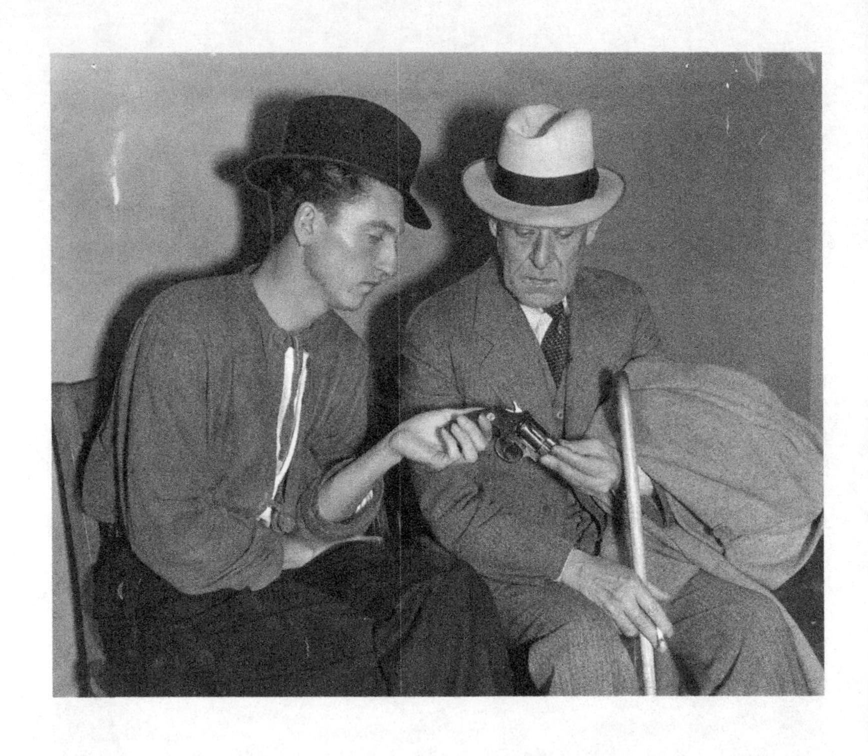

James Culver & Samuel Whittaker examine murder gun, 1936. Herald Examiner Collection, Los Angeles Public Library

Roscoe Arbuckle in San Francisco courtroom, c. 1921.
Herald Examiner Collection, Los Angeles Public Library.

Virginia Rappe. Herald Examiner Collection, Los Angeles Public Library.

Dorothy Mackaye publicity photo. Author's personal collection.

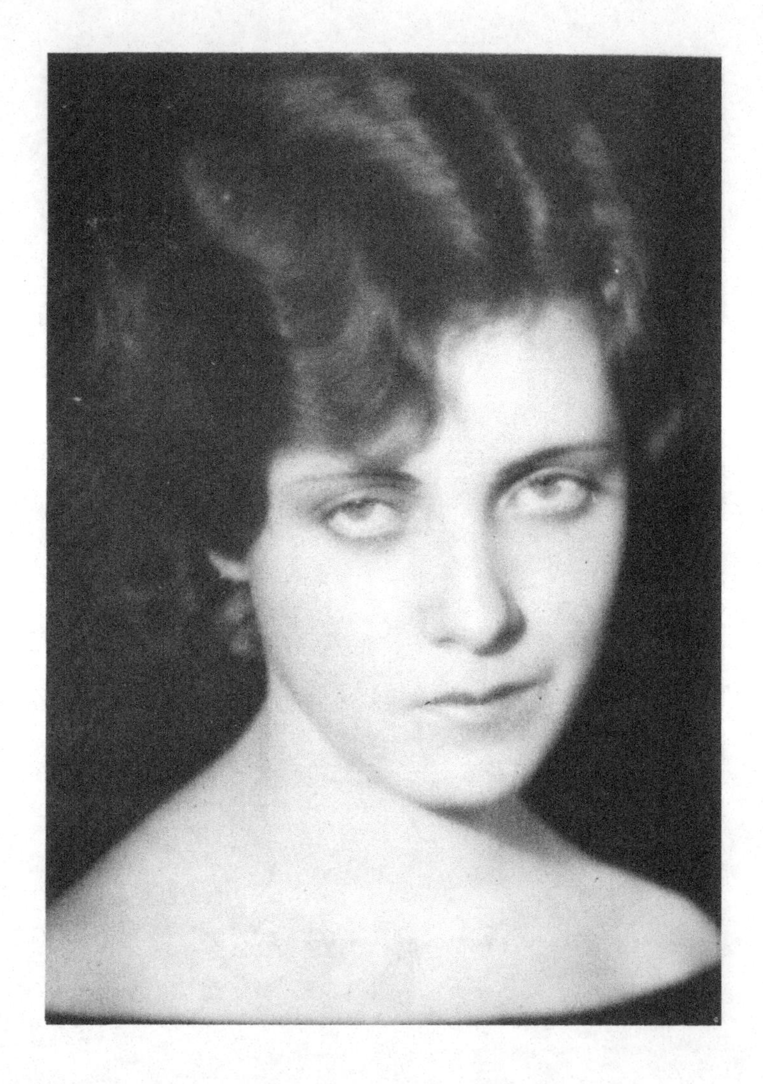

Fern Setril. Author's personal collection.

Gladys Witherell. Author's personal collection.

Extra Head Measure 7 1/4"

Height	1 m 62	6	Head length,	19	7	L. Foot	24	3	Color of Left Eye: Circle,	Age 20 Years
Outs. A.	1 m 69	—	" width,	15	6	" Md F	11	3	Periph. Z.	
Trunk,	89	—	Ear,	6	—	" L F	8	7	Haz	Born in
						" F	44	6	Pecul.	Ark

English Height 5-4 · Finger Print Classification 35 — 0 14 / 1 U 00 15 · Finger Print Reference

45041

DESCRIPTIVE.

Forehead: Incl. st · Height m · Width m · Pecul.

Nose: Profile — Ridge, rect · Base, hor shal

DIMENSIONS. Length. m · Projection. m · Breadth. m · Pecul.

Right Ear. · Teeth, fair · Chin, rid

Beard, · Hair, br · Complexion, fair · Weight 136 · Build, m

Measured at San Quentin, MAR 17 1928, 192___, by Black

Re-Measured—When and Where

William Edward Hickman, San Quentin Prison, #45036, California State Archives, Office of the Secretary of State, Sacramento, California

Fingerprint Classification 11 R 00 12 / 4 - 00 13

Fingerprint Reference

540810

Age 26

Eyes BLUE

Hair BRN

Complexion FAIR

Weight 115

Nat. Calif

Teeth FAIR

Chin RO

English Height 5-3

Build MED

Description taken at San Quentin 6-1, 1933, by [illegible]

Luella Pearl Hammer, San Quentin Prison, #54080, California State Archives, Office of the Secretary of State, Sacramento, California

Gettle kidnappers. L to R: James Ward Kirk, Larry Kerrigan, Roy Williams. Author's personal collection.

Carl Jacobson, 1925. Herald Examiner Collection, Los Angeles Public Library.

Callie Grimes, 1929. L to R: Deputy Sheriff Nettie Yaw, Callie Grimes, Attorney Leo D. Daze. Herald Examiner Collection, Los Angeles Public Library

19. Dancing with Death

From the 1920s through the 1940s, decades of poverty and war, movie theaters gave people a brief respite from their troubles. Who could worry when Ginger Rogers and Fred Astaire twirled and defied gravity in such films as *Flying Down to Rio*? If Cab Calloway and the Nicholas Brothers cannot get you up on your feet for *Jumpin' Jive*, then you must be dead.

The most creative choreographer of the Golden Age of musicals was Busby Berkeley. The kaleidoscopic numbers he created delight your eyes and confound your senses with their intricacy. Most choreographers begin as dancers with a vision. Despite being born to parents in show business, Busby never took dance lessons. His passion for complex movements performed with precision began on a parade ground during World War 1. As a lieutenant in an artillery division in the U.S. Army in 1918, Busby conducted and directed parades, sometimes with hundreds of men. His Army experience, though not traditional for his career, uniquely qualified him to direct the film sequences which made him famous.

The Hayes Code, Hollywood's way to avoid Federal censorship, proved as difficult to survive as 9.0 earthquake. Beginning in 1934, the code, named for its head, Will Hayes, governed what appeared on-screen. Hollywood suffered a series of scandals in the 1920s that left movie studios little choice. Either censor yourselves or the government will step in. The studios opted to wrestle with the issue themselves.

Musicals daringly pushed the Hayes code to its limit in a way standard narrative films could not. Many of the Busby directed sequences cleverly employed sexual innuendo. Musicals highlighted dancing girls cavorting provocatively with five-foot tall bananas; and got away with it. Audiences understood the cunning references and applauded them.

By September 1935, Busby's professional life flourished. His personal life was problematic. He married actress Merna Kennedy in 1934, but she objected to his drinking. Busby loved to down several martinis while relaxing in his bath. She filed for separate maintenance as a prelude to divorce.

On September 8, 1935, Busby attended a party with other Hollywood notables. As he did at most events, Busby drank to intoxication. He left at 10:00 p.m., and none of his contemporaries gave his drinking and driving a second thought. Most people, not only film stars, accepted the behavior as normal.

Bound for another party, he got into his car and put his foot down on the gas pedal. The big Cadillac roared recklessly down the Roosevelt Highway. On the highway near Santa Monica Canyon, he crashed headlong into a car driven by William A. Hudson, and then into another car driven by William von Briesen.

Police arrived and found several injured people and a dazed-looking Busby. He suffered a skull fracture and multiple, painful leg injuries. They rushed two victims, Laura von Briesen and Mrs. Manon von Briesen, to the hospital in critical condition. Sixty-year-old Ada von Briesen died shortly after the crash.

Doctors would not allow the police to question Busby, so they questioned witnesses instead. All of them agreed Busby was at fault. Two days after the collision, another of the victims, nineteen-year-old Dorothea Daley, succumbed to her injuries.

Busby said he was sober, and his car veered into oncoming traffic as if a tire had exploded. He denied speeding. He said he drove about 40 mph near the center of the road when he saw two cars coming toward him, one trying to pass the other.

Witnesses remembered it differently. William Hudson remained steadfast in his statement. "I was riding with my friend, Clarence Burtless of Santa Ana, when I saw the lights of a car coming around another car and the car struck us head-on. I saw a man I learned later was Berkeley, come from behind the wrecked car and I asked him if he had driven the car. He said he was the driver." Hudson smelled liquor on Busby's breath.

The Coroner's Register attributed Dorothea's death to "Shock and hemorrhage following numerous severe injuries. As the result of a three-car collision on the Roosevelt Highway about 1500 ft. N. of Santa Monica Canyon, Los Angeles. A Ford sedan driven by William Alvin Hudson and a Cadillac Coupe driven by Busby Berkeley were also involved. We (coroner's jury) find same to have been accidental and because of negligence and reckless driving by Busby Berkeley." Five days after the crash, the District Attorney charged the director with manslaughter. Joe Whitehead, head of the LAPD's West Hollywood homicide unit, said the case against Busby was "airtight."

Busby's mother, Gertrude, rushed to her son's bedside to support and comfort him. He lived with his mother longer than with any of his six wives. He found solace in her presence. What Busby needed more than his mother's love was support from his studio, Warner Brothers. If they did not have his back, he could tumble from the success of his recent film, *The Golddiggers of 1935*, into disgrace—even prison.

On Tuesday, September 17, Busby traveled in a police ambulance to court for his arraignment. Busby's doctor and attorneys accompanied him as two suited attendants brought him into court on a stretcher. Busby wasn't the only person who could choreograph a scene. Undoubtedly, his attorney, Jerry Giesler, dreamed up Busby's dramatic entrance. By 1935, Giesler had over two decades of courtroom experience. He became the go-to attorney for the famous and the infamous in Los Angeles. A celebrity in a jam bettered his odds of a courtroom victory with Giesler at his side.

At Busby's preliminary hearing, Elvin M. Anderson, filling station employee, appeared as a surprise witness. Anderson said on the night of the crash Busby whipped his car into the station at 25 to 30 mph, and wanted his front tire repaired. Anderson saw Busby stagger, and smelled liquor on his breath. "His (Busby) talk was thick, and his breath smelled of alcohol." Busby was behind the wheel, and 'gunning' his motor before Anderson could finish the repair. Busby was in a big hurry to get to the Uplifters Club to make a speech.

Judge Joseph McCall decided Busby should face two charges of second-degree murder. "I have listened closely to the testimony and I can't help arriving at the conclusion that a greater crime than manslaughter has been committed." Judge McCall said, "And I therefore have changed the charge against the defendant to murder in the second degree, which was willfully, feloniously, and without malice aforethought committed." Lying on his hospital stretcher in the courtroom, Busby fainted at the news. Second degree murder carries a more severe penalty than does manslaughter. If guilty, Busby could spend five years to life directing San Quentin's annual prisoner follies.

Two days after the judge's announcement, Busby departed for Lake Arrowhead. As he breathed the clear mountain air, in Los Angeles he faced a damage suit in the amount of $75,000 ($1.7 million in current USD) filed by Clarence Burtless Jr., one of the injured parties. William von Briesen sued. His mother, Ada, and his sister-in-law, Peggy, died in the crash. He sought $150,000 ($3.3 million in current USD) in damages.

On October 10, Busby entered a plea of not guilty to three counts of second-degree murder. Judge Schmidt set the trial for November 18, before Superior Judge Charles S. Burnell.

After fighting for his life, William von Briesen, 27-years-old, joined his mother- and sister-in-law in death. District Attorney Buron Fitts announced he would file an additional charge.

Jury selection for Busby's case began December 9. Reporters noted Busby was "pale and thin." One potential juror provided a small measure of comic relief. Grant Bilby, a realtor, got a chuckle out of the gallery when he said, "I worked for Warner Brothers' studio once, but I never heard of Busby Berkeley." Bilby made the short list of jurors. In the end, they selected eight men and four women, plus two alternates.

No sooner were the jurors seated than Deputy D.A. Di Vecchio made his opening statement. "We will show that Busby Berkeley was operating his automobile under the influence of liquor. He was driving recklessly, unlawfully, and dangerously."

In his opening statement, Jerry Giesler described Berkeley as "nervous type, high-strung and temperamental." Giesler claimed his client was "absolutely sober," and of "normal conduct," at the time of the crash. The inference being that Busby, an artist, differed from mere mortals.

Geisler told jurors, "The night of this accident, Mr. Berkeley had been invited to the home of his employer. He left there at 10:15 p.m., after a supper and musical entertainment. We will call 10 persons to testify that Berkeley was absolutely sober. We will admit that he had had just one cocktail and part of another. A half-mile from the ocean, his right front tire blew out. He stopped in a service station to have it repaired. He drove south through traffic that was especially light. Then he put on his brakes, in a sudden emergency, and the car swerved and was precipitated into the north-bound lane, sweeping him into one car, and a third car ran into him."

Fire Captain L. W. McKillip helped put out the flames that engulfed Busby's car the night of the accident. In his testimony, he said he stood near Busby and did not smell alcohol.

Only the *Los Angeles Evening Post-Record* editorialized their revulsion for the atmosphere surrounding the trial. Columnist Tom O'Connor mocked the field trips the jury took to the scene of the crash, and to visit Laura von Briesen in the hospital. O'Connor described the bus used to convey the jurors, defense, prosecution, and the judge on their field trip. He said it was "like one of those bus excursions to promote real estate subdivision sales than it did like a murder trial."

The huge number of reporters and photographers who followed the bus to the hospital offended O'Connor. It also offended him that, while in Laura's presence, people whispered. Back in the hospital elevator, everyone resumed laughing and joking.

The next stop was a little white house on Veteran Avenue in Santa Monica where Manon von Briesen, William's widow, waited her turn to be questioned. O'Connor described Manon's injuries. "Above her right eye was a jagged red scar which cut a triangular furrow in her forehead. The scar seemed half an inch deep. That whole side of her forehead was caved in. On the right side of her lower jaw was a horrible, livid swelling from an abscessed tooth. Her jaw was broken." Again, voices hushed. Manon remembered little about the accident. After a few pictures, everyone returned to the bus and the party atmosphere resumed.

Busby testified about drinking at the party. "I left absolutely sober. On the way to Santa Monica, my front right tire blew out, and I stopped at a service station to have it fixed. I was impatient and, in a hurry, and incurred the animosity of one attendant, the one who testified that I was intoxicated when I drove into the station. He resented the fact I asked him to hurry." Would anyone believe the gas station attendant was so offended by Busby's behavior that he held a grudge? Jerry Giesler hoped so.

Giesler summoned many Hollywood personalities to buttress Busby's testimony. To be in the jury box, a few feet away from people you have seen only in the movies, or read about in movie magazines, must have been a thrill. Giesler argued Busby was in shock. Shock does not smell like alcohol.

Prosecution witnesses saw a different Busby at the crash scene. L. M. Bunn, an employee of the Lighthouse Cafe, testified Busby went to the cafe, 500 feet from the crash, and tried to get a ride. "He asked me if anyone had a car to take him away. He said, 'I have to get away. They will be looking for me soon.' He talked to some people in one automobile, then climbed into the rumble seat. A minute later, he climbed from the rumble seat when the driver of the car got out of the machine. Mr. Berkeley stumbled and fell on all fours. His walk was unbalanced and wavery. Pretty soon, an officer came up and asked him why he left the scene of the accident. He said, 'I was going to phone my mother'."

Giesler closed the defense argument., "Whether Busby Berkeley is guilty of second-degree murder depends upon whether you believe he was drunk at the time of the crash. Unless he was driving while drunk, he cannot be convicted of any degree of murder. Doctors have testified that his actions at the scene of the crash could have resulted from the severe brain concussion he received in the accident. He himself has told you that he was so dazed he could remember nothing until he woke up in a hospital."

The prosecution called bullshit. "The tire was a smoke screen placed before you to take your minds away from the fact that Berkeley was driving while intoxicated and killed three people horribly."

Busby chain-smoked as he waited for the jury's decision. Late in the evening on Christmas Eve, the jury deadlocked ten to two in favor of acquittal. Jerry Giesler declared a "moral victory," and prepared for the retrial. A retrial was not Busby's only legal problem. In January 1936, he settled seven damage suits filed against him because of the crash. The out of court settlement cost Busby $95,000 ($2M in current USD) distributed in various amounts among the litigants. Busby's second trial date moved from February to April.

In the meantime, Judge Charles Burnell, assigned to the trial, received an anonymous threatening call from a man purporting to be a friend of the accused. "Busby's friends want you to give him a break." Judge Burnell responded. "Berkeley would have a fair trial, such as I endeavored to see that every defendant before me received, which was all he or any other defendant was entitled to, and that was all the 'break' I could or would give him." The caller retorted, "That is what we mean. You know damn well you can fix up your instructions and talk to the jury, so there'll be no danger of Berkeley getting in a jam." Burnell told the mystery caller to go to hell. But the stranger got the last word. "All right, if you feel that way about it, we'll see that you are yanked out of that court and someone put in who is more amenable to reason."

As the caller predicted, they removed Judge Burnell from the criminal court division. Burnell said two judges pressured him into transferring to the civil court bench. One of them, Judge Edmonds, claimed to know nothing about the Busby Berkeley case. He insisted Burnell's transfer was in the works for months because of a health issue.

Who had the power to stack the deck in Busby's favor? District Attorney Buron Fitts for one. Fitts did favors for Hollywood studios and accepted money from Paramount and MGM. Later, in 1937, Fitts used his position to block prosecution of David Ross for the rape of Patricia Douglas at the MGM Sales Convention.

On April 6, 1936, Busby went to trial for the second time. Attorneys selected eight men and four women to sit on the jury. For courtroom watchers, the defense and prosecution arguments were "déjà vu all over again." The same cavalcade of Hollywood stars who testified on Busby's behalf at his first trial, testified at his second. Partygoers said Busby was not drinking, he was, "enjoying an electric chair we had rigged up at a table." Nothing says party hearty like a full body electrical shock.

On April 19, 1936, Busby's second trial ended in a hung jury with seven votes for acquittal and five for guilty. Judge Ambrose rejected the D.A.'s recommendation to drop charges against Busby. Instead, he ordered a third trial.

On September 28, 1936, the jury acquitted Busby of second-degree murder charges.

They never identified the mystery caller.

20. Girl 27

The Golden Age of Hollywood brought to the screen many of the most beloved stars and iconic films of all-time.

Mansions, expensive cars, furs, jewelry—movie stars had it all. Or did they? The Golden Age is the period during which studio moguls called the shots, not just on scripts, but on the lives of the people under contract to them. If you were a big star and wanted to marry—the studio head could deny your heart's desire. The film contract included clauses regarding your weight, behavior, companions, and children (if the studio allowed you to have them).

Except for studio moguls, few people thrived under a system as invasive and brutal as a dictator's regime. The lucky, or smart, ones escaped with their dignity intact. Others gave their all, only to be turned into drug addicts. Uppers for weight loss and grueling schedules. Downers for sleep and zombie-like compliance. After they outlived their usefulness, studios abandoned them to perish in obscurity. What about the people who made a deal with the devil? Did they feel a twinge when they lost their soul to the studio machine?

For the troubled star or director, the studio provided a life raft. They did not save you because they gave a damn about your life. They saw you as an item in their ledger. If you were in the plus column, they went to the mat for you. If not, you were on your own.

Patricia Douglas and one hundred other female movie extras went to the studio on May 4, 1937, for a costume fitting. Patricia was girl #27. One half of them wore a cowgirl outfit, the other half wore Spanish-style outfits.

Following the costume fitting, the girls, most of them under 21, boarded studio buses they believed would take them to a movie shoot. They knew nothing about the project. Not that they cared. Douglas' mother supported her, but during the Great Depression they welcomed every paycheck. If the gig meant standing around looking cute in western garb, so be it.

The head of MGM, Louis B. Mayer, was not filming a western. He was throwing a party for studio salesmen from all over the country. The studio would treat the top earners like kings. MGM's profits doubled from the previous year. With so much to celebrate, Mayer decreed a five-day sales convention—the first in a decade—to be held in Culver City.

The conventioneers traveled to the Pasadena train station by private rail car. Most of them arrived still drunk. The 282 men began their stay in Southern California by groping starlets assigned to pin carnations on their lapels. From a make-shift stage at the station, Mayer addressed the party-ready crowd. "Our fine Chief of Police (James) Davis remarked to me a moment ago (that I) must think a lot of these men to have sent the beauty that he sees before him. These lovely girls—and you have the finest of them—greet you. And to show you how we feel about you, and the kind of a good time that's ahead of you... anything you want." An open invitation to the delegates to assault the starlets. An ambush for the unwitting girls who awaited them.

The convention opened with dinner at the Ambassador Hotel; followed the next day by a police motorcycle escort to Culver City, MGM's home. Eddie Mannix, the studio's "fixer" and "a fucking gangster" by anyone's measure, met the delegates. A marching band played "The Gang's All Here" and 4,000 MGM "family members" threw confetti.

The delegates must have felt like stars themselves when they lunched in the studio commissary with famous stars like Clark Gable, Jean Harlow, and Joan Crawford.

At 4:00 PM on May 5, 120 female dancers, plus several girls who answered an ad for MGM party hostesses, reported to Hal Roach Studios on Washington Boulevard in Culver City, one block from MGM. Camera-ready make-up deftly applied and, in their costumes, the girls boarded MGM buses to "Rancho Roachero." The buses pulled up to the ranch, and the girls went to a large banquet hall.

The movie business was, and still is, hours of hurry and then wait. Instead of a film crew and director, a herd of randy stags greeted the girls at 7:00 p.m. Loud and handsy, the group paired off with the girls assigned to their table.

Unless you paid close attention, the party appeared tame. With 500 cases of scotch and champagne, the open bar was stocked for the 282 men. The only thing missing from the Bacchanalia was a vomitorium that could rival the most debauched Roman orgy. One tent offered cafeteria-style food. Another tent held an arena in which they staged exhibition boxing matches. Laurel and Hardy provided entertainment, and so did the Dandridge Sisters, along with 13-year-old Dorothy.

By 10 p.m., the delegates turned their attention away from the entertainers and focused on the girls within their grasp.

A waiter, Oscar Buddin, later testified, "The men all became intoxicated." Buddin heard people use vulgar language and witnessed women fending off inappropriate advances.

One odious delegate, thirty-six-year-old David Ross, a bachelor from Chicago, obsessed over Patricia. Under the assumption Patricia was there to serve him, the portly, toad-man observed Patricia truckin' on the dance floor and demanded a lesson. Patricia was not thrilled. She found Ross, "Repulsive. He was slimy, with eyes that bulged like a frog." Many homely men become attractive to women because they radiate empathy, humor, and a host of other desirable traits. That night, Ross radiated only animus and lust. Mr. Hyde without Dr. Jekyll. Still, Patricia demurred in the hope a dance lesson would satisfy him. It did not. Like any woman unable to scrape an annoying, unwanted pursuer off the bottom of her pumps, Patricia excused herself and made a bee-line for the ladies' room. Safely behind the door, Patricia complained to the attendant about Ross. "I've got a man, and he's sticking."

Back at the table, when Patricia did not respond in the way Ross wanted, he and a companion held her down. She recalled, "One pinched my nose, so I'd have to open my mouth to breathe. Then they poured a whole glassful of scotch and champagne down my throat. Oh, I fought! But they thought it was funny. I remember a lot of laughter."

She got up and ran for the ladies' room, where she threw up. Unaccustomed to the uncomfortable body heat booze can produce, Patricia sought fresh air. She needed to clear her head.

Outside, Patricia saw a field being used as a parking lot for dozens of Ford sedans provided by the studio. If only she had a set of keys. As she breathed in the fresh air and tried to regain her equilibrium, a man grabbed her from behind. He put his hand over her mouth and whispered, "Make a sound, and you'll never breathe again." It was Ross. He followed Patricia outside, where he could get her alone. "I'm going to destroy you."

A mixture of terror and the alcohol that still coursed through her system caused Patricia to black out. Ross back-handed her. "Cooperate! I want you awake." The slap denied Patricia the mercy of unconsciousness. Wide awake, fearful, and humiliated, Patricia endured Ross' attack. Beaten, bloody, with her eyes swollen shut, Patricia screamed for help. Clement Soth, a parking attendant, walked toward the sound. He saw David Ross run away. He found Patricia. She said, "My god. Isn't anything sacred around here?"

The studio cover-up kicked into gear from the moment Patricia arrived at Culver City Community Hospital. Unbelievably, Patricia got a cold-water douche before Dr. Edward Lindquist, MGM's "family doctor," examined her. The douche removed any physical evidence of the rape.

One wonders where the police were during Patricia's assault, and afterwards. At least four different police departments had officers working the event. A motorcycle cop accompanied Patricia to the hospital. No one took a crime scene report. Perhaps city police deferred to the studio's own questionable force. A studio car took Patricia home, where she remained in bed, unconscious, for over fourteen hours.

The brutality of Ross' attack left her bruised and her private parts torn and sore. Patricia did not go to a doctor after her initial botched exam by Lindquist. The assault embarrassed her. She did not want to suffer the indignities of another examination.

Patricia found courage in her rage. She filed a complaint against David Ross. As a minor, Patricia needed the signature of a court-appointed guardian to swear out the complaint. A friend, Mildred Mitchell, signed on her behalf.

Patricia had everything to lose. Her career, her reputation. Some members of the public found her unsympathetic, and perhaps a bit unladylike, because she would not conceal her outrage. Even victims of violent rape were expected to adhere to certain accepted codes of behavior; Patricia refused. "I guess the Irish in me came out. You knew you'd be blackballed. Me, I didn't care. I just aspired to be vindicated, to hear someone say, 'You can't do that to a woman."

MGM, the most powerful studio on the planet, did not have friends in high-places. They were the high places. They owned cops, and they owned the district attorney, Buron Fitts. Mayer donated more money to Fitts' campaign than anyone else. The district attorney understood the *quid pro quo*.

Fitts' services were not exclusive to MGM. He did favors for other studios as well. Shady deals, pay-offs—typical of Los Angeles government officials in the 1920s and 1930s. Writer and producer, Budd Schulberg, said, "Buron Fitts was completely in the pocket of the producers. They owned *everyone*—the D.A. the LAPD They *ran* this place."

Patricia did not move in the same circles as the D.A. and his movie mogul cronies, so she was unaware of their power to crush her. She believed she would get a fair shake. Accompanied by her reluctant mother, she paid the D.A. a visit to register her complaint. They went home and waited.

Weeks went by without a word from the D.A. Rather than let it go, Patricia found an attorney, William J. F. Brown. A Los Angeles attorney straight out of Central Casting. Brown, dressed in a double-breasted suit, drove a custom Packard. His larger-than-life personality, courtroom hi-jinks and histrionics won cases.

Brown offered to represent Patricia pro bono. An offer too good to be true. He took charge of the case and put Fitts on notice. If Fitts refused to investigate Patricia's allegations, Brown would take her case to the press. Fitts ignored the threat until a headline appeared in the Los Angeles Examiner, *Probe of Wild Film Party Pressed. The Examiner*, owned by publishing tycoon William Randolph Hearst, welcomed reports of crime and cover-ups—as long as they were not his own.

In 1937, even the *Examiner* shied away from calling Patricia's attack a rape. Popular euphemisms included, attacked, outraged, and ravished. Newspapers characterized Patricia as a party girl. Her photo appeared, along with her home address. Printing victim's names and addresses was common practice, but usually they named the suspect as well. Not in this case. MGM is "the studio."

The degree to which the local authorities and press were complicit in bullying and shaming Patricia is revolting. She had the guts for a fight, but never the power to win it. Men betrayed Patricia at every turn. Louis B. Mayer, used his wealth to hire private investigators to shadow Patricia and poke around in her life. How disappointed he must have been to discover that at the time of the attack, Patricia was a teetotaling virgin.

Never mind the truth. Mayer bribed low-level actresses who attended the "party" and observed the debauchery with job offers. Eddie Mannix handled the bribes and strong-arm incentives. Mannix abused his authority and women with equal enthusiasm. During one argument, he broke his wife's back. He mercilessly beat actress Mary Nolan, his mistress, necessitating fifteen surgeries. The studio hired the Pinkerton Detective Agency in a no-holds-barred effort to control the narrative. One woman whose story contradicted Patricia's was Sugar Geise. Geise, a twenty-seven-year-old chorus girl, recalled seeing Patricia passed out at the Knickerbocker Hotel Bar. Other party-goers had similar recollections of Patricia's wanton behavior. They all agreed the evening was a "jolly old party, full of good, clean fun."

One disappointing defection from the truth came from actor Wallace Beery. Beery attended the party and "rescued" one girl from the clutches of a salesman who pawed her. Following a talk with Mayer, or Mannix, Beery denied rescuing anyone. Clement Soth, the parking attendant who saw Patricia following the rape, and saw Ross flee the scene, testified at the Grand Jury hearing that the man he saw was considerably thinner than pudgy Ross.

Patricia described the attack. Ross' attorney, one of Mayer's friends, pointed at her and asked, "Who would want *her*? Look at her!"

Patricia left the courtroom and saw Ross in the hallway, relaxed and smoking a cigarette. He was confident he had nothing to fear. MGM's power and wealth supported him. He felt guaranteed to win. Unfeeling newshounds, seeing the victim and her attacker so near each other could not restrain themselves. They pushed Patricia closer to Ross to get a photo of the two of them in the same frame. She fled.

The Grand Jury hearing was exclusively for show. On February 9, 1938, a superior court judge dismissed the case. Ross returned to his MGM sales job in Chicago.

MGM and their lackeys believed they were home free. They did not understand the depth of Patricia's rage. Within twenty-four hours of the dismissal, she sued in the U.S. District court. Patricia is the first woman to make rape a federal case based on her civil rights. Her attorney, William J. F. Brown, milked as much publicity out of the case as he could. He aspired to a political career and attempted to unseat Buron Fitts. He failed, due, in part, to his opposition to MGM.

Neither Fitts nor Brown appeared in court, so a federal judge dismissed Patricia's case. No evidence exists to show collusion between the D.A. and Brown, but their simultaneous failures to show-up suggests the fix was in.

The rape, and the subsequent ordeal of public humiliation and abandonment by her colleagues, ruined Patricia's life. She suspected her mother took a pay-off from MGM because Mildred purchased a liquor store and horses after dismissal of the case. The betrayal of Patricia reached the level of a Shakespearean tragedy.

In 2007, writer David Stenn directed *Girl 27*, a documentary about Patricia's life and the 1937 scandal and subsequent studio cover-up. The documentary vindicated Patricia and proved the truth of her allegations. At last, Patricia recognized her own bravery. "Pretty gutsy, wasn't I?"

Patricia passed away on November 11, 2003. She didn't live to see the documentary. The #metoo movement owes a debt to pioneer badass, Patricia Douglas.

PART IV. SNATCH RACKET

Dubbed the "Snatch Racket," kidnapping for profit occurred in the 1920s, but it became a cottage industry in the United States during the 1930s. Great Depression desperation inspired amateur kidnappers to take a chance to make a quick buck. Gangs, seeking an easy score, kidnapped business leaders and housewives.

Average citizens feared being snatched, but Hollywood celebrities had more to fear. The proliferation of fan magazines and the stars' own extravagant behavior made it simple for kidnappers to target them.

No matter who the victim is, kidnapping is a terrible crime. Adult kidnap victims endure, but it is particularly abhorrent when the victim is a child. The Marion Parker kidnapping and the Wineville Horror cases involved children taken by the worst kind of criminal, a child sexual predator. Was justice served in the cases? You be the judge.

21. The Pluckiest Girl in the World

Gladys Witherell was at home at 6:10 p.m. on January 25, 1921, when a man, about forty-five-years-old, knocked on her door. The man was tall, gray-haired, and smooth-shaven. He told her he saw an "auto accident" on the boulevard. A severely injured woman called for Gladys. Gladys thought the woman sounded like her mother-in-law. She pulled on her coat and took her 18-month-old son, Jack, to her next-door neighbor, Elizabeth Warden. She said she would return as quickly as possible—then she left with the man.

Otto Witherell arrived home later that evening, to find his wife gone. He spoke with Elizabeth. Something was wrong, so he phoned the police. Los Angeles Police Department detectives arrived, followed by Los Angeles County Sheriff's Department detectives. Nick Harris, of the eponymous detective agency, joined the investigation.

Why would anyone take Gladys? Otto declared, "I have no enemy, as far as I know, and Mrs. Witherell never told me of anyone who might have become infatuated with her and taken such means to take her away from me. Our married life ever since we were married in 1917, and when we were sweethearts in Hollywood High School, has always been ideal." He felt sure he would get a ransom demand soon.

Otto, the head of the Financial Loan and Investment Company, stated his willingness to pay anything for Gladys' safe return. He and his father, A. J. Witherell, offered a reward of $500 ($9,000 in current USD) to anyone who could provide information.

The Nick Harris Agency received a call from John Baldwin, a student at the Harvard Military School. He said he saw a young woman in a battered-looking five-passenger Ford on Washington between Western and Vermont. The woman showed signs of being restrained and drugged. Baldwin and his friend, Don Savage, drove toward downtown when they noticed a Ford that matched the description of the kidnap car. The engine had no hood and steam gushed out of the radiator. They followed the car, trying to get the license plate number, but when they got closer, they saw the plates were missing. At the wheel sat a swarthy man, wearing a cap. Baldwin and Savage pulled up next to the car. The man gave them a look so filled with malice they turned up a side street to avoid a confrontation.

J. E. Baumann, a gas station owner at Thirty-eighth Street and Hooper Avenue, also spotted the Ford. The top was down on the car and he saw a woman who looked like the newspaper photo of Gladys.

Some people encouraged the Witherells to engage the services of a clairvoyant or employ other supernatural means to locate Gladys. Interest in the occult was at its zenith during the 1920s. Many people became interested in the occult after losing loved ones in World War I. Local clairvoyants tried but could not communicate with Gladys. Nor could they see her in the spiritual realm. Here on Earth, dozens of people claimed they saw Gladys. A taxi driver, G. L. Cope, who had a stand near Sixth and Hill Streets, told police he saw a battered

Ford near Twenty-third and Main. Two other men saw the car on Sunset Boulevard.

The lack of viable clues in the case frustrated police. Some of the most prominent citizens in Hollywood banded together and started a reward fund, hoping that the offer of money would produce results. In less than a day, they had received contributions over $1500.

Three days following the abduction, detectives trailed a mysterious Greek merchant. They thought the man had a vendetta against the Witherell family. On the morning of the kidnapping, someone overheard him say the only way to get even was "to make the whole family suffer."

Police and newspapers distributed a description of the gray-haired man. Otto nervously waited for word from the kidnappers. Nick Harris said, "We are convinced that the time has come when some advance is to be made by Mrs. Witherell's captors, if they have kidnaped (sic) her for ransom."

Pastors of local churches, unwilling to leave Gladys' fate to police, issued a statement declaring they would pray for her safe return. As pastors and parishioners sent prayers heavenward, Chief of Police Pendegast asked the Hollywood Post of the American Legion to form a volunteer vigilance committee.

On January 30, 1921, scores of men and women gathered in the rain to search for the missing woman. Under LAPD direction they scoured the hillsides, canyons, and groves. The Los Angeles County Sheriff's Department lent a hand in the search. Hundreds of people turned over thousands of rocks, but they could not find Gladys. The young mother had been missing for about a week.

In the 1920s, Los Angeles cornered the market on firebrand preachers. Among the most vocal was Dr. J. Whitcomb Brougher, pastor of the Temple Baptist Church, who decided that a sermon on "Hell," was called for. During his fiery oration, Dr. Brougher said, "Los Angeles is suffering at the present time from a reign of lawlessness. Our mild climate invites not only tourists but also a big criminal class to spend the winter months here. Wherever good people congregate in large numbers, evil-doers go also, looking for a chance to exploit the good." The fire and brimstone sermon ended–but the search for Gladys continued. For a day or two, the police were mum. Did that mean that they had a solid lead? Was the mysterious Greek merchant responsible for Gladys' abduction?

The LAPD, LASD, and Nick Harris Agency followed leads to dead-ends. They eliminated the Greek man from their inquiries, but fake tips, rumors, and prank calls deluged them.

A demand for $20,000 ($385,000 current USD) supported the kidnap for cash theory. The Nick Harris Detective Agency received the cash demand on the day Gladys was taken; but did not make the contents of the letter public until after her rescue. The letter said upon payment of the ransom, they would release Gladys, unharmed. Unlike other crank letters they received, this one had an enclosure–a plea written in Gladys' hand. They were finally in contact with the real kidnappers. The letter instructed the family to drop a package containing the ransom near a red lantern on Valley Boulevard. They could expect a telephone call by midnight on Saturday, February 5th.

Detectives guarded the Witherell's home. Nick Harris watched Gladys' parents' home. Telephone operators monitored incoming calls to both homes.

Law enforcement sent Gladys' father a fake note demanding $50,000 ransom. They figured an out-of-the-blue ransom demand would draw out the real kidnappers. The forged note worked. Alma Bryant, night chief operator of the Hollywood exchange, said police told them about the arrangements for surveilling the wires. The operators knew about the hundreds of people in Hollywood searching the hills. They talked it over and hoped they could help. At 10:23 p.m. Bertha Heere received a call for Mr. Witherell's residence. She heard a man ask for O. S. Witherell, so she listened in. He said, 'This is the man who's got your wife" Heere contacted Bryant, who contacted Georgie Pond. She told Pond to hold the line and be ready to give the location of a number as soon as possible. Working in concert, they pinpointed the kidnapper's location as the A-to-Z Drugstore, 200 East Fifth, and informed police.

Detective Sergeants Stelzriede and Paul Meyer sped to the location and waited outside the phone booth. The man exited, and detectives approached him with a question. "Who were you talking to?" After a few seconds, he said, "Witherell."

The man identified himself as Jack Carr. He denied knowledge of Gladys' whereabouts and claimed he was a "tool" and he was working for some "higher up" whose identity he didn't know. Skeptical detectives turned up the heat for over two hours before he broke down. He confessed details of the kidnapping and implicated his cousin Floyd Carr.

Floyd and Jack held Gladys in a cabin in Corona. Detectives gathered a posse to accompany them to the hideout. Jack gave directions. The drive took two hours. Situated off a dirt road, a sheepherder had once called the place home. At 2 a.m. On January 31st, detectives crept towards the rear door of the small structure. They found the door unlocked. Deputy Anderson ran into the kitchen. He saw no one. Nailed shut, the bedroom door was easy to kick open. Gladys lay in the room on a filthy bed. She became hysterical and refused to believe the men who broke in were law enforcement until they produced their badges. She told the officers the kidnappers had not harmed her.

One officer found Floyd in a closet. Floyd pointed a .45 Colt automatic at the officer's chest, but only for a moment. The officer yelled, "Throw up your hands or I'll blow you through the wall!" Police dragged him from the closet. He fought back and got the worst of it. "For God's sake–don't kill me. I'm not at the bottom of this!"

Despite their claims to the contrary, Floyd and Jack were the sole perpetrators of the kidnapping. No "higher up" or gang existed, just two losers looking for a big payday. District Attorney Woolwine knew what to do; hustle them through the justice system and then send them to prison. They transported the Carrs from Corona to jail to court, but not without incident. A mob of people outside the County Jail shouted, "Lynch them!" "Lynch!" and "Let's string them up!" Guards ran for the doors and dragged Floyd and Jack with them. Within 12 them hours of their capture, the Carrs were in front of Judge Reeve, where they entered guilty pleas. The Judge told them they had the right to an attorney. He gave them two to five days before he sentenced them. With the clock ticking, the cousins lawyered up.

Public Defender Aggeler arrived five minutes later and consulted with his clients. Aggeler argued for leniency because Gladys was unharmed. D.A. Woolwine corroborated the Carr's statement. Judge Reeve set sentencing for Wednesday, February 2, 9:30 a.m. Sentencing was easy. Section 208 of the Penal Code offered a single option—ten years to life in prison.

At 6 p.m. on February 2nd, as they prepared to leave for San Quentin, Floyd and Jack addressed the assembled reporters with praise for their victim. Jack turned to the reporters. "Boys, before we leave, we want to let the world know that Mrs. Witherell is the pluckiest little girl in the world." Floyd echoed his cousin's sentiments. "You tell the world she's too good to wipe her feet on any man."

They had another confession to make. According to Floyd, "All that stuff about the 'Old Man' that I told you while we were coming in from the shack that morning was all the bunk. Lord, you fired those questions at me like a machine gun, and I was sore and I wasn't feeling very good, so I just doped out a bunch of lies for you. It was all the bunk."

The judge sentenced Floyd and Arthur Jack Carr to the mandated 10 years to life in prison. Police returned Gladys to her family. What about the reward? They divided it among the telephone operators, who played a significant role in the capture.

Gladys gave her story to journalists. The public devoured every word and each photo of the "plucky" young mother. She recounted how she fought her captors and attempted to escape. They promised not to hurt her, so she passed the time by playing cards with them. Sid Grauman, the theater owner, and entrepreneur, was not oblivious to the excitement generated by the case. Shortly after Gladys returned home, Grauman's Million Dollar Theater announced the appearance of the 4 telephone operators who caught Gladys Witherell's kidnappers. The ad also promised a huge switchboard scene, revealing every detail of the capture. "The most sensational act of a decade."

Grauman announced on February 9th that Gladys Witherell would present a $2000 reward to the operator heroines, to be divided among them. To Grauman's dismay, Gladys' physician said she still suffered from nerves and fatigue, so Nick Harris represented her. Her father-in-law heaped praise on the women who helped save her. "Had these girls not been on the job, nobody can tell what might have happened to Gladys. They are the most splendid examples of young American womanhood–alert, quick-witted, sympathetic, and instantaneously responsive to the call of need."

Jack Carr never made it out of San Quentin. He died there in April 1940. They released Floyd in July of the same year. He died in Orange, south of Los Angeles, in 1945.

Gladys and Otto survived the kidnapping ordeal. By 1940, the Witherells had moved to Chicago. At some point, they returned to Los Angeles. Otto died in 1967, and Gladys, the plucky girl of 1921, died in 1986. They are together at the Hollywood Forever Cemetery.

22. The Fox

William Edward Hickman, who preferred his nickname, Eddie, excelled in his studies at Central High School in Kansas City, Missouri. He served as Vice President of his class and as the President of the Central Chapter of the National Honor Society. Next to his senior class photo, the list of his accomplishments concluded with a glowing paragraph. "An excellent scholastic standing and an unequaled record in extra-curricular activities and a high standard of ideals will fix his memory in the annals of Central." His classmates and instructors were right about his memory being fixed in the annals of Central High.

Eddie succeeded in his studies, despite his dysfunctional family. His parents, William, and Margaret (known as Eva), had a troubled marriage. Mental instability ran in Eva's family. She frequently wandered out into the Arkansas fields at night. William would search for her. Many times, he found her curled in a fetal position, crying. Her symptoms worsened with pregnancy. She told William she wanted the baby out of her. William said he could do nothing to help her. She said, "All right, if you are not going to do anything, I will. I'm going to get it out of me. I'm going to take a knife and just rip myself open. You think I haven't got nerve enough to do it, but I will show you." She never acted on her threats.

Eva lost interest in sex, and she may have suffered from postpartum psychosis. William awakened many times to find her standing over his bed clutching a butcher's knife. As soon as she realized he was awake, she fled. She did the same thing to Eddie. The marriage deteriorated, and William left for good when Eddie was seven. He sent Eva support money whenever he could.

Eddie worked hard and applied himself to his studies. After their move to Kansas City, he settled in. Besides his schoolwork, Eddie pursued extra-curricular activities like the debate team. He appeared to be on solid ground. Then the cracks showed.

Eddie confided in Don Johnstone, his best friend, his desire to enroll in Park College, a theological seminary, to answer his call to God's service. Don was aware of his friend's increasing irrationality and his belief that he was aligned with a supernatural power. By the time of their June graduation, Don believed Eddie was crazy.

Welby Hunt attended high school a few miles from Eddie. They became friends, and at the end of 1926, they moved to Hollywood. They stole a car and committed burglaries along the way to pay for gas and groceries. The money also bankrolled Eddie's obsession, movies.

At midnight on Christmas Eve, 1926, twenty-four-year-old druggist Clarence Ivy Toms worked alone in a pharmacy on Huntington Drive. Los Angeles Police Department patrolman, D. J. Oliver, was in the telephone booth when two bandits came in waving guns. They failed to notice Oliver until he came out of the phone booth, gun in hand, and fired. A battle ensued. Eddie fired point-blank at Toms. He slumped behind the counter. Eddie and Welby turned their guns on Officer Oliver. Toms, a recent graduate of USC, was married for a little over a year. They rushed the wounded man to the nearest receiving hospital, where he died.

Eddie later described the incident as a miracle. "An officer of the law within three feet of me and his revolver directly aimed at my conspicuous body fired three shots and touched me not even once. This was a miracle. This great Providence had saved me and proved itself to me." The pharmacy job was their first failed heist, and it temporarily scared them straight. They took jobs after New Year's Day, 1927, at the bank where a man named Perry Parker was a senior officer.

The Parkers were a typical middle-class, white-collar family. In 1927, the family, twin girls, and a son, lived on South Wilton Place. The Parker's neighbors were professional people. The county coroner, A. F. Wagner, lived across the street.

Perry's job at the bank was usually uneventful; but when one of the bank's customers discovered his account was $400 ($7,000 in current USD) short, he reported it. The paper trail led Perry to Eddie. The authorities used Eddie's own confession as evidence to convict him of fraud. Judge Carlos Hardy sentenced him to probation in juvenile court and required him to make restitution. Not humbled by his experience, Eddie applied to get his old job back. Perry declined.

The probation department approved Eddie's return to Kansas City. He took a job at a cinema, but they let him go. He purchased a gun and committed forty-three armed robberies. After getting together a stake, he traveled west, arriving in Hollywood in mid-November 1927. He wanted one big score. Kidnapping sounded like the best way to make a lot of money fast.

Thursday, December 15, 1927, began as a typical school day for Marion and Marjorie Parker. A man named Mr. Cooper came to the school office at noon and introduced himself to the secretary, Naomi Britten. He told her Perry was in the hospital, clinging to life, following a serious car accident. Perry asked for the oldest daughter. It seemed odd to Naomi. The twins were only minutes apart, but she felt pressure to respond to the emergency.

Her shock wore off, and Naomi searched for the school's principal, Cora Freeman. She found Mary Hold, a teacher, instead. The women returned to the office and met face-to-face with the young man. Mary's impression of him was the same as Naomi's. He was well-dressed and polite. To address any fear the women had about releasing Marion, he suggested they phone the bank and verify his story. He appeared so nice; they did not bother. Marion arrived in the office, and the young man bent over and spoke to her. "Don't cry, little girl, I will take you to your Daddy." Marion's classmates watched as the man escorted her to his car and drove away.

Naomi phoned the Parker home to follow up. Did they want Marjorie sent home, too? It took a few minutes for her to realize she was speaking to Perry. As he listened to Naomi, Perry's heart sank. He turned to Geraldine and delicately tried to break the news to her. She fainted.

A telegram arrived. "Do positively nothing till you receive a special delivery letter." Signed, "Marion Parker and George Fox." Perry phoned police. The Los Angeles Police Department assigned two teams of detectives to the kidnapping. One team, Detectives Harry Raymond, and Dick Lucas, worked under the direction of the D.A., Asa Keyes. Raymond and Lucas were on loan to the D.A.'s office following their August involvement in a politically motivated plot to frame City Councilman Carl I. Jacobson.

Chief Inspector Joseph Taylor led the second team of detectives. Inspector Taylor tapped the Parker's phone and told post offices and Western Union to hold letters or telegrams addressed to the Parkers. He was a too late. Forty-five minutes after the first telegram arrived, a second one arrived. The telegram advised Perry to "use good judgement." The sender's address was phony.

A mailman delivered a special letter from the downtown post office. The note outlined payment demands. The kidnapper signed it, "Fate." It closed with the statement, "If you want aid against me, ask God, not man." A note in Marion's handwriting accompanied the letter. "Dear Daddy and Mother, I wish I could come home. I think I'll die if I have to be like this much longer. Won't someone tell me why this has to happen to me?" In her note, Marion begged her father to "do what this man tells you or he'll kill me if you don't." A heart-wrenching plea from a terrified girl.

The next day, Perry went to work and readied the ransom. At 8 p.m., he received the first of several calls from the kidnapper asking about the money. The last call came about 8:30 p.m. "I am some distance away. I will phone you again in a few minutes away and give you your instructions." The instructions were for Perry to go to Tenth Street and Gramercy. He was told to dim his headlights and not to bring the police. Perry waited for hours in the dark for the kidnapper to appear. At midnight, he gave up and returned home.

Eddie saw cars circling the block. He knew they were police. He wrote, "Mr. Parker, I'm ashamed of you! With the whole damn vicinity throbbing with my terrible crime, you try to save the day by your simple police tactics." He signed his note, "Fate Fox," again including the phrase, "If you want aid against me, ask God, not man."

Another note arrived from Marion. "Daddy, please don't bring anyone with you today. I'm sorry for what happed last night. We drove wright (sic) by the house and I cryed (sic) all the time last night. If you don't meet us this morning, you'll never see me again." Before the notes, Perry did not know that police followed him to the exchange point.

More letters arrived. The final one spelled out the Fox's terms and went into detail about the exchange. "Seeing your daughter will take a moment. My car will crawl away from yours for about a block. You wait and when I stop, I will let the girl out. Then come and get her while I drive away—and I won't go slow this time—Don't attempt to follow when you get the girl."

Perry received a telephone call with additional instructions. He checked his rearview mirror for police the entire way to Manhattan Place, the spot designated for the exchange. Thirty minutes later, a car pulled up alongside him. Eddie pointed a double-barrel shotgun out of his window. It came within inches of Perry's face. Perry saw Marion in the shadows and asked about her. Eddie said, "She's asleep."

Perry had no choice but to hand over the ransom. He did not recognize Eddie. The car drove less than two hundred feet down the block and then stopped. Perry heard the passenger-side door slam shut and saw the car drive away. He rushed to his daughter. The sight was an unimaginable horror. Eddie removed Marion's limbs and wired her eyes open so she would appear awake. Perry held what remained of his little girl and screamed.

Dozens of reporters heard the news about Marion and went to the morgue. A local photographer, George Watson, described the scene. "The body was taken to the morgue which adjoined the autopsy surgeon's office and laid on a table and covered with a white blanket." Dr. Wagner arrived, and the reporters tried to crowd into the autopsy room after him. Police kept them out. The *Los Angeles Times* sent Watson to get photos of Marion, but he would be out in the hallway waiting with everyone else in a few minutes. He had an epiphany. He approached D.A. investigator George Contreras. "For God's sake, George, tell the doctor that I'm here to shoot evidence pictures for you." Neither LAPD nor the Sheriff's Dept had a dedicated photographer. Contreras allowed him to enter.

Watson later recalled, "Dr. Wagner approached the table where the body lay. He was an older man wearing horn-rimmed glasses, tall and serious looking. His hand trembled as he took the blanket by one corner and pulled it back, exposing the torso of his neighbor's child—a child he had delivered. He shuddered and said, 'My God.'"

Watson detached himself from what he was photographing or he would not have been able to go through with it. Dr. Wagner noted what he found. "The tongue and eyes were normal, except the eyelids had been raised by a wire running through the hair and brought back and fastened to a ribbon." The next day, Wagner received Marion's missing body parts.

Police and the D.A. held back some details of the crime to verify any future confession. The information included a shirt with the name Gerber written on it, and a towel marked Bellevue Arms Apartment. They found both items packed inside Marion's body cavity. Another piece of evidence was a fragment of a Brazil nut found inside Marion's clothes.

Detectives interviewed the tenants of the Bellevue Arms. Eddie spoke with them, too. When they left, he packed his clothes, the ransom money, and three of his four guns. He dropped the suitcase at a storage locker and walked to a nearby theater to see a movie. After the movie ended, he walked about a block, then robbed a man of fifteen dollars. He stole the man's car and held him hostage for a few blocks before releasing him. Eddie retrieved his suitcase, then stole another car and drove north. At sunrise, he checked into a hotel in San Francisco using an alias.

Detective Barlow connected fingerprints found in a stolen car to those found in the Bellevue Arms Apartments. By comparing the prints to those on file, he found a match. The name was William Edward Hickman, a known criminal. Detectives found human hair and tissue in the bathtub drain of Eddie's abandoned apartment. On the carpet was a small piece of Brazil nut.

The D.A. took his case to the grand jury. The court issued a bench warrant for Eddie's arrest. On Sunday, December 20, 1927, Eddie arrived in Seattle, Washington, parked the stolen car and went into a movie theater. At 8:30 p.m., he left the theater and went to a nearby store to buy clothing. The clerk recognized him and phoned police.

Eddie continued north and picked up two hitchhikers. Several hours later, without explanation, he left them on the side of the road. Arriving at the nearest town, they saw their driver's picture on the front page of a local newspaper and called police. An hour after he dropped off the hitchhikers, Eddie reached Pendleton, Oregon, where he picked up another pair of hitchhikers, Bill, and Jack Merrill.

Pendleton's Chief of Police, Tom Gurdane, asked Buck Lieuallen, a state highway patrol officer, to join him in the search for Hickman. As they sat in Lieuallen's patrol car, Eddie and the Merrills drove past. The license plate did not match the wanted car, but the driver fit Hickman's description. Gurdane and Lieuallen stopped the Hudson and approached it with pistols drawn. Eddie played it cool. He gave his name as Peck and said he was visiting his mother and returning to his home in Seattle. Gurdane did not believe him. He had him step out of the car. He opened the door, and Eddie's pistol fell to the ground. Eddie explained he kept the gun for protection while traveling. Gurdane looked hard at the young man. "You're Hickman. I knew it was you all the time."

It took him only a few minutes in captivity to shift the blame to an accomplice, Andrew Kramer. He wove a story that absolved him from everything, except for the initial kidnapping. "Marion and I were like brother and sister. "She liked me, but she did not like Kramer, and she said she would like to stay with me all the time." He claimed he was gentle with Marion. They even went to the movies the night before he killed her.

Police followed up on Eddie's assertion that his accomplice, Kramer, was the actual killer. They did not find one Kramer; they found three. The Kramer in question had an unbreakable alibi. They exonerated the other two Kramers, which left Eddie as the murderer.

Dr. W. D. McNary, superintendent of the Eastern Oregon Asylum for the Insane, examined Eddie. In his opinion, Eddie's mind "... seemed clear. He told a straight, coherent story and never was at a loss for words. There was nothing about him to indicate insanity. He did not differ a bit from hundreds of thousands of other young men."

On December 26, 1927, on the train back to Los Angeles, Eddie confessed again. "I am ready to talk. I want to tell the whole story." Detectives said Eddie seemed to enjoy recounting details of the kidnapping, murder, and dismemberment. He confessed he had no accomplice and claimed his motive for the kidnapping was to get $1500 to pay his tuition for seminary school. He murdered Marion because, "I was afraid she would make a noise."

Displaying no emotion, he spoke about Marion's murder. He said he tied her to a chair, blindfolded her, and prepared to leave the apartment. An urge to kill overcame him. He got a rolling pin from the kitchen, then changed his mind. He picked up a dishtowel. "I gently placed the towel about her neck and explained that it might rest her head, but before she had time to doubt or even say anything, I suddenly pulled the towel about her throat and applied all of my strength to the move. She made no audible noise except for the struggle and heaving of her body during the period of strangulation, which continued for about two minutes."

Eddie removed her clothing and placed her in the bathtub. "First, I cut a place in her throat to drain blood, but this was not sufficient." He explained how he cut and removed her limbs and wrapped them in newspaper. He took off her remaining undergarments and cut through her body at the waist. "As I cut the limbs and body, there were heavy issues of blood and jerks of the flesh to indicate that life had not completely left the body."

Eddie's mother, Eva, wanted Clarence Darrow to represent her son. Darrow prevented the execution of two teenagers, Nathan Leopold, and Richard Loeb, in May 1924 for the thrill killing of a 14-year-old boy. Eva hoped Darrow could perform the same miracle for her son. Darrow cited previous commitments and recommended Jerome Walsh. Walsh took the case, but he needed help. He convinced Richard Cantillon to join him.

The trial drew enormous crowds. Emotions ran high—people wanted the defendant to hang. The sooner, the better. For everyone's safety, they searched people for weapons before they allowed them into the courtroom.

Walsh and Cantillon summoned alienists (psychiatrists) to testify to Eddie's mental incompetence. They made a strong case, using his family history of mental illness and his rapid mental deterioration over the past couple of years.

Juries are unpredictable. People wondered if twelve people could reach a unanimous decision. They waited only forty-five minutes for an answer. Judge Trabucco ordered a dozen deputy sheriffs to be present in the courtroom for the reading of the verdict. He told the audience he would not tolerate an outburst.

The jury found Eddie guilty.

The gallery was silent until one spectator got up, walked into the hallway, and exclaimed, "They got the son of a bitch."

Judge Trabucco sentenced Hickman to death and set his execution for April 27, 1928. In California, a death penalty case triggers an automatic appeal. The State Supreme Court reviewed the defense arguments for a mistrial and denied the petition.

On October 19, 1928, his last day, Hickman awakened early from a sound but short sleep. He wrote letters. In a letter to Russell St. Clair Beitzel, a former death row cellmate, Eddie told him, "I'm very comfortable here, Russ. I'm not a bit frightened, either. Tomorrow I'm going to walk up like a man. Say good-by to my friends for me and tell them I'll see them soon."

He scarcely touched his breakfast of ham and eggs, cereal, fried potatoes, hot rolls, a waffle, coffee, and milk. At his request, they placed flowers around his death cell and he listened to jazz records on an ancient phonograph.

Eddie converted to Catholicism during his last few months, so Father Fleming walked him to the gallows. Police Officer D. J. Oliver, who Eddie shot in the abdomen during the drugstore robbery in which he murdered Ivy Toms, sat in the gallery. Detective Dick Lucas, who took Hickman's confession, watched as the hangman placed the noose over Hickman's head. He fainted.

George Watson, who photographed Marion's autopsy, wrote an account of the execution.

"Hickman's eyes were focused on the shiny new rope. The rope and black cap had barely been put over his head when his body seemed to slump and he half fell to the floor. He was over the trap door, supported by the guards. One of the three cords supporting the trigger of the trap was cut by men behind a screen and the trap door dropped and the limp form of the once defiant fox half slid and half dropped through the opening, his head striking the side as he went through."

"A guard stopped the body from swaying as Dr. Ralph Blecker stepped up, tore open Hickman's shirt, and applied the stethoscope to his left breast. For fifteen minutes, the doctor stood by the side of the boy, who still hung by the neck."

"Fifteen minutes after the body of Hickman fell through the trap, the doctor, standing on a small ladder with the stethoscope to his ears, the tube end on Hickman's naked chest, nodded his head."

"The 'fox' was dead. Justice was done."

23. Wineville Horror

Prohibition was not all about flappers, sheiks, and champagne cocktails. A current of darkness ran through the 1920s and 1930s. The grimmest manifestations of post-war trauma and world-wide upheaval were crimes against children.

On March 15, 1928, the *Los Angeles Times* reported that Mrs. Christine Collins' nine-year-old son Walter had gone missing five days earlier. Christine feared her son was the victim of a kidnapping. Had a monster like William Edward Hickman taken him?

Police first focused their investigation on ex-cons because her husband, Walter, was in prison. The investigation into ex-cons with a grudge was not productive—although Christine believed revenge was the only plausible reason for taking Walter off their quiet Lincoln Heights Street.

The police rounded up local thugs and combed the Collins' neighborhood for potential witnesses. Mrs. A. Baker of North Avenue 23 saw the Collins boy in an automobile with two "foreign-looking people" and heard the boy plead to be released.

Several days prior to Walter's disappearance, neighbors noticed a man who "looked Italian" ask for directions to the

Collins home. Witnesses recalled a woman accompanied the stranger, but nobody could provide a description.

The absence of clues left police frustrated. Sightings of the boy led to dead ends, and even Walter's convict father could shed no light on a motive.

Led by Los Angeles Police Department Captain J. J. Jones, a former deep-sea diver, dozens of LAPD officers dragged Lincoln Park Lake for Walter's body. The search failed. Captain Jones and Lieutenant Hanson interviewed some of Walter's school friends. Twelve-year-old Lloyd Tutor identified a mugshot of an ex-convict as the man who asked for directions to the Collins home. The lead did not pan out. Under Jones' command, two hundred LAPD officers began a search of the northeastern section of the city. They did not find a trace of the boy—now missing for a month.

Christine could not afford the luxury of staying at home and aiding in the search. She had to go to work each day—sleep deprived and near the breaking point.

For five agonizing months, Christine waited. In early August, police notified her they found Walter in De Kalb, Illinois. The how and why of Walter's trek east was hazy. Illinois authorities put Walter on a train to Los Angeles. Christine was ecstatic at the prospect of being reunited. Christine's joy turned to shock and disbelief when the boy who stepped off the train did not look, sound, or feel like her child. The reunion should have mended her heart. Instead, it shattered it into a thousand jagged bits.

Captain J. J. Jones insisted the child was Walter. He was just a little worse for his harrowing experience. She repeated, "I do not think that is my boy." That was not what Jones wanted to hear, and he would not let Christine get away with humiliating him or his department. Jones convinced her to take the boy home and "try him out for a couple of weeks." Shaken by the public reunion and the relentless pressure from police, Christine agreed and took the strange boy home.

Eager to identify his abductor, police, and doctors questioned the boy about his kidnapping. How did he get to Illinois? Did he escape captivity or did his captors release him? The boy's story did not hang together, and psychiatrists felt he had a secret. For three weeks Christine tried to accept the boy, but how could she when she knew better? She gathered her son's dental records and, accompanied by friends, she returned the child to police.

Captain J. J. Jones was livid. He berated Christine and accused her of trying to humiliate the LAPD. Jones knew what to do with the stubborn woman. He had her committed to the psychopathic ward of the General Hospital for observation. While they held Christine in the psych ward, the mystery boy confessed to lying about everything. The shrinks were right; the kid had a secret. His real name was Arthur Hutchins, Jr. and he was a runaway. He realized he bore a resemblance to the missing Collins boy and saw an opportunity to start a new life in Los Angeles. He wanted to go to Hollywood and meet with his favorite cowboy star, Tom Mix. They released Christine from the hospital ten days following Arthur's confession.

By mid-May 1928, Christine slogged through the motions of living as she waited for word of Walter. Her job as a telephone operator kept her busy during the day, but at night, all she could do was lie in bed and stare at the ceiling. If Christine read the newspapers, she may have seen a story about two boys missing from Pomona. The boys, Nelson, and Lewis Winslow, vanished after attending a meeting of the Pomona Model Yacht Club.

Police described Nelson as 10 years of age, light hair, blue eyes, 4 feet in height, dressed in a blue shirt and knickers. They described Lewis as 12 years of age, 4 feet 3 inches in height, light hair, blue eyes, dressed in a regulation Boy Scout uniform.

Nelson and Lewis were gone for a couple of weeks when the Winslows received a note from them written on a flyleaf torn from a book issued by the Pomona Public Library. The note said that they left Pomona and were on their way to Mexico to search for gold. Pomona police sent telegrams to border authorities asking them to detain the boys if they attempted to cross the border. Nelson and Lewis never arrived there. Time passed without further clues to their whereabouts. Mr. and Mrs. Winslow joined Christine Collins in purgatory. All of them were fearful of hope and ashamed of doubt. Each dawn brought renewed heartache.

Because the Winslow's lived thirty miles east of the Collins, nobody made a connection between the missing boys. The authorities also had no reason to connect the disappearances to the discovery of the headless body of a Latino boy found on a roadside in La Puente.

The cases converged in September 1928. It began when a young Canadian woman, Jessie Clark, checked on her younger brother, 15-year-old Sanford. She was worried about Sanford ever since he left with their uncle, Gordon Stewart Northcott, two years earlier. Jessie was concerned enough to travel to Northcott's ranch in Wineville, California.

Jessie's brief stay at Wineville ranch was enough for her to realize her uncle was sexually abusing Sanford. He assaulted her, too. She returned to Canada, and told her mother, Winifred, everything. Winifred contacted U.S. authorities.

Northcott saw agents driving up the road to his ranch, so he told Sanford to stall them or he would shoot him. With two years of reasons to believe his uncle was capable of murder, Sanford did as he was told. While Sanford kept police occupied, Northcott and his mother, Sarah Louise, fled to Canada. Police soon busted them in British Columbia. California applied for extradition of the two fugitives. Sanford told police about his uncle's sexual depravity and his unimaginable brutality. Clark's statement linked his uncle to Walter Collins, the Winslow boys, and the unidentified headless body found in La Puente. Clark led detectives to physical evidence of the sadistic slayings.

Sanford led police to sites on the farm in the hunt for human remains. The police believed Northcott and his mother emptied the graves and burned the contents in the desert during the month of August.

The extradition of the fugitive mother and son was successful, and in December, the pair arrived in Los Angeles to stand trial.

On December 3rd, Northcott confessed to the slayings of Nelson and Lewis Winslow and the headless Mexican boy. Sarah confessed to murdering Walter Collins.

Before his extradition, Northcott handed his copyrighted story to the *Vancouver Daily Sun.* He wrote, "There have been a lot of stories circulated about me. They are all untrue. What awful things to say about a man. Some people have been suffering from too much imagination, and a lot of people will be sorry when this case is cleared up."

Northcott explained he had disappeared to shield his mother. "I had to protect poor little mother from this. I simply could not tell her of this. I simply could not tell her of what they were accusing me. If poor little mother had known of these charges, it would have killed her." Poor little mother? Visualize for a moment the poor little mother wielding an axe and using the blunt end to bash in Walter Collins' skull. She is the poor little mother to whom Northcott referred. He continued. "So, I kept it all from her, newspapers, and everything I was forced to hide them. I wanted to get her away to a safe place. Then I intended to go back alone and fight this thing."

True to form, Northcott's comments to the press were self-serving, but what really stood out was the way the newspapers depicted the child murderer. "Northcott is a good-looking youth and has a disarming manner. His fair hair sweeps back in an easy wave from the parting on the left and there is a ready smile on his lips beneath his well-modeled nose. His eyes alone are peculiar. They are deep blue, but possess a fixed, staring quality, as if their owner is in a thrall."

The papers gave a description of Northcott's traveling clothes. What was the well-dressed child serial killer wearing in 1928? "On the train he wore a smartly cut brown tween suit with a dark brown stripe. His tie was brown with cream-colored spots, and there was a thin brown strip in his shirt." The reporter failed to note Northcott's primary accessory, shackles.

Dressed impeccably, and delighting in his notoriety, Northcott shared his thoughts with the press on a variety of topics. The pre-trial publicity infuriated him. "The newspapers, especially those in the South, convict a man before he comes to trial. I do not think there should be so much publicity about crimes before the man charged with them goes into court. I don't blame the newspapers so much. They are in a competitive business. But I do blame the administration that permits the practice." They cited the Hickman case to him as an example of his contention. "Oh, that was different. Hickman deserved all he got."

Back in Los Angeles, Northcott and his poor little mother confessed. Then recanted.

The most bizarre twist in the case was the meeting between Christine and Northcott in the County Jail where she confronted him about Walter's murder. Christine really wanted to believe Walter was still alive, so after her meeting with Northcott, she was convinced he was innocent of the murder. Christine was Northcott's most unlikely supporter.

Arrogance and stupidity ruled when Northcott discharged his counsel and represented himself. As the saying goes, "every man who is his own lawyer has a fool for a client."

Northcott's cross-examination of Sanford Clark was so inept, the prosecution offered no objections. Despite his abysmal performance, Northcott appeared pleased with himself. "I am not such a bad attorney after all, am I?"

Gordon's mother surprised everyone when she pleaded guilty to Walter Collins' murder. She took responsibility for all the atrocities committed in the Wineville chicken coop. Nobody believed her to be the sole villain. They sentenced Sarah to life in San Quentin for killing Walter.

The jury found Northcott guilty of the murders of Lewis and Nelson Winslow and the unidentified "headless Mexican" boy and sentenced him to hang.

Northcott went to the gallows on October 2, 1930, at San Quentin. He required support to climb the thirteen steps. He collapsed on the platform. They rolled him through the trapdoor, and he strangled to death at the end of the noose.

Wineville residents were so traumatized by their connection to the infamous child killer, in 1930 they changed the city's name to Mira Loma.

24. Amateur Night

Widespread lawlessness and violence characterized the U.S. in the 1930s. Bank robberies, gangland killings, and kidnappings made headlines. The most infamous kidnapping of the period was the abduction of the twenty-month-old Charles A. Lindbergh, Jr. on March 1, 1932. There were many other victims, all over the country.

Early in the afternoon of January 27, 1933, a man telephoned the Smith home in Pasadena asking after twenty-nine-year-old Isabel. The maid told the caller Isabel was out. When he called later, Isabel answered. The man said, "This is Mr. Johnson of the church." Isabel assumed he referred to the church where her father, Rev. Merle N. Smith, was pastor. The caller continued. "We are arranging a surprise party for your father and mother and there is to a committee meeting tonight and we would like you to attend. We'll pick you up."

Suspicious, Isabel asked the man to hold the line. She turned to her aunt, Anne Wolfe, and told her about the man on the phone. Wolfe was leery. "Find out who he is. You won't go until you are sure of his identity."

The caller arrived a short time later to collect Isabel, but Anne would not allow her niece to go alone. The two women accompanied "Mr. Johnson" to a medium-sized sedan parked at the curb. A woman waited in the car. Anne asked, "Is this

Mrs. Johnson?" The woman nodded in acknowledgement and buried her face deep into the fur collar of her coat.

The man threw open both doors of the sedan and reached into the back for a lap robe. He grabbed Isabel's arm to assist her into the car. The drizzle had loosened the spirit gum by which Mr. Johnson had attached a false mustache to his upper lip. Isabel looked at the cockeyed mustache and said, "I don't know you. I'm not going with you. And besides, your mustache is slipping." Isabel pulled her arm free. She and Anne dashed for the house. They ran inside, slammed the front door, and listened as the sedan disappeared into the night.

Isabel and Anne were lucky. The survived a close encounter with two of the ineptest kidnappers in criminal history.

The kidnappers learned a valuable lesson from Isabel's thwarted abduction. Invest in better glue.

Failing to kidnap Isabel, they implemented Plan B. On February 5, 1933, Mrs. Mary Bosworth Skeele, the 65-year-old wife of Dr. Walter F. Skeele, Dean of USC's College of Music, received an anonymous call. "Dr. Skeele has been injured in an automobile accident. They have taken him to the North Side Emergency Hospital at 287 San Fernando Road. We're coming in a car to take you there." While she waited for her ride to the hospital, Mary phoned her son Franklin and told him where she was going and why. "A car has just stopped in front of the house and someone is knocking at the door. I suppose they've come to get me. I'll meet you at the hospital."

Franklin rushed to meet his mother. He arrived to find his father was not a patient. He waited for Mary, but she never came. Worried, he telephoned the church where his father played organ on Sunday evenings.

Franklin breathed a sigh of relief when his father answered the phone, but after speaking for a few moments, father and son realized Mary was in trouble. They notified the police.

The first clue was the address on the envelope containing the ransom letter. The kidnapper cut it from a page in the College of Music yearbook. Based on the wording, detectives concluded Mary was not the kidnappers first choice. Police learned of the attempted kidnapping of Isabel Smith. Thanks, in large part to her aunt, Anne, Isabel escaped. Mary fell for the bogus family emergency. Luckily, she called Franklin before she left the house, otherwise it may have taken longer for her family to realize she was missing.

The stranger accompanied Mary to a car parked in front of her home. As with Isabel, a woman waited. They seated Mary between them and drove off. The car took a turn away from the hospital. Mary demanded answers. The mysterious couple remained silent. Mary screamed and fought until the man stifled her with a blanket.

While they drove Mary around Los Angeles, Walter and Franklin arrived home and found a ransom note pinned to the front door. The note was weird. The kidnappers recycled it from the note used in the aborted kidnapping of Isabel. They altered the wording to reflect a change in the victim, "wife" replaced the word "daughter."

The note led police to Isabel. She told detectives about the man and his fake mustache. They realized the kidnappers were bumbling amateurs. Amateurs are unpredictable and often volatile.

Another ransom note arrived. It was a novella compared to the usual concise demands made by kidnappers. The gist of the note instructed Dr. Skeele to deliver $10,000 ($233,000 in current USD) in unmarked bills to a place on Montecito Drive. "Your wife will be held twenty-four hours to see if you have met these requirements. Remember, we are watching your every move and it is necessary that you BE CAREFUL. You might make a move that would seem to you to be O.K., but it might prove fatal. Be wise, be careful." Dr. Skeele said, "I cannot understand why my family should have been singled out for this. I'm only a schoolteacher, and teachers never have money."

Dr. Skeele described himself as "only a schoolteacher." He did very well as Dean of the College of Music, earning about $4,000 per year ($88,000 in current USD). You can't blame him for his reluctance to advertise his wealth; especially with the average annual salary hovering around $1,370 per year ($28,187 in 2023 USD). Despite being affluent, Dr. Skeele's family was an unusual choice for kidnappers. The Skeeles were not newsmakers or Hollywood stars.

During the 1920s and 1930s, stars often carried guns for personal protection. Bing Crosby had a gun to thwart any attempt made to steal his children. Mae West was the target of a kidnap/extortion plot. Police foiled a plot to kidnap Mary Pickford in 1925. Other kidnap plots include a 1930 threat against the daughters of famed film comedian, Harold Lloyd. Stars were vulnerable then, just as they are today. Fame comes with a dark side.

The police thought the kidnappers were amateurs because they got scared before getting the money. Career criminals, or a gang, would not surrender willingly. The high-profile nature of the case may be why they abandoned the plan, and Mary. They dumped her within walking distance of her home.

Investigators peppered Mary with questions about her time in captivity. Despite being blindfolded and gagged, she noticed important details about her kidnappers and the place where they held her. She slyly peeked underneath her blindfold and saw a throw rug on the floor. She heard a clock chime every half-hour—and it made a distinctive sound. Mary knew she could recognize it. Another detail Mary noticed was a train whistle blowing. She told detectives the noise seemed to be a mile away. Her kidnappers kept her near a station or a railroad crossing.

After Mary returned home, a postman and his wife, who lived near the ransom drop, alerted police to suspicious activity in their neighborhood. The tip led to the arrest of a couple, Luella Pearl Hammer and W. D. Howard, for questioning. Police transported Luella and W. D. to the Highland Park Police Station.

A police search of one of Luella's homes uncovered the Royal typewriter used to create the ransom note, and they found the clock with the unusual chime. A Santa Fe railway spur was nearby. Among the items seized in the search was an envelope in Luella's desk upon which she had scrawled the names and addresses of several Hollywood stars. One wonders why she and her accomplice abandoned the stars in favor of a college professor. It turned out Louella was once a student in the music department. Likely some imagined offense put the school's Dean on her list.

At first, Luella claimed ignorance about a list, but then said, "If there was such a list, it meant nothing at all to anyone but me." Louella and W. D. confessed. W. D. assumed most of the blame. "Well, I'm just in the middle again. And over a woman, too. A woman put me on the spot before. But I felt sorry for her because she was out of dough. I know I'm due for a 'rap,' so I'll plead guilty." Luella denied making a confession. "I will plead not guilty to this charge. I don't know where anyone got the idea. I will plead not guilty by reason of insanity, because I never said and I haven't any lawyer yet, so I authorized no one else to say so for me."

One of Luella's brothers-in-law hired Nathan O. Freedman to represent her. Freedman was best known for defending Daisy De Voe. In 1930, they prosecuted De Voe for stealing money and clothing from her employer, the "It Girl" actress Clara Bow. Freedman gathered a team of psychiatrists to assess Luella's mental condition. The team concluded she was under the influence of her partner in crime, W. D. Howard, whose real name was E. H. Van Dorn, a recent Folsom Prison parolee.

Luella worked overtime to sell her mental instability to the media and to potential jurors. While in jail, she went to solitary confinement for hurling a bowl of soup at a fellow prisoner. Clearly bad manners, but not mental illness.

The shrinks came back with a report declaring the kidnapper legally sane. Well, maybe not entirely sane. One expert diagnosed Luella as having a "hysterical nature," while another said she was "constitutionally psychopathic." Luella and her attorney went forward with an insanity plea.

Luella may not have been insane, but she acted the part in court. She laughed out loud several times during Mary's testimony. She laughed and waved her arms, but because she studied music, not psychology, she did not realize how it affected the jury. A welcome counterpoint to Luella's histrionics, Mary was calm and made a favorable impression on the jury.

Every trial worth the bother needs a surprise witness, and Luella's trial did not disappoint. The clock with the distinctive chime appeared in court. It testified in the only way it could; it chimed the half-hour.

At his turn, E. H. stood up in court and announced he wished to plead guilty. Luella moaned, wildly gesticulated, and created such a ruckus they removed her from the courtroom, causing a delay in the proceedings. Luella's reaction was so dramatic, Freedman called doctors to re-examine her.

E. H. had a caveat before entering his guilty plea. He wanted to read a prepared statement. Judge Aggeler granted the request. He told the court that the kidnapping was all his idea and Luella was innocent. E. H. said Luella was sick and in bed during the time he kidnapped Mary. While E. H. made his grand gesture, four psychiatrists examined Luella. Again, they determined she was legally sane. In their opinion, her desire to manipulate the jurors motivated her courtroom antics. Luella did not know how to read a room.

E. H.'s misguided attempt to play Sir Lancelot to Louella's demented Guinevere proved an utter failure. The bungling kidnappers received sentences of ten years to life.

Because of Luella's double plea of not guilty and not guilty by reason of insanity, they put her sanity on trial following her conviction. She gave her last performance as a madwoman. She hummed a tune, made meaningless motions with her hands, and waved goodbye to a group of curious spectators.

E. H. Van Dorn appeared before the parole board in 1941, but they denied his request for release. He applied for parole again in 1944. If they paroled him, it did not make the newspapers. By 1950, Van Dorn was a janitor for a bank, living in the Mark Twain Hotel in Stockton. He passed away in San Luis Obispo in 1973.

The 1940 Federal census shows Luella, age 45, as a patient in the Mendocino State Hospital for the Insane. The hospital closed in the early 1970s. Luella may have gone to another facility or to a private home. She passed away in Mendocino in 1990.

25. William Gettle is Missing

Retiring with a fortune by age 40 is a common dream. Most people never get further than dreaming. William Gettle pursued success with single-minded focus and determination. He ran slightly behind his self-imposed schedule; he retired at 42.

Born in Davis, Oklahoma, on October 9, 1887, William began his career at the J. C. Penney Company in Wyoming in 1913. A natural leader, he climbed the corporate ladder, finding his place in the company's executive hierarchy.

William realized if he was going to attain his retirement goal, he needed to diversify. During the summer of 1929, when the stock market peaked, he liquidated many of his holdings. He sold his interests in the J. C. Penney stores and some of his oil and mining properties. Incredibly, with thousands of people facing financial ruin, William's savvy investing plan amassed over $3 million dollars ($53.5M in current USD) in assets.

The years William spent making money were busy and productive, but he found the time to meet a woman and get married. He and Fleeta Reston, the sister of one of his colleagues, married in 1924. They had four children. Twins Billy and Betty (8), Bobby (5), and Jimmy (4), a house in Beverly Hills, and an estate in Arcadia. The Arcadia estate boasted a swimming pool and a recreation room.

On Wednesday, May 9, 1934, James Wolfe, Albert Hitchen, and their wives spent the day at the Gettle's Arcadia estate. The pool party wrapped up at 10 p.m. when the women went to bed. William and James walked toward the recreation room while Albert escorted the women to their quarters. William went behind the bar to fix cocktails, and James seated himself on a stool facing his host. They were talking and laughing when James felt, "... a poke in the back." He saw a second man with a handkerchief over his face point a revolver at William. "Stick 'em up." William and James complied and raised their arms over their heads. The bandits led them out of the room and walked them beyond the pool. James felt the man prodding him along. William and his captor were out in front. As they walked alongside the pool, the man whispered. 'This is no stick-up. This is a kidnapping."

James thought the kidnapping might be an elaborate joke. He knew William's reputation as a prankster, but he was not sure enough to resist. He surreptitiously dropped his wallet, containing $200, in the swimming pool as they walked by. They came to the wall surrounding the property and stopped for a moment so the abductors could bind James' hands behind his back. William's hands were bound in front of him at the wrists so he could use them to climb the ladder over the wall. James heard William moving up the ladder, then he heard a thud as William dropped to the other side and groaned.

James' said his captor, "bound my mouth and nose with adhesive tape. He did a good job of it, too. Only my eyes were left open. Then he bound my feet and sat me down on the ground." The man leaned over and whispered, "Stay where you are for an hour or we'll kill you." James heard the man climb the ladder, and then he heard a car drive away. He said, "My tennis shoes were not tied and I wiggled my feet out of them. Soon I worked the binding from my ankles—they weren't very tightly bound, as it was done in a hurry—then I worked myself over to a small tree. Working against this tree for a few minutes, I was able to stand on my feet. Then I hurried to the recreation room where I ran into Alber. He jerked the adhesive from my face and untied my hands."

James told Albert everything. The abduction, which seemed like it took hours, took only ten minutes. They phoned police.

A weird telephone call came in about 15 minutes after the kidnappers took William. Albert Hitchen answered the phone. "Did Gettle get that special magazine he ordered today?" Albert was about to reply when the caller hung up. Sheriff's investigators figured the call was a way of checking that the kidnapping had occurred.

Through the family attorney, Ernest E. Noon, Fleeta issued a statement. "To the kidnapers (sic) of my husband. I beg you not to harm my husband and father of my four children. Please realize that I am ill and that this tragic turn of events has seriously aggravated my condition. Realization of the detention of their father has seriously and pathetically affected our four children. I urge you to communicate with our personal attorney. He is E. E. Noon, Bank of America Building, Beverly Hills, telephone Oxford 7075. Mr. Noon is authorized by me to meet your ransom demands. Any contact you make with Mr. Noon will be treated confidentially by him. He is working independently and exclusively in our interests."

Ernest issued a statement to the press about the situation. "We want Mr. Gettle back at once. We are prepared to deal confidentially, honestly, fairly, with the kidnapers (sic) and we shall meet any reasonable ransom demand. The money will be forthcoming as soon as the ransom demand is made, provided we have sufficient money to meet it. We are willing to follow instructions of those who are holding Mr. Gettle. Mrs. Gettle is on the verge of collapse and in no condition to face the nervous strain of negotiations with the kidnapers (sic)."

Captain William Bright of the Sheriff's homicide detail reconstructed the crime. Captain Bright deduced that William's assailants knew his habits. They were also familiar with the layout of the estate. Bright believed the kidnappers climbed the wall at the rear of the property and waited for an opportunity to snatch William.

The dirt road behind the property yielded little in the way of evidence. Workers used the road constantly to deliver material to complete the swimming pool. Police found tire tracks near the curb on Foothill Boulevard outside the home. Someone had turned a car south toward Pasadena. Hoping the tracks might be important, the crime lab technicians made sketches, took photographs, and made imprints.

The agony of waiting was relieved when Ernest received a telephone call from the kidnappers. They demanded $75,000 ($1.7M in current USD), but they cut the call off before Ernest could ask questions. Several hours later, Ernest's office received a second call. The caller left instructions for the attorney to put an advertisement in a morning paper stating his willingness to do business.

In between the two phone calls, a letter, postmarked in San Bernardino at 6 p.m. on Thursday, the day following the abduction, arrived at the Arcadia home. The letter demanded a ransom of $40,000 and the writer promised to contact Mrs. Gettle. Ernest's office received a third telephone call while he was at dinner and the caller asked for $45,000 instead of the original $75,000. The kidnapers likely feared imminent capture if they did not take a quick payoff and run.

The Los Angeles Police Department and the Los Angeles. County Sheriff's Department held a joint conference at the Gettle's Beverly Hills mansion. Local law enforcement officials, District Attorney Buron Fitts and a representative from the Department of Justice, addressed reporters. After they finished, they issued a joint statement. It read, "We feel that William Gettle is still alive. Our first concern in this case is the welfare of the victim and therefore, we are thoroughly willing to co-operate with his family by withdrawing our officers if by their presence he is endangered, or so that negations can be made with the family for the return of the victim."

Late Thursday evening, May 10, a letter arrived at the Beverly Hills Post Office. Addressed to William Drews, one of William's friends, the postal authorities knew to deliver the letter to Ernest's office. They called police, who opened the note. It read, "Have $60,000 ($1.4M) ready. You may get the money from the Gettle trading account at Hutton's. If not, try the Bank of America." Ernest looked at the signature, but a telltale flourish used by William was absent. Not convinced of the letter's authenticity, he waited.

Another note addressed to Ernest arrived on Friday. It directed him to get a Ford coupe, remove the passenger side door and the door of the trunk. The kidnappers did not want anyone to hide there. They told Ernest to get $40,000 of the payoff money in $10 bills and $20,000 in $5 bills and place a note in the personal column of a newspaper. Ernest still doubted the note's authenticity.

On Saturday morning, Ernest received a call from someone calling himself Percy. "Did you get the letter?" Ernest said yes, but the signature seemed wrong. He asked Percy a few questions only William could answer. "What did I play with on my one and only trip to the ranch, and who was there?" Percy hung up. At 2 a.m. on Sunday, Ernest's phone rang. Percy was on the line with the answers to the questions. "You played with a green parrot, and Dan Richards and George Lutzi were there." Ernest then knew the caller was legitimate.

Percy said to expect a call from Mr. E. F. Fox, a friend of William's. Within minutes, Fox called and told Ernest to hurry over to his Beverly Hills home. He, too, received a call from the kidnappers. They wanted to deliver a note to Ernest at his office, but they were afraid because the place was "too hot." Ernest hurried to Fox's home. The mysterious caller, Percy, instructed Fox to drive to the Community Church on Santa Monica Boulevard in Beverly Hills and pick up a note. Addressed to Ernest, it read, "Dear Ernie—Our friend Percy said you aspired to be sure I am alive. If I don't get out of here, I won't be. Give me results."

Ernest got a call from Percy at 1 p.m. on Sunday. "Be ready to start with the money at 8 tonight." He agreed but was sure the cops would trail him. Percy said to get a substitute. The substitute was Blayney Matthews, Chief Investigator of the District Attorney's Office. Blayney picked up the car at a garage on North Highland Avenue. The Bank of America supplied the ransom money. Matthews carried it in a small black satchel.

The kidnappers marked the route to the ransom drop with stakes. The first of them had a white handkerchief tied to it and there was a note with directions to Firestone and Alameda Boulevards. Attached to the note, as proof of authenticity, was William's 1932 membership card for the Al Malaikah Masonic temple. Matthews located the second stake at Firestone and Alameda and another note which told him to drive east on Firestone to a park. Behind Blayney, spread out in a fan shape, were 65 radio cars. The authorities did not know if they were dealing with two men or a large gang, so they opted for a fan shape rather than a line of cars. If Blayney was under observation by the kidnappers, the police did not want them to see him leading a parade. Approaching the park, Blayney heard gunshots. He could not pinpoint their location, and he did not know who was firing. He aborted the mission.

As efforts to rescue him continued, William sat bound and blindfolded at the mercy of his captors. He did not know where he was. They had kept him trussed up with his eyes covered ever since his abduction. His mind constantly turned to Fleeta and his children. He was frantic about Fleeta's condition. Fleeta was an invalid, and under a doctor's care, so she was unable to attend the pool party at their Arcadia estate. She waited for William with their four young children in their Beverly Hills home. If he survived his kidnapping ordeal, she might not.

One kidnapper, whom the others addressed as the boss, stood out from the rest. Whenever he came into the room to dictate a note, he covered himself with a white sheet. He looked ghostly and menacing. William could glimpse him out of a loose corner of his blindfold, but did not recognize him. The only thing William knew for sure was he was somewhere that got scorching hot during the day. He used the ebb and flow of the heat to keep track of time. William calculated it was Sunday when the boss came into his room and told him negotiations were ending. The ransom pay-off fell through and the boss was furious.

At 4 a.m. on Monday, Ernest received a call from Percy. The botched ransom drop-off annoyed him. Worse, he seemed to know about the radio cars. He told Ernest he better find someone else to deliver the ransom—then hung up. Percy called later in the day and advised Ernest to go to Fox's home again. Percy was about to say something when Ernest heard a click on the line. He knew the cops had tapped his phone, and he also knew that Percy would know what the click meant. Ernest told Percy that they had better talk over another phone. Percy agreed, and Ernest went to Fox's home to wait.

A few weeks before William's kidnapping, LAPD Detective Lieutenants William C. Burris and Harry Gearhardt installed a Dictaphone in the apartment of a man named Kirk. They suspected him of band robbery. The detectives eavesdropped, hoping to overhear something incriminating. Days went by, and they heard nothing of value until Monday, May 14, when they overheard a conversation between Kirk and two women. One woman said, "I'll bet you're scared about that phone call." Kirk replied, "Oh, no I'm not. I know a call from a pay station can't be traced." Kirk had it wrong. Investigators traced his calls to a phone booth in a drug store at Pico and Western. The same phone booth used by Percy to phone Ernest about the ransom drop-off. They found Kirk in an apartment on Harvard Street.

Early on Monday morning, detectives picked him up. They broke into the apartment where they found two young women. Kirk refused to talk. Detectives frisked him, and found a card for N. W. Zimmer, a real estate man in La Crescenta. On the flip-side of the card, they found William's name along with an address and phone number.

Detectives located Zimmer. They asked him if he remembered renting a house to, "... a little man with a red neck." "Sure," Zimmer said. "I rented a house at 4256 Rosemont Avenue to such a man. He paid me $30 in advance. Said he wanted it for his invalid mother and that it must be quiet."

LAPD relayed the information to the Sheriff's Office. Deputies Harry Brewster, Ernest Sichler, Ray Rowe, Claude Morgan, and Investigator Jack Southard of the D.A.'s office, all heavily armed, sped to the La Crescenta address.

The small bungalow sat behind an American Legion clubhouse. The occupants heard police arrive. A man ran out of the back door and disappeared into the brush. A second man leaped from an open window and ran through a hedge. Guns drawn, Southard and Sichler pursued the fleeing men. Other deputies smashed in the front door of the house. They found William. He was on a bed in a room with the blinds drawn. He was still bound and had a table napkin taped across his eyes. The deputies removed his bindings and helped him to his feet. William smiled. "Well, here you are."

They captured Roy Williams near the scene. The other man, Larry Kerrigan, escaped on a bus bound for downtown. A telephone call interrupted Sheriff Department Captain Norris Stensland's dinner. The caller asked, "Do you want Kerrigan?" Stensland responded, "Do I want Kerrigan? Don't be silly. Where do I go?" The caller directed Stensland to a café at College Street and Broadway. Minutes later, he found Kerrigan sitting on a stool at the counter—he was the café's only patron. Stensland walked up to him. "I want you, brother." On the drive to the Hall of Justice, Kerrigan told Stensland, "... you wouldn't have me now if it hadn't been for a dirty stool pigeon ..." Unruffled Stensland just smiled. "That's what all you crooks say. You never give us officers any credit."

The first thing William did was phone Fleeta. Word of his release spread faster than a summer brushfire. Thousands of people thronged to his Beverly Hills home to witness his return. Calling it a "bedlam of cheers," the *Herald* likened the scene to the ovation Charles Lindbergh got after his historic

Atlantic crossing. “Women wept. Strangers embraced each other. It was as if everyone was victorious, as if humanity stood there epitomized in the person of William F. Gettle, triumphant over the powers of darkness.” The *Herald* was fond of hyperbole—and this situation demanded nothing less.

Instead of William’s joyful homecoming, the press turned its attention to the fates awaiting his kidnappers. The gang members, James Kirk, the boss, and his co-conspirators Roy Williams, aka Roy Tate; Larry Kerrigan; Loretta Woody, aka Ann Williams and Joan Burke, aka June Ward, faced decades in prison.

To no one’s surprise, two of the kidnappers had previous brushes with the law. Kirk was a former bootlegger. Kerrigan, who based his operations in Long Beach, had charges of bootlegging, burglary, and petty theft against him going back to 1925.

Captain William Bright concluded one kidnapper was familiar with the Arcadia property. Roy Williams worked there, under an alias, several months prior to William’s abduction. The link between the victim and the kidnappers became stronger when they discovered Gettle purchased illegal booze from Kirby.

The Sheriff’s department and LAPD worked together to question the suspects in Sheriff Biscailuz’s office. Kerrigan and Williams caved in, leaving Kirk the last man to be grilled. Stensland took the lead. “Now Mr. Kirk, these men say you’re the brains of this kidnapping and that you fingered this man Gettle and outlined what to do.” Kirk denied everything until Stensland had a stenographer read Kerrigan’s and Williams’ statements. The men denied their female companions played any part in the kidnapping.

Deputy District Attorney Percy Hammen chimed in during the questioning and declared the state would seek the death penalty. William suffered an injury when he fell over the fence during the first few minutes of the kidnapping. Under California's Little Lindbergh Law, a state enhancement to the Federal kidnapping statute, any injury to the victim qualified the conspirators to death by hanging.

Crowds of people lined up outside the house where kidnappers held William. The place was a destination for curious people who stripped the roses from the bushes outside and took them home as souvenirs. A local entrepreneur tried to get an option on the house so he could charge admission before public interest waned.

In fewer than twenty-eight hours following their arrests, the grand jury indicted Kirk, Kerrigan, and Williams. All three entered guilty pleas to the charges of kidnapping for ransom and robbery, and for stealing $26 from William's wallet. Fourteen minutes later, Judge Fricke accepted the guilty pleas and sentenced the men to life in prison. The D.A. and the citizens of Los Angeles felt cheated by Fricke's ruling. They wanted the kidnappers to hang, but Judge Fricke said they failed to meet the requirements for the death penalty.

The speed of the indictments and sentencing of the kidnappers was dizzying. The gavel came down and moments later, the men were on a north-bound train for San Quentin to serve 42-year sentences. Henry Dennison, the deputy in charge of transporting the convicts, expressed his opinion of his charges. "Three more saps who thought they could outsmart a flock of cops." Kirk, the leader of the gang, agreed. "We thought we were smart. We turned out to be dumb."

Because Judge Fricke's decision made the kidnappers' parole eligible, the Feds stepped in to prosecute them for sending ransom notes via the U.S. mail. Also tried in Federal court were the two female co-conspirators, Loretta Woody, and Mona Gallighen. Even though Kirk, Kerrigan, and Williams denied Woody's and Gallighen's involvement; conversations recorded on the Dictaphone planted in Kirk's apartment proved otherwise.

The court convicted Woody of conspiring to send ransom demands through the U.S. mail. As a result, Judge McCormick sentenced her to two years in prison and ten years on probation. Gallighen received a similar sentence of eighteen months, followed by ten years of probation.

The frenzy surrounding William's kidnapping was so intense that he agreed to a radio interview the day after his homecoming. Braven Dyer, a *Los Angeles Times* sportswriter, and Carroll Nye, a radio editor, also of the *Times*, quizzed William about his days in captivity. They broadcast the show from the tower of the *Times* over radio station KMTR. Adding to the media frenzy, the radio drama *Calling All Cars* wrote and aired a show featuring the case within 48 hours of the William's return.

The euphoria in the Gettle home was short-lived. A year after William's kidnapping ordeal, on July 29, 1935, Fleeta passed away. Hundreds of people attended rites conducted at the Little Church of the Flowers. They entombed her in the family's section of Forest Lawn Mausoleum, next to an infant son who died in 1931.

On December 13, 1941, William, surrounded by his four children, joined his beloved wife in death.

26. Dangerous Curves

"Cultivate your curves–they may be dangerous but they won't be avoided," so said legendary blonde actress Mae West. Mae's remarkable curves inspired WWII allied soldiers to name an inflatable life vest after her. A popular prank at parties was to ask a male guest if he wanted a 'Mae West cocktail.' If he said yes, they would serve him a glass of Alka-Seltzer and water in a glass with a condom on top. The effervescence of the Alka-Seltzer would cause the condom to inflate.

Mae took the tongue-in-cheek tributes with grace; after all, she built her career on her shape and her bawdy sense of humor. She had a gift for turning an innocent remark into sexual innuendo. Her impact on popular culture is profound. With a nod, a wink, and a razor-sharp wit, she lampooned stuffy and hypocritical attitudes about sex. Her humor shone a light on social wrongs, like the criminalization of homosexuality.

Mary Jane West was born in Brooklyn, New York on August 17, 1893, to a corset model and a bare-knuckle boxer. Her career began at age five when she performed at a church social. At fourteen, using the stage name Baby Mae, she performed on the vaudeville stage.

As Mae developed into an outspoken and raunchy adult stage performer, her mother, Tillie, gave Mae unwavering support. Tillie believed in Mae, and Mae believed in herself. Mae pioneered a career path through territory unexplored by any performer. Much of the material Mae performed was too tame for the rebellious young woman. She could not find what she wanted, so she wrote it herself.

Using the pen name Jane Mast, she got her first starring role on Broadway in the 1926 play *SEX*, which she wrote, produced, and directed. Panned by conservative critics, loved by Jazz Age crowds, if for no other reason than its scandalous title, SEX did well at the box office. City officials lacked the chutzpah to fend off self-righteous religious groups. Police raided the theater and arrested Mae and her entire cast. Sentenced to ten days for corrupting the morals of youth, Mae had the option of paying a fine or doing the time. Ever the savvy publicist, Mae did the time.

Incarcerated on Welfare Island, now Roosevelt Island, Mae dined with the warden and his wife. The star-struck warden caved in to Mae's demand that they allow her to wear her custom silk undergarments rather than the scratchy burlap ones worn by the other female prisoners. Mae served eight days, with two days off for good behavior. Her short stint in jail bolstered her career. She became the girl who "had climbed the ladder of success wrong by wrong."

Mae looked out at the audience while she was performing and saw that most of them were men. She wanted to get women in the seats. In 1928, *Diamond Lil,* debuted on Broadway. It was her first bona fide hit. Set in the 1890s, Lil is a bawdy barroom singer. Women flocked to see the play. Many theaters offered women only performances that sold out. Women loved her wardrobe; even though Mae's look was as far from the flapper aesthetic as one could get. Glamorous, curvy, and bejeweled, *Diamond Lil* is the iconic Mae West we know and love. She sauntered across the stage in platform shoes so high they threw off her center of gravity, thus producing her unique rolling sway, Mae captivated her audiences. The play brought her to the attention of Hollywood. She was not keen on making movies; she preferred the theater, but when she realized she could reach more people in a single film performance than a full season of a play on Broadway—she hopped a westbound train.

Arriving in Los Angeles, Mae never shied away from asking for what she wanted. When she met with Adolph Zukor at Paramount to discuss her salary, she asked him how much he made. He told her. She said she wanted a dollar more, and she got it. The only person in the United States making more money than Mae—newspaper magnate William Randolph Hearst. She got the salary she asked for, and full approval of her scripts and co-stars. An unheard-of amount of control for an actor, male or female.

In 1932, Mae made her film debut in the Paramount film, *Night After Night*, starring George Raft. Mae scanned the script and promptly made revisions. The revisions improved everyone's part, but it was Mae who stood out. George Raft said of her performance, "She stole everything but the cameras." Achieving such a feat was remarkable for anyone, but especially for a woman approaching 40.

Movie magazines exhaustively examined the lives of the stars. Women adorned in diamonds, swathed in furs—men in top hats and tails driving exotic cars. The people in the movie colony rivaled European royalty. Mae frequently graced the covers of *Modern Screen, Picture Play, Screenland, and Movie Classic.* Anyone could go to a neighborhood newsstand and thumb through the pages of the magazines and dream of wearing an expensive gown and satin shoes rather than a threadbare skirt and shoes lined in cardboard. Average people dreamed. Crooks plotted.

In August 1932, burglars ransacked the apartment of Zeppo Marx, of Marx Brothers' fame, and stole over $37,000 ($863K in current USD) worth of jewelry and personal effects. Fortunately, Marx and his wife were not there, having spent a few days at their Malibu beach home.

In August, the Sheriff's department announced that they believed an eastern syndicate stole over $100,000 worth of gems from local celebrities. A photo on the front page of the *Los Angeles Evening Citizen News* showed some of the loot recovered in the arrest of two men, Harry Hight, and Edward Felnan. Along with jewelry, detectives found a "modern" burglar kit: three passkeys capable of opening nearly any knob lock (the type usually found in apartments), a small screwdriver, and long nail file, and a small chisel.

The arrest of Hight and Felnan did not stop the crimes. In mid-October, police suspected many gangs were working in the Hollywood and Beverly Hills area. Mae became a victim, losing over twenty thousand dollars in jewels and cash in a bold curbside stick-up.

Mae sat in her car near her apartment at 570 North Rossmore Avenue, waiting for her chauffeur to complete an errand. She said a "blue jowled" man stepped up to her car, brandished a gun and told her to "Toss out that poke (handbag) and those rocks." Mae knew better than to resist. She gave the man sixteen thousand dollars in jewels and four thousand dollars in cash.

Two days later, Mae received an anonymous telephone call. The caller directed her to a vacant lot in the middle of Hollywood, where she recovered her empty handbag. Mae contacted the District Attorney, and investigators from his office covertly worked to expose the underworld gang they suspected of the crime.

On December 5th, the grand jury indicted three men—one of them, Harry Voiler. Voiler, a friend of Mae's, was in the car with her during the robbery. Mae may have been unaware that Voiler was once associated with Detroit's notorious Purple Gang. The two men arrested alongside him, Edward Friedman, from Chicago, whom police claimed confessed, and Morris Cohen, were his purported accomplices. In a newspaper photo, a smiling Mae poses with S. S. Stone, chief of the police hoodlum squad.

According to Friedman, he and Cohen staged the robbery and then "cut Voiler in on the loot." Voiler, the finger man, knew where she would be and when.

Friedman went to trial in January 1934. He confessed to police, and he also confessed to Mae. His attorney, W. J. Clark, vigorously cross-examined the actress. He seemed to believe he could get the better of her. Clark held up photos of Friedman, nude from the waist up, and asked her if she had ever observed the alleged bruises on his stomach. "You know, Mr. Clark," she drawled, "that I have seen nothing but this defendant's face."

Friedman went to San Quentin for his part in the stick-up.

Despite Mae's claim that only her manager and Voiler knew about the money in her bag during the hold-up, the authorities cleared Voiler of charges in February 1938 due to insufficient evidence. Mae remained convinced Voiler was in on the robbery.

Mae moved on from the robbery. Her career thrived, but being rich and famous has its drawbacks, including becoming a target for kidnappers and extortionists. This was especially true during the 1930s.

Outrage over the death of Little Lindy rocked the nation and led to the expedited passing of the Federal Kidnapping Act. President Hoover signed it into law it on June 22nd. Several states added enhancements to the law for kidnappings that did not cross state lines. We know these enhancements as Little Lindbergh laws, and in some states, California, among them, a kidnapper could receive the death penalty.

In May 1934, a column in the *Los Angeles Times* reported on the massive, multi-agency search for Beverly Hills financier, William Gettle. Several Hollywood notables, like comedian Joe E. Brown, lived near Gettle. According to the article, "Their (Hollywood stars) private lives are an open book and stories of their fabulous salaries paraded before the eyes of the world. These men and women, and members of their families, are ready prey for gangsters and racketeers who work outside the law."

Many stars received threats and paid up to stay safe. Fearful of retaliation, they never reported the crimes. They bought kidnap insurance and turned their homes into fortresses. Silent film superstar Harold Lloyd and his family lived on an estate in Beverly Hills surrounded by a high wall. Armed guards stood ready to challenge any visitor. Others who employed security guards were Bing Crosby and Marlene Dietrich.

Mae's brother Jack, toting a sawed-off shotgun, accompanied her everywhere. Boris Petroff, her dramatic advisor, and her chauffeur, lived in an apartment adjoining hers. Mae's security measures could not keep her out of a predator's sights.

On September 2, 1935, Mae received a special delivery letter. It read, "Acid is a horrible deed to throw in one's face so beautiful in the heights of her career for the small sum of one thousand dollars. We could have did [sic] it many times already, but we want to see what you would say first. We had your chauffer's automatic last Friday, but put it back. Ask him if he left it in the car and then come back for it an hour later. You can tell the police if you wish. But then you will be sure to get acid and a little lye in the eyes as good measure. We want one thousand dollars in 5s, 10s and 20s, unmarked or copied. If so, you shall never be afraid again of this threat as we keep our promise. We told you two yrs. [sic] Ago you would get it some time, so kick in if you don't want to lose, lose your career and beauty. We are going to give you a little fact [sic]."

A letter signed "Acid Burns," advised Mae to place a personal ad in the morning paper

Mae rushed to Buron Fitts with the letter. Fitts devised a scheme to have one of his investigators, Harry Dean, impersonate Mae, blonde wig, high heels, slinky clothes, and all, to make any money delivery. Several attempts to trap the suspects failed. Dean did a credible impersonation of the actress—if you squinted through a piece of cheesecloth.

The final letter instructed Mae to put to one thousand dollars in a pocketbook and place it in a palm tree near the Warner Brothers lot at 7:00 p.m. Accompanied by former boxer Albert Chalky Wright, standing in for her chauffeur, Mae made the delivery. Six members of the D.A.'s investigation team, armed with machine guns and sawed-off shotguns, hid near the tree, and waited. Their orders were to shoot any person attempting to get the money.

At 7:30 p.m., investigators observed a man sauntering down the street. He got to the palm tree and reached in and grabbed the pocketbook. Within seconds, three members of the squad surrounded him. Other squad members arrested six men found loitering near the scene. Innocent of any wrongdoing, police released them. The man who picked up the pocketbook identified himself as George Janios. He denied being anything but curious. He said he saw something in the palm tree and reached for it.

Blayney Matthews, chief D.A. investigator, grilled Janios, a busboy at Warner Brothers studio. They detained Janios for two days until Buron Fitts acknowledged they were mistaken. A Greek immigrant, Janios could neither read nor write English.

Fitts eagerly handed the case off to Joseph Dunn, head of the local department of justice. Dunn hesitated to take the threats to Mae seriously, which makes it likely the investigation was superficial at best. "Acid Burns" vanished.

Fitts told reporters, "If Miss West has any further information, we'll be glad to have her come up and see us—any time."

PART V. LAW AND DISORDER

In Law and Disorder, you will meet bootleggers, cop killers, and a killer cop. The lure of Los Angeles' picture postcard perfect days and nights drew retirees weary of shoveling snow, and it also drew conmen and killers. From early Italian mobsters, like Joe Ardizzone, to snowbird gangsters like Chicagoan Ralph Sheldon, Los Angeles was the place to enjoy life. For as long as it lasted.

Crooked politicians ruled Los Angeles during the Prohibition Era. They formed a subversive shadow government, The Combination. The Combination was a group that included politicians, law enforcement officials, and criminals. They made money from illegal activities like gambling, bootlegging, and prostitution.

One reformer, councilman Carl Jacobson, found out first-hand how dangerous it could be to cross The Combination.

27. Death of a Society Bootlegger

The barking of her dog, Rex, awakened Isabel Betts at about 11:30 p.m. on a chilly February night in 1923. Isabel pulled on her dressing gown, gathered it around her and cautiously approached the closed porch in the front of her house where Rex slept. Rex was so agitated that he pushed open a door to the yard and ran off in pursuit of something or someone. Had Rex caught the scent of a nocturnal animal visitor or, worse, a human intruder? She dismissed the idea that Rex was barking at her next-door neighbor, Earle Remington. Rex was familiar with Earle and never paid the neighbor's late-night comings and goings any mind. Cautiously, Isabel searched the perimeter of her home and found nothing. Relieved, Isabel started back for the house. She heard a loud sound. She froze for a moment, but then thought she recognized it as the backfire of a passing car and took a breath. Isabel called for Rex and went back inside.

At 6 a.m., February 17, 1923, Rex awakened Isabel Betts again, but this time she knew the cause. Charity Dawson, the Remington's maid, was standing in the driveway of 1409 South St. Andrews Place, screaming and sobbing. Prone on the driveway was the body of aviation pioneer and electrical engineer, Earle Remington.

Charity's screams had awakened Virginia "Peggy" L. Miller Stone Remington. She rushed outside to determine the cause of the shrieks and saw Earle's body on the driveway. Someone called the police.

LAPD detectives arrived, and they recognized the name of the victim. People in Los Angeles knew Earle for his involvement in aviation and his work as an engineer. What was not common knowledge was Earle's other job, bootlegging. Police at the scene constructed a plausible scenario for the crime. According to them, the murder went down this way. Earle pulled his small coupe into the driveway of his home and exited on the passenger side, then he walked around the back of the vehicle. One or two killers materialized from behind a hedge. Did Earle recognize them? Did they speak to one another? Nobody heard anything except for the sound that several near neighbors described as a car backfiring. A car did not make the sound. A double-barreled, sixteen-gauge shotgun did. Earle watched his assailant raise the weapon to fire and instinctively clutched his large briefcase to his chest. The briefcase proved worthless as armor. One shot penetrated Earle's chest just above his heart. The blood trail showed the wounded man staggered toward the house. He didn't make it. He was likely dead before he hit the ground.

At the autopsy, the coroner determined that someone had shot Earle, and stabbed him with a bayonet.

Detectives turned their attention to Earle's wife of six years. Peggy Remington met with attorney Jerry Geisler to discuss representing her in a divorce. A private investigator had confirmed Peggy's suspicions that Earle was having an affair, and she wanted out of the marriage. Peggy knew about the affair with a married woman, but did she know Earle was juggling several extra-marital relationships simultaneously?

Was Peggy angry, or broken-hearted enough to kill? What about the other women in his life? A jealous husband? Earle had promised one of them he would divorce Peggy and then marry her. Until she discovered Earle was also cheating on her, she had believed him.

The suspect pool expanded when investigators took a hard look at Earle's finances. It is possible that Frank Champion and Earl Daugherty, who were his partners in the Day and Night Electric Protection Company and Night Safe Deposit Company, were the ones facing financial difficulties and blamed him. An employee, Harry Miller, thought Champion and Daugherty were responsible for the crime, but refused to provide details.

Earle's bootlegger acquaintances had to be located and questioned. Earle did not handle small quantities of booze. His most recent purchase was 100 cases of the stuff. In the illegal liquor trade, Earle would rub elbows with career criminals and others who would not hesitate to end a dispute with a bullet. Had Earle double-crossed one of his sources? And what about Earle's double-barrel shotgun? Someone stole it from his office a few weeks prior to the murder. Could it be the murder weapon?

With more questions than answers, detectives had their work cut out for them.

Earle Remington made a name for himself as an aviator and businessman on a national and local level. On the surface, he wasn't the sort of man to get himself murdered. He was more likely to be injured tripping over a Persian rug at one of the exclusive clubs he frequented. Further investigation by the police revealed Earle had a secret life that could have made him a victim.

The widow had at least two motives to murder Earle. His infidelity was one. Another, and perhaps even stronger motive, was life insurance. Earle had a policy in the amount of $27,500 (equivalent to $300K in current dollars). Ten thousand dollars were to go to his sister, and the rest would go to Peggy. Detectives reasoned Peggy did not have to kill Earle herself; she could have hired someone to do it for her.

Where would a well-to-do matron find an assassin? Her friend and acquaintances were not shady, like some of Earle's. Ironically, Peggy's good works put her in touch with a pool of killers. She worked with veterans of WWI, some of whom were not only physically but also psychologically scarred. Peggy knew dozens of men who could use a weapon, but would any of them be unstable enough to go through with a murder-for-hire?

The suggestion that one of the wounds in Earle's chest was made with a bayonet or trench knife lent credibility to the theory that a vet, either on his own or enlisted by Peggy, had done the deed. How far was Peggy willing to go to get out of her marriage?

Two veteran LAPD officers, Captain George Home, and Detective Sergeant Herman Cline, headed the murder investigation. Captain Home had 20 years on the job, and he served as chief of police in 1919 and 1920. Detective Cline worked many high-profile cases–most notably, he was involved in the investigation into the mysterious slaying of film director William Desmond Taylor in 1922.

Many criminal acts were attributed to veterans from the end of WWI until the beginning of WWII. If vets misbehaved, then maybe they suffered from shell-shock, the original term for Post-Traumatic-Stress-Disorder (PTSD). T. E. Milster, Peggy's brother, spoke on his sister's behalf. As a WWI vet, he suspected another veteran of the crime and concluded Peggy was not involved in Earle's murder. Detectives were not as sure. They suspected Peggy of withholding information.

Earle kept a little red book containing the names, addresses and telephone numbers of many women. Detectives hoped the book would lead them to Earle's killer. All Peggy would say is for at least two weeks prior to the murder, Earle appeared to be in fear of his life. She said he never revealed to her the reasons for his unease.

Less than a week into the investigation, police discovered Earle was the victim of extortion. A blackmail scheme run by a man and woman. The woman seduced Earle, then told him he must pay for her silence.

In 1933, crime novelist and chronicler of Los Angeles noir, Raymond Chandler, published his first piece of crime fiction entitled "Blackmailers Don't Shoot." Chandler was right, why would blackmailers kill the golden goose?

Earle was hemorrhaging money, and when the blackmailers tried to tap him again, he told them they were out of luck. Were they angry enough to kill?

Police identified the couple, but they would not share their all their information with the press. They admitted they heard from informants about the night before the murder. The blackmailers were at a party in a cabaret on the outskirts of Chinatown. Earle was there with another man and three women. No one had seen the blackmailers since then. Or had they? Neighbors of Earle's saw a couple necking in a coupe near the murder scene. They also saw another coupe, driven by a woman, arrive at the Remington home, followed by a touring car with two men inside. Both automobiles circled the block several times before disappearing. Nobody knew the whereabouts of the amorous couple. Were Earle's killers conducting reconnaissance before they struck?

Adding to the complexity of the case, Aimee Torriani, an actress and acquaintance of the Remington's, came forward. Aimee told detectives that two weeks before his death, she bumped into Earle at a downtown club. Earle confided in her that his marriage to Peggy was in serious trouble. He seemed nervous.

Aimee told police she had a special insight into the Remington's marriage because she was a childhood friend of his, and she was a psychic. Aimee Torriani's self-proclaimed psychic abilities were underwhelming. She put forward the same theory Earle's brother-in-law had suggested; that the killer was a veteran of the world war. According to Aimee, the mystery vet's motive was simple. He respected Peggy Remington for her work with veterans and felt her husband was doing her dirt with his constant string of affairs.

Aimee also offered her opinion on the Remington's relationship. "Peggy and Earle loved each other with a love which was so possessive that it was destructive." Aimee said, "I was surprised when Earle told me, more than two weeks ago when I met him downtown by chance, that an estrangement might occur. I have been away from Los Angeles a lot and have only seem him infrequently since I came here to enter pictures almost three years ago." "I never knew Mrs. Remington well. She used to ask a number of my girlfriends to assist her in giving benefit affairs for disabled war veterans, but I never was able to take part in any of the functions arranged by her."

Detectives asked about the parties Earle attended in the company of other women, Aimee claimed she never attended parties with him. She reiterated Earle was "...never more than a big brother to me."

The investigation into Earle's murder became more complicated with every interview. Far from shining a psychic light on the slaying, Aimee succeeded only in casting more doubt on the widow.

Peggy was so stressed she collapsed. Her doctor ordered her to bed. Captain Home and Detective Sergeant Cline questioned her. This time, she had more to say.

Peggy hoped people would not judge Earle too harshly. She said, "He started (bootlegging) in a frantic effort to recuperate his fortunes. That was a long time ago. I begged him to quit. At first, he said it was impossible. Recently, however, he promised he would get out of the terrible business. But—he didn't."

According to Peggy, Earle's personality changed as he became more involved in bootlegging. Peggy didn't like his new friends. "And they were so different. In the mornings they would call at the front door, perhaps. Then a few would seek to gain admittance at the rear door of the house. Trucks would drive up to the house and unload the terrible stuff. And again a truck would be driven into the driveway to take whiskey away. I was compelled to give up entertaining. I couldn't bear to bring my friends into the house. The odor of liquor was noticeable in every room. It was just one long nightmare."

Most of the men who came to the Remington's home were strangers to Peggy. She told investigators Home and Cline, "The telephone would ring. They would ask for Earle. A long conversation concerning 'prices,' 'deliveries' and 'grades' would follow. Sometimes Earle would get angry and, following the calls, say terrible things about the party with whom he had just conversed. I never made it any of my business to ascertain the identity of the party in question. All I wanted was his promise to quit the thing."

Earle's new friends brought out the worst in him. Earle drank excessively. Peggy said, "His business affairs were in a chaotic condition and this, combined with the dangers and worries involved in his activities as a bootlegger, made him drink." Earle also became obsessed with money. Peggy felt Earle lost sight of everything in his life but his desire for money.

On the day of his death, Peggy overheard Earle talking on the telephone. Peggy was convinced that he would have started a fist fight if the caller had been in the house. Earle swore at the unknown caller and when he hung up, he continued to rage for hours. If Earle had a falling out with a bootlegging partner or rival, the situation may have escalated from verbal threats to murder.

Detectives pulled on multiple threads, hoping to unravel the tangled case. A search of Earle's personal papers revealed the names of scores of people to whom he had sold liquor.

Dr. Wagner, the autopsy surgeon, surprised the detectives by stating that the fatal wound was not made by a dagger, bayonet, or trench knife. A freak discharge of the shotgun or another unidentified weapon caused it.

Earle's will made police take a second look at Peggy. Earle was not destitute, as they had thought. He left an estate of over $150,000 (equivalent to $2.1M in current USD). That sum of money is one hell of an incentive to murder.

Peggy may have been a suspect, but detectives believed Earle died because of a dispute with another bootlegger. That theory gained credibility when, about a week after Earle's murder, police learned during the three months prior to his death, he was in fear of his life. Earle contacted some of his business associates, informing them he was in a jam and that someone might kill him. Earle did not name them.

The chances of solving Earle's murder got better when his sister, Blanche Remington, reported being followed by four people. She told the District Attorney Thomas Woolwine and Deputy District Attorney Asa Keyes; she noticed the stalkers after Earle was killed.

During her meeting with Woolwine and Keyes, Blanche revealed what she knew of her brother's finances. According to Blanche, she loaned Earle money for various enterprises over the years. She knew about his legal business dealings, but nothing about his bootlegging sideline. Woolwine told reporters, "Miss Remington arranged the conference through her attorney. She believed that she might be able to help us in our investigation, but she has told me nothing that can be used in apprehending Remington's slayer."

Was Woolwine telling the truth about Blanche's ignorance of her brother's bootlegging scheme? Or was he equivocating, hoping it would prevent her from being targeted by people who might fear her disclosures? Reporters turned up at Blanche's home on West Twentieth Street to get more information, but the frightened woman refused to talk.

Three weeks following Blanche's meeting with the District Attorney, prohibition agents and Long Beach police carried out a significant raid on a bootlegging outfit. They arrested eight men, two of whom were millionaires thanks to the Eighteenth Amendment. The raid resulted in the seizure of 160 cases of whiskey, two trucks, four automobiles, and a Japanese fishing launch. The authorities thought they could make a connection between the bootleggers and Earle's murder. Earle had likely conducted business with Claude V. Dudrey, one man being held on charges stemming from the raid. Claude did not deny his association with Earle. He admitted under questioning he attempted to get the lease on a building Earle was preparing to vacate. He also admitted to selling seven cases of booze to Earle. He denied involvement in the murder.

On April 30, 1923, after months of frustration and dead ends, the *Los Angeles Times* reported on a lead. A young woman who remained nameless had a story everyone hoped would resolve the case. The woman did not approach police first. She took her story to a local defense attorney, S. S. Hahn. Hahn acted as the messenger. He met with Assistant District Attorney Asa Keyes and repeated what the woman had told him.

Hahn said the woman, an attractive 28-year-old brunette, stated that she and Earle had been lovers for over eighteen months, but he lost interest in her. She tried to hold on to him. "I loved Remington and expected him to marry me. I first began to share his love more than a year and a half ago. I had been married. I knew he was married, but he promised he would obtain a divorce and marry me. For a year, we were happy. He and I lived together for a time at the beach in Venice. Then gradually his love seemed to cool. He missed his appointments with me and I saw less and less of him. At first, I suspected, and then I knew that there were other women in his life. It became more and more difficult for me to see him and finally I realized he was out of my life. I wanted to talk to him but was unable to meet him. Time after time, I sought an interview with him at his office without success. Then, on the day of the shooting, I trailed him. I saw him meet the other woman. I followed them. They had dinner together in a restaurant. I waited outside while they dined and followed them to the Los Angeles Athletic Club, where I lost track of them. That day I carried with me a bottle of acid with which I planned to forever disfigure both of them. After losing trace of them, I got in touch with a man I knew I could trust and asked him to help me. He brought another man with him.

With them, I drove to the Remington home and waited for Earle. I wanted to talk with him."

According to the mystery woman, she never got the chance to speak with Earle. She waited in the car for her two men friends to bring Earle to her. She saw him drive up and then there was a scuffle. Two gunshots and the woman's screams shattered the evening quiet.

From the murder scene, the woman said the killers drove her to aunt's home. She stayed with her aunt for the first few weeks following the murder. The woman confessed details of Earle's murder to her aunt; but told no one else what she had witnessed.

According to Hahn, she was so conscience-stricken, she came to him to unburden herself. He told reporters, "The woman came to me as a client and said she was wanted for the slaying of Earle Remington. She said she would disclose the details of the murder if the District Attorney's office would assure her that she would be allowed liberty on bail pending the trial. She was nervous, hysterical, and exhausted."

The D.A. would not make the deal. Hahn refused to name his client.

The Remington case stalled again in early May. LAPD Captain Home said, "we are no nearer a solution of the mystery than we were two months ago."

Two months turned into two years, then twenty. Finally, a WWI veteran, Lawrence Aber, confessed. His reason? He said he was angry at Earle for selling liquor to veterans. Aber lied. He was not being malicious, he suffered from severe mental issues and he was in a hospital at the time of the slaying.

For several years following her husband's death, Peggy Remington suffered a series of tragedies. She lost three brothers to various ailments including paralysis and Bright's Disease. Most of her money vanished due to "sharp practices of asserted friends." She was undeterred. "It means I am going to work; I am going to be hostess of a country club at Rye, N.Y." She smiled at reporters and said, "Oh, I'll get along."

Despite the dozens of suspects identified early in the investigation, detectives never got the break they needed.

28. The Last Mile

A heavy fog blanketed Luther Green's westside Los Angeles neighborhood. Damp and cold outside—a perfect night to stay in. Green sat in the living room of his home, relaxed, and read a book.

Outside, several men waited in the darkness in a large, black touring car. At 7:00 p.m., one man gestured. Time to go. Using tools they brought with them, they broke into Green's cellar. They were after a stash of pre-war liquor worth over ten thousand dollars ($172,000 in current USD). The Volstead Act, enacted in 1919 and effective in 1920, made the sale, manufacture, and transportation of liquor illegal. As counterintuitive as it seems, the Volstead Act did not make the consumption and possession of alcohol illegal. Green's cellar was legal.

Moments later, frantic cries for help from his cook, Leu Chung, startled Green into action. He tossed aside his book and leaped from his chair. Without being told, he knew what was happening. Hijackers. He grabbed the .22 rifle he kept nearby. The weapon jammed. He threw it down and retrieved a shotgun, then stormed outside to confront the robbers. He got off one shot, wounding a man who limped toward the getaway car. The other men opened fire. Ten rounds ripped into Green's body, and he dropped to the ground, bleeding profusely.

Hearing the melee outside, Robert, Green's eighteen-year-old son, took up his BB gun and ran to his father's aid. A brave but rash act. Neighbors, attracted by the sound of gunfire, came out of their homes. They saw Green on the lawn and several of them carried him to his sister-in-law's house a couple of doors down from where he fell. Tenderly, they laid him on the sofa and tried in vain to find a pulse.

Police arrived. From descriptions given by neighbors, they identified Harry Thomas as a suspect. Thomas arrived in Los Angeles in the mid-1920s and gained a reputation as "King of the Hijackers." Stealing liquor from bootleggers is crazy dangerous. Many of his contemporaries and rivals ended up on a slab in the county morgue. Word on the street gave better than even odds that one day soon he would wear a toe tag. He had another nickname, "Mileaway," and it stuck. He earned it because on a dozen different occasions, when he was a suspect in a crime, he provided an alibi proving he was at least a mile away from the scene.

The attempted theft of Green's stash, and his murder, fit Thomas' modus operandi like a glove. LAPD issued bulletins to be on the lookout for Thomas and his known associates. Local law enforcement regularly declared crackdowns on bootleggers and hijackers. LAPD formed a squad dedicated to eradicating the crime wave accompanying illegal booze.

Another enormous problem for police was the annual winter migration of crooks to the area. Bitter cold weather in Chicago, Detroit, Cincinnati, and points east drove criminals to seek warmer weather. The migration was not a recent phenomenon; it went on for decades. The biggest difference in the current flock of uninvited guests was they arrived more heavily armed than in previous years. Many of them brought "Chicago Typewriters" (Thompson submachine guns) with them. LAPD and the Sheriff's department had to update their armories to keep pace.

On February 4th, three days following the murder, the Los Angeles Stock Exchange closed from 10 a.m. to 11 a.m. to allow its members to attend Green's memorial service. The exchange announced it would offer a $5,000 ($89,000 in current USD) reward to anyone with information leading the arrest and conviction of the killer.

Police kept to themselves that one of Thomas' lady friends, Betty Carroll, was in custody. Police arrested her in Thomas' apartment two hours after Green's murder. Betty stood amid half-filled suitcases. It appeared she intended to flee. Police took her in for questioning. Within two days of Betty's detention, defense attorney S. S. Hahn arrived with a writ of habeas corpus. LAPD Captain Joe Taylor clarified Betty was not under arrest. Police kept her under surveillance in a downtown hotel with her promise she would stay put and be ready for questioning.

Della Lee, Thomas' other girlfriend, accused him and some of his henchmen of the Green murder. Della's statement was enough for Captain James Bean to secure the right to arrest, or shoot, the accused hijackers. Two men wanted with Thomas had lengthy police records. George Elmer "Curly" Fifer, under a suspended 180-day sentence for suspicion of robbery, and Warren Reeder, aka Jimmy Dundee, an ex-con and bootlegger. The other suspects were unidentified, so they issued John Doe warrants.

The complaints against Thomas and his compatriots activated squads of police who combed the city for the suspects. Police search efforts focused on the women behind the men—

cherchez la femme. Locating the suspects' wives and girlfriends could break the case.

Determined not to let Thomas weasel his way out of the Green murder, police hunted him in every corner of the city. Newspapers broke the story that Green's liquor, the booze he died to protect, was not entirely legal. Prohibition headquarters examined it and determined most of it was, in their words, "rank moonshine." Green's cellar held only 38 bottles of bonded liquor, vermouth, and 18 bottles of champagne. The tragedy of Green's death compounded.

S. S. Hahn's effort to gain Betty's release worked—contingent on an agreement with police. Betty would serve as bait to lure Thomas into the open. The trap sprung on February 15. Police arrested the couple. They claimed ignorance of Green's murder.

A witness who saw the hijackers flee described Thomas except for his hair color. The witness said the man he saw had light hair. At his arrest, Thomas sported dark brown hair—he dyed it from its natural silver.

To the disappointment of police and prosecutors, Thomas once again lived up to his nickname. Nine days following his arrest for murder, Thomas walked free. Reporters called out questions as he walked from the courtroom. They asked him about his hair. "Sure, I dyed it myself." They asked if he was worried about his arrest. "Oh! I wasn't worried much."

While he collected his belongings from his cell, Thomas called a cheery goodbye to his jail mates. "So long, everybody. See you again sometime." If his record of 13 arrests, 3 of them for murder, was any sign of his future, Thomas would see them soon. Cold comfort for the Green family.

Not long after his release, Thomas got a tip on a liquor stash kept in a garage at 1408 West 35th Street. The home belonged to the movie actor Jack Dougherty. Thomas told Betty about the tip; she warned him against going. He insisted it was okay. Accompanying him would be a former cop, who Thomas said he could trust.

At 8 p.m. on April 22, Thomas arrived at the garage. He hoped for a big score. He wrenched the padlock from the garage doors and opened them. Flashlight in hand, he stood ready to take in the sight of dozens of crates filled with bottles. He heard, "Stick 'em up!" He fired twice toward the voice. Three LAPD detectives, Lucas, Bowers, and Hoy, opened fire with a shotgun, a Thompson machine gun, and a revolver. Thomas staggered and fell into a bloody heap. A police ambulance rushed the injured man to the receiving hospital. He died a short time later.

People never doubted that Thomas would die with a gun in his hand. Still, the obvious overkill of the police ambush left a foul taste in the mouths of some citizens. The detectives' account of the incident downplayed the ambush. They said they had no choice but to shoot.

At the coroner's inquest three days later, the detectives said they acted on an anonymous tip that the garage was to be hijacked. They staked out the garage for three days before Thomas arrived. Coroner Nance asked the detectives if they knew who they were shooting at, they said no. Because the police controlled the narrative; it is impossible to know exactly what transpired that night.

One problem with the detectives' statements is Detective Lucas was a shady character who was in and out of the police force a few times. Once for "political shenanigans"—another ambush scenario. His credibility was questionable, but his brutality was not. LAPD Chief Davis took heat for returning Lucas to the force to head the reconstituted gangster squad. Davis ignored the criticism. Lucas fit Davis' model of the kind of cop needed to deal with crooks, especially out-of-towners. Davis answered his critics. "You can't stop gangsters by slapping them with a powder puff."

One unanswered question raised eyebrows. Jack Dougherty's chauffeur, Charles Lawson, rented the garage three weeks before the shootout, to a man named Williams. Is it a coincidence that the man in charge of the ambush was LAPD Captain Williams? The questions did not bother the coroner's jury. It took them twenty minutes to find the officers justified in shooting Thomas.

Betty planned Thomas' funeral. She buried him at Forest Lawn in Glendale under his true name—Fred Thomas Owen. The chapel at the Gulick funeral parlor downtown drew a crowd. At 10:30 a.m., a car pulled up to the curb and stopped in front of the chapel. Betty, dressed head-to-toe in black, supported by two men, stepped onto the sidewalk. Police held back the crowd to allow her to enter the mourner's section. Reverend Parnell Huff, pastor of Our Saviors' Church, conducted the service. Midway through the choir's rendition of "Love's Old Sweet Song," Betty collapsed. Several women in the crowded chapel sobbed.

Outside, scores of men and women from all walks of life stood in silent wonder at the city's first gangster funeral. A hearse pulled up to convey the casket to Forest Lawn. The crowd dispersed. Thomas wrote his own epitaph in the ambulance on the way to the hospital following the ambush. Detective Lucas told him he was dying, Thomas replied, "Everybody has to fall sometime."

29. Hall of Justice Shootout

On October 17, 1918, his eighteenth birthday, Robert E. "Zeke" Hayes entered Folsom Prison on a robbery charge. His time in prison gave the fifth-grade dropout an opportunity to learn from older, harder men. He applied what he learned, and by November 1923, he found himself in the Los Angeles County jail, where he met Jack Hawkins. The like-minded 23-year-olds had long rap sheets and seemed determined to see them grow.

In 1926, feeling the heat after one-too-many jobs in Los Angeles, they drifted to St. Louis.

Upon their release from the county jail, they committed penne ante crimes in Los Angeles for a few years until they realized their luck would not last forever. In 1926, they left LA for St. Louis.

In October, they got into a gunfight with three policemen over a stolen car. They shot and wounded Patrolman John Kaiser. Police arrested them under the aliases, James Elmer Fox (Hawkins) and Robert E. Williams (Hayes). They held each of them on a $45,000 ($777,000 in current USD) bond for wounding Kaiser.

At 4:40 p.m. on December 12, seven prisoners, led by Hayes and Hawkins, rushed Deputy Sheriff Rudy Baumer when he unlocked the bull pen. Baumer struck Hawkins in the face with his keys, knocking him to his knees. The other prisoners grabbed Baumer and the trusty who accompanied him and threw them onto the floor of a cell. Hawkins pushed the door shut.

At 8:30 p.m., police found an abandoned commercial dry-cleaning truck hi-jacked by the escapees. A shirt, believed to be stained with Hawkins' blood, lay on the seat.

The next morning, they arrived in Kansas City and registered in a hotel on 15th Street. Exhausted, they slept until evening when they took a southbound train and got off in Wichita. Hayes wired a friend in Oklahoma City. He claimed that he had been seriously injured in a car accident and needed money. The friend came through. They bought train tickets for Oklahoma City. Hayes said, "Our program was to keep traveling fast, and we didn't try to pull any jobs to get money, as that would have drawn attention to our trail. We stayed in Oklahoma City a day, and at night bought tickets for Dallas, Texas, where we arrived the day before Christmas. We put in the day going to a couple of picture shows, had supper, and went to our hotel about 7 o'clock."

It turned cold and snowed. They had no overcoats. Hawkins volunteered to get them something. According to Hayes, "Burglary was Jack's long suit. I've known him to break into a house and rummage through it without ever taking a thing. He really enjoyed it. But it was never my game, so I went to bed." Hawkins returned about 10 p.m. and knocked on the door. He said, "Santy Claus is here." He carried two suitcases, two handbags, and a Christmas tree. Hawkins stole a car and broke into a house where the residents had their tree up with presents stacked underneath. He stuffed suitcases with clothes, fruit, candy, and three quarts of whiskey. He even remembered the overcoats.

Returning to Los Angeles in 1927, Hawkins and Hayes established new aliases, Robert, and J. C. Allen, brothers. Hayes hi-jacked bootleggers and Hawkins committed robberies. Hayes got so comfortable he regularly stopped in at a local gas station. They even took phone messages for him. The station owner introduced Hayes to a police officer stationed at the nearby school crossing. He still carried a gun, and he always kept a bottle of liquor in his car. He carried a badge he took from a deputy sheriff during a gas station holdup. A wanted man, he went about his business with little worry until, "One afternoon, they finally got suspicious of me. When I drove in to stop at the pump, one of the fellows in the station slipped me a warning that I was in a trap." Police surrounded the gas station at Third and Hobart. Hayes said, "My car hadn't come to a full stop when I got the warning that the station was surrounded. I threw her back into gear and stepped on the gas. My quick dash out was a surprise to the police, who came chasing after me with a Dodge car in the lead. I drove through the stop signal at Third and Western, six blocks later I had lost the police cars."

The police only surrounded Hayes because they thought he was William Edward Hickman. They wanted Hickman for the kidnapping and mutilation murder of twelve-year-old Marion Parker. Getting out of town seemed prudent. Hayes joined Hawkins in Lake Tahoe, where they and their girlfriends spent several weeks relaxing and playing in the snow. One night, Hawkins got a long-distance call from a friend; a wholesale bootlegger named Mac. He had a job for them. "Don't ask any questions, but come. It's something worthwhile."

Neither Hawkins nor Hayes was thrilled when they heard the details of the job. Police pay-offs, made it a six-way split. They declined to take part and stayed several more weeks in Tahoe. Their girlfriends got homesick for their families, and they returned to Los Angeles. Hayes and Hawkins registered at a hotel on Flower between Seventh and Eighth. They went to see Mac. He said, "I'm in a fine jam." One robber got arrested and confessed. He involved everyone, including Zeke and Jack. Mac advised them. "You boys had better get out of town. Don't stay here." They took Mac's advice, purchased a new Marmon touring car, and left for Tahoe. They stayed just a few days before leaving for San Francisco, where they robbed a jewelry store, and a revenue collector for Standard Oil.

A few days after the crime spree, they left their rented house and agreed to meet at 4:00 that afternoon. Hayes took a streetcar to Sixth and Market and window shopped. Because he intended to try on suits, he left his gun at home. He said, "About the middle of the block I felt a hand laid on my shoulder, and somebody said, 'Hello there, Hayes.' I haven't used the name of Hayes for several years. Who could this fellow be?" It turned out the man was a fellow ex-con from San Quentin who was going down the street with police officers, identifying people he knew. He told the police Hayes was a parole violator. Hayes slugged an officer and ran. The police caught and searched him, and they found $400 in cash, a stickpin from the Bastheim jewelry store holdup in Los Angeles, and a $150 wristwatch. Police also found a receipt for a new telephone Hayes ordered for the house. The address on the receipt led them to Jack.

Hayes and Hawkins returned to Folsom to serve 5-year-to-life sentences. They arrived on May 27, 1928. They had little time to get into their prison routine when Los Angeles put a hold on them. Two Los Angeles deputy sheriffs arrived at San Quentin and took charge of them.

Hayes and Hawkins found out they were being returned to Los Angeles to face eight counts of robbery, assault, attempted murder, and kidnapping. The authorities assigned Hayes and Hawkins to the "high-power" tank in the county jail. The authorities designated the area for maximum-security to house prisoners who were highly likely to attempt escapes or cause disturbances.

On January 21, 1929, Deputy Sheriffs Ames Randolph "Casey" Jones and Tom Higgins accompanied the pair of crooks to a courtroom a few floors below their cells. Only a sworn member of the Sheriff's department could operate the jail elevator, which often transported dangerous felons. Robert Pope was on duty that day. Following a hearing in Superior Court, Jones and Higgins stepped into the elevator with the prisoners handcuffed to each other. Hawkins and Hayes were to be returned to their cells. As the elevator started for the tenth floor, Hawkins drew an automatic pistol. He pointed it at Higgins and said, "Down with the elevator. Stick 'em up!"

Pope whirled and knocked Hawkins' gun to one side just as he fired. Higgins tried to disarm Hawkins, but Hayes blocked him. Hayes reached for the officer's gun. Higgins stepped back just as a bullet struck Jones in the neck. The battle ended. Hawkins lay on the floor with five bullets in him. Pulled to the floor by his fallen partner, Hayes pleaded for his life. Fate intervened and saved Hayes from death. A bullet fired by Higgins struck the muzzle of Hawkins' pistol, it jammed the gun. Hawkins threw it at the deputies and collapsed. Pope escaped injury when a bullet penetrated his sweater and shirt in the left shoulder, grazing him.

Bail bondsman, James Cochrane, crouched in a corner of the elevator while bullets flew around the tiny enclosure.

Hearing the gunshots, jailer Frank Dewar, and Charles Catlin, assistant jailer, ran to the elevator. They found Hawkins dying, Hayes with a broken wrist, and Deputy Jones severely wounded. Pope took the elevator to the jail hospital on the fourteenth floor. From a gurney, Hayes said, "I wish I had a rod. I'd have gotten some coppers, too." Everyone wondered where Hawkins got his "rod."

Despite an inquiry, decades later, how Hawkins got the gun is still a mystery. Hawkins succumbed to his wounds, but Jones survived. Elevator operator Pope received a Carnegie Hero Medal for heroism. Tom Higgins became captain of the Sheriff's Department sub-station in San Dimas.

Jones' injuries left him in pain and unable to speak above a whisper for the rest of his life. He remained with the Sheriff's department until his health forced his retirement. Zeke Hayes' was the first man in California to be sentenced under the habitual criminal act to natural life in prison.

At 3:00 a.m. on September 21, 1947, Henry Whitfield, aka Henry Warren, sat in a café in Glendale. He turned to the man seated next to him.

"I didn't think I had the nerve to do it."

"Do what?" asked the man.

"Murder a man," replied Whitfield.

Whitfield got up and went to telephone police. He wanted to turn himself in.

As Whitfield spoke to police, Detective Sergeants R. E. Stevens and H. I. Brown leaned over a body that lay next to an expensive sedan in Whitfield's driveway. Whitfield identified the dead man as Robert E. Hayes, a prison buddy from Folsom. The same Robert Hayes who survived the elevator shoot out in 1929. The same Robert Hays who should have spent his life in prison. Earlier in the evening, Whitfield and Hayes fought over a woman; but the shooting was over money. Whitfield fired five times at Hayes and hit him twice. "I'm glad I did it. My conscience doesn't bother me." He went to prison for two to twenty years.

Police wondered why Hayes had more than $2300 ($30K in current USD) on him, and a receipt for a cash purchase of the car, a 1941 Cadillac. In a bizarre twist that could only happen in Hollywood, actress Mae West befriended the career criminal and employed him at her San Fernando Valley ranch. She gave him money and sold him the car. West allowed him to register the car in her name to avoid questions from the parole board.

For those of you who believe in Karma, A. R. Casey Jones outlived Hayes, dying in February 1949.

30. The Black Hand

If you search online for the *Black Hand*, one of the first hits you get is the life story of Mexican Mafia defector Rene Boxer Enriquez. On his chest is a black tattoo in the shape of a human hand stamped with the word eMe—the symbol for the Mexican Mafia. The Black Hand of Death is neither a new symbol nor a new concept.

People confuse the Black Hand with the American Mafia or Cosa Nostra. They are not the same. The Black Hand is not an organization, it is a means of extortion. A victim receives a letter or other warning to either pay the amount demanded or face the kidnapping or death of a loved one, or their own murder. The extortionists stamped the warning with a Black Hand, or a skeleton's head, dagger, hangman's noose, smoking gun, or a knife dripping blood. The racket targeted Italian immigrants—especially the successful ones—people just trying to get ahead in their new home.

At the turn of the 20th century, Black Hand schemes flourished on the East coast; however, any city with an Italian population experienced the same problem. On May 18, 1905, a *Los Angeles Herald* headline proclaimed, "Murder Society Does Not Exist: No Black Hand or Mafia in Los Angeles." The declaration was premature. Crooked politicians and their minions ran Los Angeles crime throughout the city and county. But that did not keep other organized criminals from establishing a presence. Crime bosses like Charles Crawford, Farmer Page, and Tony Cornero worked with politicians and police to control vice. Maybe they were so busy building their own empires, they did not notice Italian gangsters moving into the area.

In June 1906, Joe Ardizzone, future boss of the Los Angeles mafia and the owner of a local fruit ranch, had a beef with George Maisano, a fruit peddler. Supposedly, there was a long-standing vendetta between the Ardizzone and the Matranga families. Masiano was a close confederate of the Matranga's. Old Country hostilities followed them across the ocean.

To settle a business dispute, Ardizzone sought the counsel of his cousin, Joe Cuccia. Cuccia, another local farmer and horse trader, often mediated issues in his community. After hearing both sides, Cuccia ruled in Ardizzone's favor. Enraged, Maisano swore vengeance.

On the evening of Saturday, June 2, 1906, near the Mathie brewery, Ardizzone shot Maisano twice in the back, leaving him for dead. Doctors tried to save Maisano, but his prognosis was grim. To ease his fear, they told him Ardizzone was in custody. They lied. Ardizzone had vanished. Three months after the shooting, Maisano succumbed to his wounds. Ardizzone remained missing.

The feud was not over. At noon on September 25, 1906, Cuccia drove his wagon along North Main Street. A young man on a bicycle rode up behind him and fired four shots. The horses took fright and bolted down the street. Two blocks from where the shooting occurred, the team of horses stopped at the Main Street bridge. They abruptly halted, causing the force to launch Cuccia from the wagon. Witnesses rushed to his aid. A Good Samaritan pursued the shooter, but stopped when the man drew his weapon and said, "Let no one try to follow me." He peddled away toward the Italian neighborhood. They found the bicycle abandoned on a front lawn.

A police patrol wagon rolled to the scene. Injured, but still breathing, Cuccia suffered from a gunshot wound and lacerations from his fall. He died enroute to the hospital. Police theorized Cuccia was a target of the Black Hand but lacked evidence of extortion. More likely, Cuccia was a victim of revenge. Witnesses described the killer as young, about 25, 5 feet 7 inches, with light hair and a light stubby mustache. He wore a dark suit and a light-colored hat. Cuccia's murder went unsolved.

On May 23, 1914, on a tip that Joe Ardizzone was back in town, deputies surrounded the ranch in Sunland, where they believed he lived. They approached the house with caution and saw Joe's brother Sam holding a rifle. Another family friend, Jack Garana, armed with a shotgun, scouted the perimeter at the rear of the house. The deputies evaded detection and entered the premises from the front, where they found their suspect. He surrendered without incident. They arrested him for murder.

Where was Ardizzone for eight years? After the shooting, he visited his attorney, who disguised him as Captain J. D. Fredericks, and sent him to Louisville, Kentucky. Under the Fredericks name, Ardizzone worked throughout the East. In 1912, he returned to the Los Angeles area and bought a farm in Sunland. He became enamored with his neighbor's fifteen-year-old daughter, Elsie Ellenberg. It did not thrill her parents that a man almost twice her age was sleeping with their daughter. They contacted police.

The D.A. dropped the murder case because of the lack of evidence and the reluctance of witnesses to testify against

Ardizzone. Elsie wanted to be with Ardizzone. It is evident why. Wrapped in the arms of a handsome lover known as Iron Man, must have made Elsie feel safe and special. Her parents relented, and the couple married.

The L.A. mob never had the power of their eastern brethren, but the Volstead Act offered new opportunities. Local Italians, declaring themselves to be fruit farmers or peddlers, found themselves ideally situated when Prohibition went into effect. Many wineries stayed in business making wine for religious purposes. They turned their grapes into raisins. They sold them to average citizens who, under the Volstead Act, could produce up to 200 gallons of wine annually for personal consumption. Wine bricks were a way for wineries to package grapes for consumers. With little effort, the bricks, boxes of compacted grapes, turned to wine.

Gangsters from the East and Midwest wanted to gain a foothold in Los Angeles. Legal wineries were a huge draw. Among the gangsters to visit Los Angeles was Al Capone. On December 7, 1927, newspapers reported that from his headquarters in the Metropole Hotel, Capone announced his departure from Chicago. "I'm leaving for St. Petersburg, Florida. Let the worthy citizens of Chicago get their liquor the best they can. I'm sick of the job—it's a thankless one and full of grief. I don't know when I'll be back, if ever. But it won't be until after the holidays, anyway."

Al's pity party continued. "I've been spending the best years of my life as a public benefactor. I've given the people the light pleasures and shown them all a good time. And all I get is abuse—the existence of a hunted man—I'm called a killer. Well, tell the folks I'm going away now. I guess murder will stop. You won't be able to find a crap game even, let alone a roulette wheel or a faro game. I guess Mike Hughes (Chief

Commissioner of Police) won't need his 3000 extra cops after all." They asked why he wanted to go to Florida, the land of the rumrunners. "I've got some property in St. Petersburg I want to sell. It's warm there, but not too warm. I wish all my friends and enemies a merry Christmas and a happy New Year."

Capone never intended to go to St. Petersburg. He arrived at Los Angeles' Santa Fe station on December 11. Roughhouse Brown, a Los Angeles police detective, met him at the station and gave him an ultimatum. Get out, or else. Perplexed by his less-than-cordial greeting, Capone sighed. "I came here with my boyfriends to see a little of the county. We are tourists and I thought that you folks liked tourists. I have a lot of money to spend that I made in Chicago. Who ever heard of anybody being run out of Los Angeles that had money?"

Capone was clueless about how crime worked in the City of Angels. The politicians and their cronies had their own empires to protect. They did not want to share with a mobster from out-of-town. The local Italian faction felt the same way. They controlled their own wineries, without interference from the east.

Capone rebounded. "I am coming back. I've found out what to do. When I get a little business done in Chicago, I am going to send out a lot of money here and have some real estate and buy me a large house. Then I will be a taxpayer and they can't send me away." Ironically, the Feds busted Capone in 1931 for income tax evasion. They sentenced him to 11 years in federal prison. He went to Atlanta. In 1934, a federal prison opened at Alcatraz in California. The notorious thug was right. He returned to the Golden State.

By the time the Volstead Act went into effect, Ardizzone had positioned himself for a leadership position in the Los Angeles mob. New Orleans mobster Vito DiGiorgio came to the city and thwarted Ardizzone's rise. Influential mafia leaders from the east, who tasked him with keeping the peace between Ardizzone's and Matranga's gangs supported DiGiorgio. On July 18, 1921, DiGiorgio was on his way home from the beach with his family when someone shot him in the leg in his front yard. He survived.

On May 12, 1922, someone gunned down DiGiorgio and a colleague in a Chicago poolroom. Whispers circulated Ardizzone was responsible for the murders. DiGiorgio's death restored Ardizzone to power in Los Angeles.

In the mid-1920s, Ardizzone partnered with fellow gangster Jack Dragna in the Italian Protection League. Dragna was the League's president, and Ardizzone was its treasurer. The purpose of the league is murky. Ardizzone and Dragna probably used it as a cover for their bootlegging activities. Although rarely in the news, the league got positive press for an event which even the mayor attended. He heaped praise on Ardizzone and Dragna for supporting Italian culture and heritage.

By 1931, constant in-fighting and "rum wars" among local Sicilian factions threatened Ardizzone's leadership. According to the Los Angeles Police Department's *Gangland Killings 1900-1951*, five gangsters died in 1931. In March, the body of Dominic Di Ciolla, found lying in the 200 block of Arleta Street, had obvious signs of a gangland execution. Someone meant the shotgun blast to his face to send a message. Nothing as lucrative as bootlegging could continue without violence. Disputes over territory became bitter blood feuds. Bootleggers preyed on each other. Those who did not manufacture liquor hi-jacked it from those who did. Bullet-ridden bodies turned up in abandoned cars and along roadways. Sometimes people simply vanished.

Two weeks after the Di Ciolla hit, someone shot Ardizzone and "Little Jimmy" Basile while they were leaving the home of Rosario DeSimone, former leader of the Los Angeles mob. DeSimone handed the boss' job to Ardizzone. Basile died, but Ardizzone, with several gunshot wounds in his back, survived. LAPD Detective Lieutenant Jerry Hickey asked Ardizzone who shot him. He shook his head. "I don't know. We'll wait and see." Released from the hospital in late April, Ardizzone said, "I'm going for a long rest."

On October 15, behind the wheel of his 1930 Ford Coupe, carrying a .41 caliber Colt revolver, Ardizzone left his home to visit a cousin in Etiwanda (now Rancho Cucamonga). He never arrived. His family reported him missing three days later. Lt. Hickey described the missing man as one who "settled" many differences among local Italians. He said he believed Ardizzone, through his actions as an arbitrator, may have "incurred the enmity of certain factions in Little Italy."

After seven years without a word from her husband, Elsie had him declared dead.

The question in Ardizzone's disappearance is *cui bono*. Who benefits? No one stood to gain more than Jack Dragna and his eastern bosses. The consensus at the time was Ardizzone was a "mustache Pete," a man with an antiquated mindset. In 1931, when he disappeared, the "Young Turks" of the mafia, like Charles "Lucky" Luciano and Vito Genovese, wanted the organization to fully embrace future opportunities. Rather than fight endless personal vendettas, the Young Turks saw the mob had the potential of a Fortune 500 company, and they wanted to manage it in the same manner. Jack Dragna shared their vision of the future.

As Ardizzone's bones decayed in an unmarked grave and his reputation faded, Dragna built the Los Angeles mob. He reigned as boss from 1931 to his peaceful death of a heart attack on February 23, 1956.

31. Taken for a Ride

Santa Fe Railroad switch tender, William Hopkins, navigated the dirt road to the shanty near the 9th street viaduct bridge for his 11:00 p.m. to 7:00 a.m. shift. Between 12:30 and 1:00 a.m., two gunshots, a few seconds apart, disrupted the early morning silence. Hawkins looked, but saw no one; however, he heard a car. He could not see the car in the darkness, but it had the distinctive sound of a Model T Ford. The car stopped, then it started again. Hopkins heard the car pass within 25 to 30 feet of the shanty. He stayed at his post and did not investigate.

About 7:00 a.m. on the morning of August 6, 1921, Phillip Bomar, a twelve-year veteran of the Los Angeles Police Department, found the body of a man lying on his back. The body lay on East 9th Street, about 200 feet east of the bridge. Bomar recognized the dead man as Mike Mucich, a local bootlegger. Mucich had two visible gunshot wounds to his head. Bomar called in his find.

Mucich cheated death at the hands of rivals five times over the past several months. In November 1920, two assassins entered his home, shot him, and left him for dead. Doctors gave him a slight chance of survival. Miraculously, he pulled through. His luck did not last. County coroner, A. F. Wagner, performed the autopsy. He noted two gunshot wounds. One bullet entered the left cheek four inches in front of the external opening of the right ear. The second bullet entered just behind the left ear at an upward angle. Wagner did not bother to cut open Mucich's body—either of the head wounds was lethal.

LAPD detectives questioned Mucich's wife. She told them her husband left home on Saturday evening with a man; a stranger to her. Mucich and the stranger were going to a house Mucich maintained on Kearney Street for his bootlegging activities.

Police questioned two suspects, Phillip Stickels, and LAPD officer Charles Stevens. On the day of the murder, Stevens and Stickels argued with Mucich. The argument broke out at the home of Tony Panzich, owner of a notorious local bootlegger's hangout, Tony's Café, on East First Street. Stevens claimed to know Mucich only because he knew most of the bootleggers in his patrol area.

Steven's colleagues inspected his service weapon and determined that it had been fired recently. Stevens said he went target shooting in the nearby mountains and cleaned the gun when he returned home. They assigned him to the investigation, and he attended Mucich's autopsy.

Four previous attempts on Mucich's life offered police several suspects. Rival bootleggers may have wanted to take over Mucich's business. Detectives chased the leads they had, but nothing panned out. No one on either side of the law wanted to get involved in a murder case. Police ran out of leads by the end of 1921. The investigation went cold.

Eight years passed without a break in the case. In March 1930, a woman named Addie Minser offered a shocking story. She said she knew who murdered Mucich because she witnessed the slaying.

Questioned by LAPD Captain of Detectives Cato, Minser accused two men of Mucich's murder. She named two of the original suspects, Phillip Stickels, and former LAPD officer, Charles P. Stevens. Minser said she attended a party at Mucich's Kearny Street home. After the party, she accompanied Mucich, Stickels, and Stevens to a picnic near Chatsworth Lake. On the way home from the picnic, Stevens drove and Stickels occupied the front passenger seat. Minser and Mucich sat in the rear. Minser sat behind Stevens with Mucich seated beside her. As they crossed the 9th Street bridge, Stevens shouted, "Hey, look," and pointed to the right. She and Mucich turned their heads. She heard a gunshot. She saw blood running down Mucich's face. She turned to prop her feet against Mucich to keep him from falling on her.

Minser's chilling first-person account of the murder led to the indictment of Stickels and Stevens. Police had no trouble locating Stickels. He was in the Lincoln Heights jail under the alias Frank Harris severing a sentence for possession and sale of liquor. Stickels had an extensive rap sheet: Wright Act violations, vagrancy, and drug offenses. Delays kept Stickels out of the courtroom until June, when he faced the murder charge alone. Stevens eluded capture.

Minser's testimony failed to sway the jury. After deliberating for less than two hours, they acquitted Stickels of first-degree murder. Maybe the jury wondered why it took years for Minser to come forward. Did she have an agenda, or a guilty conscience? According to Stickels' statement to reporters, Minser acted out of jealousy. Whether of him or Stevens, Stickels did not say. Stickel returned to bootlegging and narcotics. Minser got a divorce.

In January 1935, Los Angeles police received a tip that Charles Stevens was alive. A former LAPD colleague saw him in Sacramento. The man approached Stevens to say hello; Stevens claimed to be someone else. The man knew better. He told his story to detectives, and they believed him. Owen Kessel and Harry Hickok, inspectors for the state division of criminal investigation, searched for the fugitive. They found him on April 11 as he lounged in the plaza near the state capital. He admitted his identity and surrendered without resistance.

Stevens' trial began its first full day on June 7, 1935. Prosecutor Eugene Williams made a brief opening statement in which he outlined the events on the night of the murder. Stevens' attorney, Charles De La Fond, deferred his opening remarks.

The state called its first witness, railroad switchman, William Hopkins. He testified about hearing a car he tentatively identified as a Model T Ford, and about the two gunshots he heard.

The people called A. F. Wagner to the stand to describe his findings at Mucich's autopsy. He described the head wounds, and said he concluded that either one of the wounds would be fatal, and the victim would die within a few minutes of being shot.

Spencer Moxley, a police department ballistics expert, testified Stevens could have stopped his car and shot Mucich in the head. He based his opinion on the direction and force of the fatal bullets.

The most damning testimony came from eyewitness Minser. She recalled how she and Stevens met in 1914. She admitted to being in love with him for several years. Each time she brought up the subject of marriage, Stevens demurred. Stevens' defense seized on their past relationship to portray her as a woman scorned.

Minser testified that, close on the heels of the murder, Stevens moved in with her and her young daughter in the rooming house she owned. She said Stevens pressured her to maintain her silence. Even after he moved out, Stevens continued to threaten her. He occasionally walked by or dropped in to intimidate her. He told her he would kill her and her daughter if she ever talked. He pulled a gun on her, and he shot up her home.

Despite professing her fear of Stevens, Minser admitted she went on a few drives with him, even after her marriage. She claimed he would drive to the spot by the 9th Street bridge where Mucich died and park his car. He would sit for a moment and then hum. As she sat next to him, she wondered if he would kill her, too.

The defense tried to impeach Minser's testimony. They brought up the woman scorned angle, and they accused her of running a brothel, even though no evidence supported their claim. The defense also blamed others in Mucich's circle for his murder. As a known bootlegger with a fiery temper, he made enemies. They argued Stevens had no incentive to kill Mucich. The cause of tension between them was unclear.

Stevens' conduct as a police officer showed he was a violent bully and a mean drunk. In May 1914, he got into a fight during which he viciously injured several men, leaving them on the verge of death. In 1916, someone accused him of brutality, but they exonerated him. He was such a liability to the department that LAPD discharged him in late 1921, just months after the Mucich murder.

In his closing statement, prosecutor Williams demanded the death penalty for Stevens. Just before noon on Wednesday, June 12, 1935, the case went to the jury. They returned the next day with a verdict of guilty of first-degree murder, without a recommendation. No recommendation from the jury meant he would hang.

After several reprieves, Governor Frank Merriam commuted Stevens' death sentence two days before he was to hang at San Quentin. Among his reasons for the commutation was Addie Minser's five-year delay in coming forward.

Paroled in July 1949, Stevens returned to Los Angeles where he lived in obscurity until his death of natural causes in a cheap rooming house at 333 Clay Street in the now lost neighborhood of Bunker Hill. Scattered around him were newspaper articles and true detective magazines. They had one thing in common: each contained an account of Steven's criminal career. The pathetic scrapbook of a wasted life.

32. Murder at the Roost Café

George Leslie Bruneman, Les to his friends, grew up in San Francisco at the turn of the 20th century. One of five children, his family moved several times from 1900 to 1930. His father, Fred, worked as a butcher and his mother, Mary, was a housewife. With each move, they stayed close to the Embarcadero. Les and his siblings attended parochial school at St. Brigid.

In March 1918, Les signed-up for the Merchant Marine. He served two years sailing up and down the Pacific Coast before leaving San Francisco for Los Angeles. The move south served Les well. By 1923 he was co-owner, with Jesse Orsatti, of the Cabiria Club at 745 North Main Street. Serving liquor and offering a variety of entertainments, the club boasted an upscale crowd of Prohibition scofflaws.

Lieutenant Bert Massey, head of LAPD's vice squad, also known as the purity squad, cruised downtown streets seeking the places where vice thrived. He saw expensive cars parked in the seven hundred block of Main Street near the Cabiria, he had a hunch. He and a small squad of officers entered the building. His hunch that the club sold bootleg booze was correct. He and his men did not detain the smartly dressed patrons who pushed toward the exit. Les was the last man standing. In his possession, they found three large barrels of beer. He paid a fifty-dollar fine, and they released him.

Two weeks later, Massey and his squad raided the club again. Les avoided arrest. They carted Jesse off to jail for possession of a dozen, nearly empty, bottles of Scotch. He paid a fifty-dollar fine, and they released him. Maybe the busts made it impossible to keep the Cabiria running. The club closed later that year.

In early August 1925, Les got involved in a pitched gun battle in Long Beach. Someone shot C. H. Munson three times as he drove a truckload of liquor from Seal Beach toward Los Angeles. One bullet pierced his lung. Also wounded was Jake Barret, aka Jack Collins, from San Francisco. Barret, with four bullet wounds, landed at Seaside Hospital. Police found Munson in the Clara Barton Hospital. The police apprehended Les and his accomplice, Jack Martin aka E. H. Schultz. Police took Martin into custody after he ran into the home of a Long Beach police officer a mile from the scene of the shooting, begging for a glass of water. They arrested Les when he took Munson to the hospital.

LAPD and the Sheriff's department searched in vain for the missing truck. Long Beach police found a "large, enclosed car pierced by thirty-five bullets" parked in front of the hospital where Collins was located. Police suspected the hijacking was part of an ongoing conflict between rival bootleggers, Farmer Page, and Tony Cornero.

Officers conducted a sweep of the city and arrested or warned dozens of known bootleggers. The Combination, the city's shadow government, instigated the crackdown to get rid of their rivals, like Cornero. They busted him and told him to leave town or face the consequences.

Les worked his way up the ladder of local crime, providing muscle for a "piece of the joint." To keep his ambition in check, his bosses rewarded him with control of the beach districts.

In 1930, E. L. Zeke Caress, a well-known gambler, part owner of a racetrack in Agua Caliente, Tijuana, Mexico, and mentor to Farmer Page, was the victim of a kidnapping. Three masked and armed men kidnapped Caress, his wife Helen, and their Japanese servant from their home in the Hollywood Hills. Kidnapping was still considered a state offense. The men told Caress they were "taking him for a ride." Fortunately for the victims, the ride ended not in a hail of bullets, but at a home in Alhambra.

The kidnappers jammed a gun in Caress' ribs and threatened him with death if he refused to give them $100,00 ($1.9M in current USD). The masked men underestimated Caress. He talked them into accepting half of what they originally demanded, with a caveat. They had to accept checks. Two each for $10,000 and two for $15,000 each, made out to Les. He told them Les would accompany them to deliver the checks to a gambling ship, the Rose Isle, anchored off the coast of Long Beach. Les would vouch for the checks. The men agreed.

Les met the men at Sixth and Spring streets. They drove to Long Beach and parked near the P. & O. docks. Suspicious of the men, two cops, William H. Waggoner, and C. A. Jenks, started toward their car. Officer Jenks went to one of the car windows and spoke to Les, who told him they were gamblers waiting for a water taxi to take them to the Rose Isle.

A gangster in the backseat opened fire. Wounded, Jenks stumbled and fell backwards. Officer Waggoner came to his aid. All the men in the car, except for Les, who tossed his pistol out of the window, fired at the officers. Waggoner charged. Shot twice, he collapsed. Patrolling nearby, officer W. E. Slaughter heard the gunfight. He captured one man who gave his name as James J. Sherman, a gambler living at a local hotel. Another of the gunmen, pursued by Slaughter, escaped. The smoke cleared. Police found Les attending to Waggoner.

Following the gunfight, the kidnappers watching Caress, his wife, and his servant released them. Caress went to the Hollywood police station and reported to the Captain of Detectives. Caress offered little information. He said he did not recognize his abductors and did not know why they chose him as their victim. He expressed concern for Les, sitting in a jail cell. Caress said he would post bail. Police said they needed Les as a material witness.

Despite Les' lack of cooperation, the police identified James Sherman as Ralph Sheldon, a former Chicago gangster associated with Al Capone. Police held Sheldon on two counts of assault with intent to commit murder. Officer Waggoner survived against the odds, but the incident left him paralyzed.

Sheldon's trial began on March 18, 1931. Joining him in the dock were Ray Wagner, Louis Frank, and Les. Despite support from Caress, and that fact that he helped Officer Waggoner, the district attorney believed Les to be involved in the kidnap and extortion plot.

At 3:45 p.m. on April 19, the jury acquitted the defendants. Blayney Matthews, the chief investigator for District Attorney Fitts, said, "I consider the acquittal a blot on the judicial record of the Southland. We believe the evidence against the four men was irrefutable, but the jury found them not guilty. From the information I have received, I understand there was a question in the minds of the jurors whether the police or the others fired the first shot." In a second trial, Sheldon's luck ran out. The judge sentenced him to 10 years to life in San Quentin. On July 4, 1944, 45-year-old Sheldon died of a heart attack in the record clerk's office of the prison.

Les fled the country to avoid a retrial, but life on the run did not suit him and he surrendered himself to Los Angeles police on February 26, 1934. He hired every felon's favorite attorney, Jerry Giesler, to represent him. Tried in 1934 and re-tried following an appeal, a jury acquitted him on October 21, 1935. Les kept a low profile throughout 1936, operating the Surf Club in Redondo Beach.

On the evening of July 19, 1937, Les and twenty-eight-year-old Patricia Eatone, a hostess at the Surf Club, took a leisurely stroll along the strand. They were on a well-lit section of sidewalk near the Fox Theater when two gunmen loitering near a bench fired into Les' back. Patricia watched in horror as he staggered up the street. She ran with him. The assailants fired twice more. She heard one gunman say, "Now we've got you." Bleeding profusely, Les whispered to Patricia, "If you think I'm gone, get a priest." Les lurched into the lobby of the Fox and collapsed. An ambulance arrived and took him to the Torrance Hospital. One bullet entered his left shoulder and deflected downward into the lung and abdomen. Doctors gave him a 50/50 chance to survive.

Sheriff's department investigators arrived. Les claimed not to know the identity of his assailants. In a statement to the press, Captain William Penprase said, "Gang hoodlums invariably use .45's when they put someone on the spot." Penprase was right. They found a .45 caliber automatic, three shells and a pair of men's gloves near the scene of the shooting. Nobody doubted it was a gang hit, but Les was in no condition to talk. Not that he would have, anyway. Men from his crew arrived at the hospital to guard his bedside day and night in case the assassins came to finish him.

Hysterical, Patricia hid out in fear of her life. Typical of newspapers then, they printed the address of Mr. and Mrs. Grover Hill, where Patricia was in seclusion. The unknown gunmen found her and telephoned a threat, to “keep quiet or else.” Patricia got the message.

Believing he would die, Les called for a priest to administer last rites. Doctors gave him several blood transfusions. Les improved, but his rally was short-lived. By August 10, doctors declared him to be on the verge of death.

Les defied the odds and survived. Doctors transferred from Torrance Hospital to the Queen of Angels’ facility to convalesce. An attractive blonde nurse, Alice Ingram, supervised his recovery. Detectives investigated but could not find the suspects, described as “Italian.”

Les and Alice grew close. On October 25, Alice got off duty at 7 a.m. She and Les drove out to a ranch in Montebello. They spent the afternoon at Les’ apartment, then the couple went to the Montmartre for a few high-balls and dinner. Not ready to call it a night, Alice suggested they meet her sister and her sister’s boyfriend at the Roost Café on Temple Street.

Alice introduced Les to the Roost’s owner, Roy Huddle, who seated them at a table near the center of the room. Just before 1 a.m., five men in a large sedan pulled up near the front door of the café. Two men armed with automatic pistols came through the front door. They opened fire. Les carried two guns, a loaded .25-caliber in his right hip pocket, and in his belt a .32-20 automatic, but he never used them. One round struck him in the left eye, shattering his glasses. He pitched backward in his chair. As he lay on the floor, the assassins fired seven times more. Alice took four shots to her legs; one round shattered her shin bone.

Hoping to get a license plate number, Frank Greuzard, a café employee, rushed out the front door on the heels of the shooters. Elaine Huddle, Roy's wife, screamed, "For God's sake, don't go out there!" Frank either did not hear her, or he ignored the warning. He paid with his life.

Les knew his chosen life would be the death of him. Several weeks before the shootout, Les visited LAPD Lieutenant Detective Warren Hudson. He knew the finger of death was still pointing at him. "I'm living on borrowed time." He said, "I hate to think that I went through the suffering of that other attack only to be heading straight for another rain of lead. I've got about six weeks more to live at the most. They'll get me the next time. They won't use the same pair, though. That other pair bungled the job. They'll send experts after me the next time."

The murder investigation went cold until 1940, when police busted a small-time crook, Peter Pianzelli, for the slaying. Pianzelli, an ex-con, asserted his innocence. He told the truth, but the jury did not believe him. He spent thirteen years in prison for a crime he did not commit. If not Pianzelli, then who murdered Les?

In the late 1970s, mobster Jimmy "The Weasel" Fratianno turned government informer. He turned on his mafia brothers to save himself. Out of the mob life, he told his story to Ovid Demaris for the book, *The last Mafioso: the treacherous world of Jimmy Fratianno*.

Jimmy remembered a conversation with Leo Moceri several years after Les' murder. Moceri said, "Let me tell you about Bruneman. See, Jimmy, in those days Johnny Roselli was with

Gene Normile and they controlled Nationwide, which was the only wire service coming into California. Bruneman was bootlegging it, and he and Johnny got into a beef. The word got out that Bruneman was going to hit Johnny. When Jack Dragna heard that, he gave Bomp the contract." The contract was for the first botched hit of Les in July 1937. A Sicilian born mobster; Frank "Bomp" Bompensiero served as a capo during Jack Dragna's regime.

Moceri continued his story. "Bomp heard Bruneman was getting passes from the hospital and taking his nurse out to the Roost Café. The same joint they hit him the first time." We know they first attempted to murder Les in Long Beach, not at the Roost Café. Moceri's mistake could be a memory lapse.

Moceri described the hit at the Roost Cafe. "Bomp said, 'Okay, Leo, you take him this time and I'll cover you.' Now listen to this, Jimmy. I've got a forty-five automatic and the place's packed with people. I walk right up to his table and start pumping lead. Believe me, that sonovabitch's going to be dead for sure this time. Bomp's supposed to be by the door, watching my back to make sure nobody jumps me. I turn around and I see this football player, his name was Frank Greuzard, coming at me. Bomp's nowhere in sight. Now I'm going to clip this Greuzard, or he's going to knock me on my ass. So, I blast him and run out, and there's Bomp already in the fucking car, waiting for me."

Neither Moceri nor Bompensiero died peacefully. Bompensiero died on February 10, 1977, on orders from Dominic Brooklier. Brooklier replaced Jack Dragna as the boss of the Los Angeles mob at Dragna's death. The killer shot Bomp at close range with a silenced .22 caliber handgun as the mobster walked alone in San Diego. Leo "Lips" Moceri became the underboss of the Cleveland mob. A rival gang murdered Moceri at the beginning of that city's mob war in 1976.

33. The Battle of Santa Monica Bay

Born in Italy, Antonio Cornero Stralla's family immigrated to the United States and settled in San Francisco. As a young man, he dropped Stralla and called himself Tony Cornero. When the Volstead Act became law, he saw the opportunities available to a man with ambition. Living in San Francisco, with the Pacific Ocean on his doorstep, he got into the rumrunning business.

Cornero assembled a small fleet of freighters and, using a shrimping business as a front, he imported high-quality whiskey from Canada. Running whiskey up and down the California coast made Cornero a millionaire by the time he turned twenty-five. During his early days as a rumrunner, people knew Tony "The Hat" for his colorful personality and his signature 10-gallon hat. Even as he grew older and wealthier, his nickname remained.

In 1926, five years before they arrested Chicago gangster Al Capone for tax evasion, Cornero faced the same charge. The government alleged the rumrunner owed thousands of dollars in taxes on his 1923 and 1924 earnings. He played it coy. He had "overlooked" paying the IRS.

Cornero's legal woes turned to a possible criminal prosecution for the shooting death of Walter Hesketh, a rival bootlegger. Cornero and his brother, Frank, landed in a Los Angeles jail to await results of Hesketh's inquest. When the coroner failed to find evidence to connect the brothers with the murder, they went free. For Cornero, the Los Angeles jail had a revolving door. Out in March, back in early April — 'round and 'round he went. Police knew he and several of his contemporaries were involved in bootlegging, and worse crimes. Trying to pin anything on him was like trying to nail Jell-O to a fencepost.

By early August 1926, rumors spread that Cornero, known as the Czar of Rumland, planned to sell everything and get out of the business. Los Angeles Chief of Detectives, Herman Cline, said, "Several weeks ago Cornero told me he was going to quit the game in Los Angeles. Tony then declared that things were breaking bad, and it was getting too hot for him."

Cornero was not the only inhabitant of "Rumland" to feel the heat. LAPD created a squad under the leadership of Inspector Finlinson and Captain O'Brien to wipe-out bootlegging in the city. Two days before Christmas, grand juries in Seattle and Los Angeles handed down indictments against fifty-six people. The roundup of bootleggers on the Pacific coast was dubbed the greatest since Prohibition began, and Tony and Frank Cornero were included in the list of names. Tony fled. Local police and government prohibition agents searched for him for three years.

To everyone's surprise, at the end of October 1929, days before the stock market crashed, the fugitive walked into the office of S. H. Hamer of the Special Intelligence Unit of the Internal Revenue Service and surrendered. He said, "I am out of the racket. My family is here and I want to do something worthwhile." Cornero said he would reveal his plans once they released him from McNeil Island federal prison.

Once freed, Cornero opened the Ken Tar Insulation Company. It sounded legit until the feds learned it was a cover for a large bootlegging enterprise. So much for getting out of the booze business. After a raid, Cornero moved Ken Tar to Culver City, where he produced 5,000 gallons of alcohol a day. The feds raided the Culver City facility but found no evidence of bootlegging. Everyone assumed someone tipped him off.

Cornero got another money-making idea. On March 19, 1931, Nevada governor Fred Balzar signed into law Assembly Bill 98. The bill legalized card games and other forms of gambling. Besides gambling, Nevada made it easy for people from anywhere to get a divorce. The residency requirement was only six weeks. Cornero saw potential in the dusty cowboy town and partnered with his brothers Frank and Louis to build the Meadows, one of the first Las Vegas hotel casinos. His major miscalculation was creating the Meadows as a luxury hotel. Most Las Vegas residents, and visitors to the town, came for the casual atmosphere of sawdust floors, spittoons, gambling, and prostitution. They had no interest in dressing for dinner. Cornero had the right idea at the wrong time. Even if the cowboys in Vegas had not balked at wearing a suit for cocktails, the Depression still made the hotel project risky. Two months after it opened, the Cornero brothers sold it to Alex Richmond, but a fire on Labor Day 1931 put the hotel rooms out of commission. The brothers kept the casino until early 1932.

Cornero never ran out of ideas. In 1936, he opened a gambling ship in international waters off the coast of Southern California. He bought two large ships and converted them to floating casinos. The remodels cost him $300K ($6.5M in current USD). He christened the ships the S.S. Rex and the S.S. Tango. The Rex, the pride of Cornero's "fleet," was roomy enough to host 2,000 gamblers. It had a crew of 350 waiters, waitresses, gourmet chefs, a full orchestra, and a dance floor. Also roaming the decks was a small squad of gunmen.

Ostensibly to keep the peace, they occasionally followed high-rollers to shore and relieved them of their winnings.

Cornero's success made state lawmakers apoplectic. Most of the public embraced the gambling ships. Cornero realized positive PR would go a long way in bringing new revelers to his venues. In October 1939, the Los Angeles Zoo needed money to stay open. Cornero offered the zoo one day's proceeds from the Rex—$300,000. The zoo wanted to accept, but political pressure forced them to decline. They had to find another way to feed the bears.

Pressure on Cornero to close the casinos mounted, but the money was too good. Besides, it gave "The Admiral," his latest nickname, a perfect opportunity to thumb his nose at state and local officials.

California Attorney General, and future U.S. Supreme Court Justice Earl Warren, wanted to crush Cornero. To accomplish the ruination of Cornero's gambling empire, Warren, complicit with local authorities, redrew the Santa Monica coastline so the international boundary changed. The alteration made the Rex subject to California law. If Cornero anchored the Rex beyond the new international line, a water taxi ride would take longer and, as Earl Warren said, "gamblers would be too seasick to gamble."

Cornero showed no sign of quitting the ocean for land. Outmaneuvered at every turn, Warren charged Cornero with being a public nuisance, and issued a notice of abatement. He claimed the ships, "contributed to the delinquency of minors by openly glorifying...gambling and the evasion of the laws of the state, and by inducing them to lead idle and dissolute lives." Officers served a notice, which Cornero ignored. Enraged, Warren ordered a secret raid on the Rex and other gambling ships in the area. Warren peered through binoculars from a beach club as three ships yielded peacefully to law enforcement.

When the police got to the Rex, they encountered a defiant Cornero. He manned a bullhorn and announced he would repel anyone who attempted to board. Like any captain, he would go down with his ship. He and his crew grabbed fire hoses and doused all boarding craft within range. At the time of the raid, 600 passengers were aboard the ship. Cornero would not let them off, nor would he allow the raiders to board. Warren called the gamblers on the ship Cornero's "temporary prisoners." Eight hours after the ill-fated raid began, Cornero negotiated for his passenger's release.

On the third day of the Battle of Santa Monica Bay, Cornero exchanged bullhorn greetings with Captain George Contreras of the Los Angeles County Sheriff's Department. Contreras asked if the Admiral was ready to leave his ship. "What good would that do me? I been told by the Coast Guard that no one can come aboard here unless they are invited by Capt. Stanley ... You can say for me that we've got plenty of provisions and we're having a good time. I haven't got any immediate plans and I'm not worrying none."

Cornero refused to surrender on anyone else's terms. On the eighth day of the battle, he allowed officers to confiscate the ship. Reporters asked him why he gave up. He quipped, "I need a shave and a haircut, and the only thing the ship does not have is a barber."

The courts allowed the questionable redrawing of the Santa Monica coastline to stand. Cornero agreed to pay for the destruction caused by deputies taking an axe to the tables and slot machines. Cornero left his seafaring life behind in 1944 and moved to the desert sands of Las Vegas. He and several partners opened a small casino, which he named the S.S. Rex, inside the Apache Hotel on Fremont Street. The business arrangement fell apart, and Cornero returned to Los Angeles where he tried to establish another gambling ship off Long Beach. The Coast Guard seized the ship, and Cornero hung up his admiral's hat for good.

Back in Las Vegas, Cornero started work on his dream casino, the Stardust. Learning of his criminal past, the Nevada Gaming Commission refused to grant him a license. Not to be denied his dream, he partnered with another former Los Angeles gambler, Milton B. "Farmer" Page. Page leased the Stardust's hotel and casino for $500,000 ($6M in current USD) per month.

On July 2, 1955, while the Stardust was under construction, Cornero lost $37,000 at a craps table at the Desert Inn. Chump change for someone in his bracket, but that did not prevent him from getting into an argument with a dealer over a $25 chip.

During the argument, Cornero suffered a massive heart attack. The coroner said he was dead "before he hit the floor."

34. I Did Not Have Sex with That Woman

During the Prohibition Era, Los Angeles politicians promised to clean up vice in the city; but vice paid too well for them to keep their promises.

City councilman Carl Jacobson promised his constituents a crusade against vice and corruption, and he meant every word. Born in Norway in 1877, Jacobson resembled Washington Irving's fictional character, Ichabod Crane. Washington described Crane as a goofy old scarecrow who escaped the cornfield, tall and lank, with narrow shoulders. Jacobson's gaunt face and his round Coke-bottle glasses gave him a serious demeanor, and lent credibility to his promises. The councilman was not to be trifled with.

Jacobson ran for the thirteenth district council seat in 1925. He lost by twelve votes. They convicted his opponent of accepting bribes on a tunnel project. The council appointed Jacobson to fill the vacant seat. His opponent's corruption proved Jacobson's point—city government needed cleaning up.

Jacobson ranted against the vice czars in town. He named Charlie Crawford, Albert Marco, Milton "Farmer" Page, and members of the police department. He believed they were all part of the city's shadow government run by Kent Kane Parrot.

Jacobson accused Marco of offering him a $25,000 bribe ($250,000 in current USD). Marco called it a contribution to parks and recreation. Jacobson refused the money, and Marco became the subject of a federal tax evasion investigation. Found guilty, Marco paid a $250,000 fine. Marco waited for a chance to get even.

Jacobson's accusations did not affect gamblers, bootleggers, or pimps, but harmed law enforcement's reputation. In 1926, Police Chief Robert L. Heath resigned, and Vice Squad commander James E. Davis replaced him. The District Attorney's Office came under Jacobson's scrutiny. In 1929, caught up in the Julian Petroleum scandal, a classic Ponzi scheme, a jury found District Attorney Asa Keyes guilty of accepting a bribe. He spent nineteen months in San Quentin and died less than three years following his release.

Jacobson may have felt invincible, waving his sword of righteousness in council chambers. But local vice lords, and the politicians who benefitted from their crimes, took note. In a council meeting on August 3, Jacobson called for a comprehensive investigation into gambling. On August 4, he doubled-down. He said a camp run by a United Spanish War Veterans group on South Main Street was a front for gambling run by Farmer Page. Jacobson described the camp as a "regular Tia Juana gambling place." William Baxter, quartermaster of the camp, denied the allegations. Police Lieutenant Hoy, a member of the vice squad, paid Baxter a visit and suggested the camp be shut down until "we get this thing figured out." Baxter fired back. "Farmer Page was never in the place, to my knowledge." Jacobson riled up his constituency, who pressured police to close the camp pending an investigation. Whatever the truth, the persistent attacks by Jacobson earned him powerful enemies. If they could not bribe him, perhaps they could find another way to shut him up.

On Friday, August 5, Jacobson took a call at home from a constituent. She gave her name as Hazel Ferguson and said she needed to speak to him about an issue with a county assessment at her home at 4732 Beagle Street. He told his daughter he was going to the woman's home, and then he would attend a nearby school meeting.

The debate about what happened after Jacobson arrived at the house is still ongoing. Jacobson's version was he stopped by the home to discuss a property assessment the homeowner thought was excessive. She greeted him with a bottle of whiskey and two glasses. Jacobson refused the offer. He said he had not taken a drink in 30 years.

The woman walked around the home, and then she asked him to look at her bedroom. According to the councilman, "The lights went out, and shortly thereafter, [police] officers turned on the flashlight and grabbed me."

The next morning, United Press picked up the story and ran the headline, "Councilman is Taken in Police Raid. Jacobson, Found with Woman, Charges he was 'Framed." The headlines became more lurid. "Police Break into Bedroom Surprise Jacobson with Undraped Beauty."

In his defense, Jacobson claimed it was a set-up. "It was a trap, and I walked into it." M. O. Graves, Jacobson's attorney, declared, "We will fight it to the finish, but I believe the perpetrators of the frame-up will ask that the case be dropped before it is even started."

The D.A. presented the case to the Grand Jury. On advice of counsel, Jacobson took the fifth—so did Hazel Ferguson. When they investigated, police discovered Ferguson's name was Callie Grimes. George Wallhaus, the jury foreman, read a prepared statement. "The Los Angeles County grand jury called in a special session to investigate the charges of Councilman Jacobson that he was framed in connection with his recent arrest, made an investigation and heard witnesses. Mr. Jacobson was called and given an opportunity to testify, which he had a legal right to do. No evidence of any kind supporting Mr. Jacobson's frame-up charge was presented to us and the grand jury closed its investigation without any action."

A disappointing outcome for Jacobson, but not a shock. District Attorney Keyes agreed with Wallhaus. Because Jacobson declined to testify, they would take no further action in connection with the frame-up charges. If Jacobson was right about a frame-up, then why his reluctance to testify? His attorneys said if he testified, he would have to make public the names of his sources in his vice crusade. Perhaps a more personal reason for the councilman's reluctance to take the stand was he knew Grimes' family and had met her several years earlier.

Jacobson's September trial drew hundreds of Angelenos. They knew from the headlines the testimony in the case would be titillating.

Detective Richard Lucas testified how he and the other detectives knew to go to the Beagle Street house. He said a man who refused to give his name called in a tip about a wild party in progress. If the tip was accurate, why would four senior police officers take the call? An out-of-control party in Los Angeles in 1927 was commonplace. Surely, two or three uniformed officers could handle it; and, if they did not know Jacobson was there, why did they bring two newspaper reporters with them? If the Combination wanted to silence one of their most vocal critics, a frame-up made perfect sense.

In a complaint issued by Chief Deputy City Prosecutor John Concannon, they charged Jacobson with "resorting." Named as witnesses on the complaint were Det. Lucas, Capt. Wallis, Capt. Williams, District Attorney Asa Keyes, Police Commissioner Rodney Webster, and Det. Harry Raymond. Callie Grimes entered a plea of not guilty to a charge of being a dissolute person. Her counsel stated Grimes would repeat the same story from the witness stand that she gave to police.

Support from local churches poured in for the beleaguered councilman. Reverend Robert "Fighting Bob" Shuler, known for his attention-seeking behavior, solicited money to support a recall movement against Mayor Cryer and District Attorney Keyes. He charged them with being allied with the underworld against Jacobson. Shuler slung a lot of mud from his pulpit over the years. This time, he may have got hold of the truth.

Despite the innuendo-filled headlines, many local newspapers believed Jacobson. Other newspapers slyly hinted that the councilman, outwardly a teetotaling, Bible-thumping zealot, might have a repressed sexual complex.

Courtroom spectators got an earful from the witnesses on both sides. When Captain Wallis began his testimony, the defense went for his jugular. They made a chilling accusation when they confronted Wallis on the stand. "Isn't it a fact that you gave him (Jacobson) two alternatives: to commit suicide or sign a confession?" Wallis responded, "Why, that is ridiculous," and never answered the defense's yes or no question. Regarding the gun, Wallis said, "Detective Lieutenant Lucas was standing against a dresser after he had entered the place and turned on the lights. Councilman Jacobson was sitting on the bed when he said to Lucas, 'Let me have your gun, will you?" When Lucas asked him why he wanted it, Jacobson reportedly said, "I'll put a bullet in my brain, because I realize I'm through."

To bolster the defense argument of a frame-up, Jacobson's counsel asked a witness, Fern Carlin, a neighbor of Grimes, if she ever saw Grimes with Harry Raymond. She said she saw them talking in front of Beagle Street house at 5:00 p.m. August 5—several hours before the raid. Carlin also said Grimes introduced her to Raymond on Sunday, a week before the raid. The prosecution assumed only a crazy person would testify for Jacobson. That is why they asked Carlin if she had been in a mental institution as a teenager. She denied it.

R. J. Francour, a law student visiting a nearby service station on the night of the raid, testified he noticed "three well-built men" discussing something in a car parked near Grimes' home. Jacobson did not take the stand, and neither did Grimes.

On September 23, forewoman Ida C. Creitz announced the jury of eleven women and one man deadlocked at seven to five for acquittal. The sticking point for the five hold-outs hinged on Jacobson's intent when he left his home to go to Beagle Street.

Judge Blake dismissed the panel. "Apparently, your minds are not all in the same frame. I can see no reason to send you back over the paths you have traversed, only to reach a disagreement, so you are now excused." Reporters hounded Jacobson for a statement, but he would not speak. He left the courtroom on the heels of his counsel.

The plan to retry Jacobson in October never came to fruition. The district attorney dismissed all charges against him. Callie Grimes never went to trial either; they quietly dropped the charges against her.

What happened that August night in 1927? A plausible explanation is that Albert Marco, "King of the Bootleggers," and a member of the Combination, held a grudge against the councilman for costing him a fortune in back taxes and fines and sought revenge. If he could get Jacobson in a compromising situation, Jacobson might either slink off into oblivion or commit suicide. He needed an attractive woman for the plan, and he found Grimes through her brother-in-law, Frank Cox, an LAPD vice cop. Cox was on the take and worked for Marco. The plan to bring Jacobson down came together.

For a price, Grimes agreed to be the bait. They settled on a $2,500 down payment. Marco promised to pay her a monthly stipend of $100 for the rest of her life. His promise to her ended when he shot and wounded a patron in a drunken brawl at the Ships Café on the Venice Pier. Her continued comfort in jeopardy, Grimes came clean in 1929. She admitted she helped Marco put Jacobson in the frame. The district attorney reopened the case with new defendants. Among those to be tried were Albert Marco, Charles Crawford, Callie Grimes, and the police officers who had made up the raiding party. The trial ended in a hung jury. Politically savvy Angelenos were not surprised by the outcome. They knew not to bet on justice.

What happened to the principals in the case? They tried Abert Marco twice on charges of assault and attempted murder for the Ship's Café debacle. A jury found him guilty. Eventually, the government deported him to Italy.

In 1931, someone shot Charles Crawford and his business partner, Herb Spencer, to death in Crawford's Hollywood office on Sunset Boulevard.

An unprecedented order forced Captain Bert Wallis and 22 other high-ranking LAPD officers to retire in 1939 after 20 years of service. In November 1939, *Liberty Magazine* ran an article entitled, "*The Lid Off Los Angeles, A Study of Corruption and Vice in a City.*" In the expose, they recall Carl Jacobson's arrest in 1927.

According to the article, M.O. Graves, Jacobson's attorney, arrived at the jail. He looked at Jacobson through the bars. "We've got to get you out of here." Jacobson agreed. He asked Graves how he knew of the arrest. Graves said a policeman who appreciated Jacobson's tough stance on corruption called a doctor, who phoned Graves. "You see, Carl, what has happened so far, as I get it, is only the beginning of the plot. Do you know a woman named Mary---?" Jacobson he did; she operated one of Albert Marco's bordellos on Main Street. Graves said, "Right. Well, the story is that there's a plan to inject some of her blood into your veins." Stunned, Jacobson said, "In heaven's name, what for?" Graves replied, "She has syphilis, Carl."

Carl Jacobson remained on the city council until he lost an election in 1933.

35. Politics is a Dirty Game

On Thursday, May 21, 1931, corner newsboys shouted out the day's biggest story: Charles H. Crawford, and Herbert F. Spencer, were dead. Murdered in Crawford's Hollywood office. Killer or killers, unknown.

Crawford, nicknamed "The Gray Wolf" and "Good Time Charlie," was a saloonkeeper who was part of the city's shadow government known as the "Combination." He claimed to be in the insurance business, but his true sources of income were gambling, prostitution, and bootlegging.

In June 1930, following an indictment on bribery charges, Crawford turned his back on the Combination, and turned his face toward God. He joined Reverend Gustav A. Briegleb's congregation at St. Paul's Presbyterian Church. To celebrate his baptism, Crawford placed a ring set with two enormous diamonds on the collection plate. In November 1930, he gifted the church $25,000 ($475,000 in current USD) to build a parish hall. He asked that they name it after his mother, Amelia.

Because of his religious conversion, he funded Herbert Spencer's newsletter, *Critic of Critics*. The newsletter threatened to expose government corruption—a risky proposition in 1930s Los Angeles.

Spencer took a bullet to the heart and was dead when police arrived at his Sunset Blvd office. Crawford clung to life with a bullet in his abdomen that ruptured his liver and one of his kidneys. An ambulance rushed him to the hospital where he received blood transfusions. He regained consciousness for a few moments and detectives asked him for the name of his assassin. In classic underworld style, Crawford said his secret would accompany him to his grave. When death came for Crawford, two surgeons, nurses, his wife, and sisters-in-law, his brother George, and the Rev. and Mrs. Gustav Briegleb surrounded him. Crawford's final thoughts were of his family. "I love my wife and babies."

Herbert Spencer, a former police reporter, founded the *Critic of Critics*, a weekly publication, to uncover the city's corruption. On the day of his murder, Spencer and his wife, nicknamed Frankie, left their home at 2446 Kenilworth Avenue in the Los Feliz hills early. Herbert needed time to drop Frankie off at a Hollywood hairdresser and still be able to make it to a meeting with Crawford on Sunset Boulevard.

A home in the hills? A Hollywood hairdresser? How could a journalist make enough in 1931 to afford such a lifestyle? Simple. Despite the *Critic of Critics*, which may have been a front for other activities, Spencer milked the rackets for what he could get. He never expected to meet an end like that of *Chicago Tribune* newsman, turned crook, Jake Lingle. Lingle died in gangland style on June 9, 1930—shot down on a Chicago street.

Whispers in the corridors of City Hall pegged Crawford as the target of a hit ordered by his former employee, Guy McAfee. McAfee and Crawford engaged in a bitter feud for months before the slayings. McAfee appeared to be winning a power struggle to control the city's vice. A local newspaper referred him as the Capone of LA

McAfee was a former police captain who had commanded LAPD's vice squad–which was how he met his wife, a former madam. Many people believe McAfee is the model for Raymond Chandler's suave mobster Eddie Mars in *The Big Sleep*. People assumed Crawford was the target, and Spencer was collateral damage. The theory went nowhere when police found out McAfee had an iron-clad alibi.

The murders panicked some members of the Combination. One man turned up at the city jail and begged to be locked up for his own safety. Other Combination members fled the city in terror, some of them stayed away for years. Some never returned.

When the suspect surrendered one day after the slayings, the city was stunned. The shooter was David H. Clark, a former deputy district attorney running for a municipal judgeship. Clark, known around town as "Debonair Dave," was a rising star in the D.A.'s office.

The murders of Spencer and Crawford revealed to Angelenos another layer of corruption in the city's government. Only two years before, Albert Marco and the Combination, with the help of some crooked LAPD officers, engineered a frame-up to destroy city councilman Carl Jacobson.

During his first trial, David Clark argued he shot Herbert Spencer and Charles Crawford in self-defense. He claimed they were trying to involve him in a plot to frame his friend, Police Chief Steckel. He referred to the victims as skunks.

On August 23, 1931, the jury deadlocked and a second trial began on September 22nd. The second trial culminated in an acquittal, owed in part to the eight women on "Debonair

Dave's" jury who could not believe the dapper former assistant district attorney could commit murder. One juror, Mrs. Florence H. R. Gorham, was more impressed with Clark's wife, Nancy, than the defendant. She approached her following the verdict. Gorham gushed, "I loved you from the first time I saw you."

Following his acquittal, Clark left the legal firm where he worked and set up his own practice. His primary client was Guy McAfee. The Combination paid Clark well for his loyalty. He remained with them for a few years and then, in January 1937, people reported him missing. After two months, he surfaced in Nice, France. The U.S. Consul described him as "... insane and without the courage to commit suicide." McAfee paid $800 ($17,000 in current USD) for Clark's ticket home.

Dave's wife Nancy divorced him in 1939, and his life spiraled downward. His law practice foundered. For a time, he lived in obscurity running a small store near Costa Mesa, a Southern California beach town.

Only a few friends remained loyal. George Blair, a friend from his USC days, and his wife Rose, nicknamed "Toots," took him in through the summer and fall of 1953.

On Armistice Day, November 11, the Blairs threw a party. George passed out drunk on the sofa. "A kind of an explosion, like a backfire," awakened him. When he sat up and looked around the room, he saw Dave sitting in a chair. George asked, "Where's Toots?" Dave looked at him. "I killed her." They found Toots in the kitchen, dead of a shotgun blast. It happened after an argument when she accused Clark of mooching off the family.

Clark pleaded guilty to murder in the second degree. On February 20, 1954, three weeks into his sentence of five years to life, he died of a brain hemorrhage.

36. A Bomb in Boyle Heights

Private investigator, Harry Raymond, removed the padlock from the door of his garage at 955 Orme Avenue in Boyle Heights. As Harry prepared to start his car, his wife, Beulah, walked over to a neighbor's home to let her know Harry was ready to take them on their shopping errands.

As Beulah and her neighbor waited, a massive explosion shook the ground and shattered windows up to a mile away. They saw the Raymond's garage reduced to kindling, and the motor of Harry's car lying on the pavement in front of their home belching smoke. Neighbors rushed into the rubble. They saw Harry struggle to free himself from the wreckage. Neighbors pulled him out and dragged him to the front lawn. He suffered from a broken right forearm, a broken right ankle, and multiple lacerations. As he waited for the ambulance to arrive, he said, "This is a rotten way to try to get a man. They didn't know, but what my wife or some other person would be the first to enter the car this morning."

He remained conscious in the ambulance to Georgia Street Receiving Hospital. He stayed awake for the next four hours as surgeons removed 40 pieces of metal and wood from his body. Harry required one hundred stitches to close his wounds.

The police identified the explosive device as a six-inch pipe bomb filled with black powder and packed tight with oakum.

The bomber rigged it to detonate with the car's ignition switch. Joe Taylor, LAPD chief of detectives, and a friend of Harry's, disputed the belief the bomber meant the device to kill. He felt the bomb maker grossly underestimated the power of the explosives. Jack Parsons, a founder of the Jet Propulsion Laboratory, disagreed with Taylor's assessment.

When asked who wanted him dead, he did not equivocate. "That sonofabitch Kynette. They told me they would get me. They put Kynette on me. He and his boys were shadowing me. I've known for weeks. They had my phone tapped. Somewhere in the neighborhood, you'll find where they had their listening devices. Kynette takes his orders from City Hall. He's the one who rigged the bomb. I want you to promise to get him for me." Who was Harry Raymond? Who was Kynette, and why did they want Harry dead?

Harry Raymond was born in Kansas in 1881. He married Beulah Early in Denver, Colorado, in 1903. By 1906, the couple lived in Los Angeles, where Harry worked as a salesman. Three years later, he began working as a detective for the Citizens Detective Agency on Spring Street. He worked as a detective off and on for the rest of his life.

In 1917, Harry became chief of police in Venice, California. The job was tougher, and more political, than he could have imagined. His trouble began with the 1918 arrest of James Alexander Johnston, a rich Canadian who had lived in the area for over a decade. One night in a beach café, Johnston got belligerent and defamed American soldiers fighting in Europe. He claimed the U.S. was in the fight just to wave the flag and throw parades. A local patriotic group, the Venice Vigilante Committee, took umbrage, and dragged Johnston off to Harry's office.

Harry placed him under arrest. Johnston's arrest may seem out of proportion to his crime in our modern eyes, but at the time they jailed him for violation of the Sedition Act of 1918. Police arrested thousands of people for "disloyal, profane, scurrilous, or abusive language," about the government, the flag, and the military. Johnston claimed Harry violated his right to liberty. He said he paid a $300 fine, and an additional $400 to an attorney who appeared to be in league with Harry.

Harry answered the charges in court flanked by an armada of the most powerful attorneys in Los Angeles, Jerry Giesler, Paul Schenk, and half a dozen others. District Attorney Thomas Woolwine put several of his detectives on the case and assigned more to guard Johnston from retaliation by Harry. Johnston stated he faced physical threats and the possibility of federal prosecution if he didn't abandon his case and leave town. Johnston left town for a brief stay in San Diego. When he returned, two men stopped him outside his hotel. They threatened him again and warned him Harry's attorney would "trim. every cent" he had. He sent word to the D.A. of the threats and implored him to speed up the trial. Johnston failed to appear in court as promised, He checked out of his hotel and fled to Canada. Judge Gavin Craig dismissed all charges against Harry.

Harry faced misconduct accusations more than once during his career. He played both sides of the fence—enforcing the law and breaking it when it suited him. By January 14, 1938, Harry was working with local cafeteria owner and political reformer, Clifford Clinton, to investigate graft and corruption in City Hall.

Clinton, the son of Christian missionaries, took his civil duties as seriously as his faith. Like many Angelenos in the 1930s, he grew disgusted with the in-your-face corruption in City Hall.

He formed a group, Citizen Independent Vice Investigating Committee (CIVIC), to hold officials accountable. The committee also investigated brothels and gambling. To aid his mission, he became a member of the county grand jury. When the jury failed to address the problems within City Hall, Clinton, and a few of his supporters, submitted a minority report to the jury. Submitting the report was a bold move, but it came at a cost. CIVIC had not even had the time to order letterhead before LAPD Chief Davis called Clinton a "crackpot reformer." Clinton's cafeteria, Clifton's, was the subject of an attack by the health department. The accusations of filth were untrue—his enemies filed false claims of food poisoning to ruin his business.

Mayor Frank Shaw was no kinder in his comments about Clinton. Shaw ousted George Cryer's crooked mayoral regime in 1933. He ran on a reform ticket, but here was no actual reform, only a change in bagmen. At the time of the bombing, Harry worked to link Frank Shaw's administration with local crime bosses. A disgruntled former Shaw employee, Ralph Gray, paid Harry's fee. Gray worked for Shaw's mayoral campaign, and Harry Munson, the campaign manager, owed him $2900 ($67,500 in current USD). Gray established a direct link from Shaw to crime. He observed Munson accepting a $20,000 campaign contribution from Bob Gans, known as the Slot Machine King.

In 1938, many of the crime bosses who worked with Kent Kane Parrot and the Combination during George Cryer's administration departed for Las Vegas. Legal gambling made the desert town attractive. Despite the exodus, dozens of gamblers, bookmakers, and pimps remained in Los Angeles. Enough of them to line Frank Shaw's pockets with cash.

Earle Kynette, the man Harry accused of planting the bomb, also played on both sides of the fence. In 1927, Kynette worked as an LAPD detective, while Harry worked as a private investigator and as a special detective for LAPD. He and Kynette were among those involved in the sex scandal set-up of crusading councilman Carl Jacobson.

Harry's frenetic career continued. He briefly held the position of chief of police in San Diego. He served on LAPD's gangster squad, and in 1934 he became chief of the Automobile Club of Southern California's Auto Theft Bureau. A brilliant detective, Harry failed as an administrator.

Mayor Shaw and Police Chief Davis formed an intelligence squad headed by Kynette. The squad's mission was to focus on "subversive elements." By that, the mayor and the chief meant anyone who opposed them. By January 1938, the mayor and the police chief faced their biggest challenge from Clifford Clinton and, by extension, detective Harry Raymond.

As Harry predicted, investigators located Kynette's spy squad in a home one hundred-twenty-five feet away from his front door. From their vantage point, they observed Harry's house around-the-clock. A search of Kynette's home turned up a length of pipe matching that of the bomb. They also found suspicious wire, which Kynette dismissed as being nothing out of the ordinary. The police built a case against him.

Neighbors of Harry's offered stories of mysterious goings-on in the house occupied by Kynette's spy squad. George Sakalis, a produce vendor, came forward and talked about being approached by two men, one of whom he identified as Kynette. They warned him against getting involved. They advised him to "take care of his children," and to stay out of politics. To make sure he understood, an LAPD detective, Roy Allen, beat Sakalis, while Kynette watched from a car.

In mid-February, D.A. Buron Fitts took his case against Kynette to the grand jury. They issued indictments against Earle Kynette, Roy Allen, and Fred Browne. Their trial began on April 12. In a rookie attempt to change his appearance, Kynette grew a mustache. It only made him look seedier.

Chief Davis did not fare well on the witness stand. He described the intelligence squad as responsible for investigating criminal political elements in the city that harass the police department and undermine morale. On his way out of the courthouse, a crowd jeered and booed him.

The jury found Kynette and Allen guilty of the malicious use of explosives. They convicted Kynette of attempted murder and assault to commit murder. From his hospital bed, Harry expressed his joy at the convictions, although he said it disappointed him when they acquitted Browne. Clifford Clinton ramped up his campaign to recall mayor Shaw. After the spy squad trial, thousands of disgusted Angelenos signed a recall petition.

Shaw argued evil forces aligned against him because he was a true reformer. Except for the *Los Angeles Times,* which had its own agenda, few believed anything Shaw said. Some of Shaw's supporters circulated fake petitions and tried to destroy legitimate ones. It was not enough to keep Los Angeles voters from recalling him. Shaw holds the dubious distinction of being the first recalled U.S. mayor in history.

Judge Fletcher Bowron stepped forward to accept the nomination for mayor. He won the election by a 2-to-1 margin. Bowron got to work and replaced most of the city's police commissioners, and the entire police board. Chief Davis retired before he could be removed. In March 1939, the newly appointed police commission forced twenty-three high-ranking LAPD officers to retire.

The Prohibition Era began with George Cryer's corrupt administration and ended with Frank Shaw's recall in 1939.

ACKNOWLEDGEMENTS

I realize I am intense when I talk about crime. My choice of topics for dinner conversation often horrifies people, or their eyes glaze over and they drift away. My family does not do that. Well. I'll be honest, they do, but they are sensitive, loving people who don't want to hurt my feelings. I appreciate them and love them for their kindness.

Scott Holderman, my husband, whom I've known for most of my life, has little interest in crime. His disinterest doesn't stop him from finding new, ever-more horrible shows for me to watch. He knows to search keywords like deadly, evil, buried, nightmare, and homicide. I am grateful for his unconditional love and support.

By the time I was three, I knew I wanted a brother. Imagine my surprise when my parents obliged me twelve days before my fifth birthday. Imagine their surprise. I'm not sure I'd have made it through childhood without my brother, Rick Renner. We did it, little brother—and we continue to thrive. Our plan to live long enough to become a burden on society is on schedule.

Jill Vidas is as close to a blood sister as I could have. I am sure my brother has no idea that we are not actually related to her by blood. She is smart and hilarious. She is always in my corner—even when she knows I am wrong. I could never find a friend as loyal or caring.

My daughter Lori, granddaughter Melissa, and great-granddaughter Emilee think I'm cool for my advanced age. They are strong, wonderful women. I am very proud of them.

I can't thank Kim Cooper enough for fishing me out of her spam folder in 2007 and giving me the opportunity to write for her seminal Los Angeles crime blog, the *1947 Project*. Through the blog I met some phenomenally talented people. Author and historian Nathan Marsak, for one. Nathan and I volunteered together at the Los Angeles Police Museum. Kim and her husband, Richard Schave, continue to encourage me to take chances. I'm lucky to have them in my life.

Glynn Martin and Mike Fratantoni are my kindred spirits. Hanging out with them is like taking a master class in Los Angeles crime history and police procedure. We've worked together on various museum projects since 2009. We are cooking up a book proposal. I can't wait to get started. Their friendship and respect mean the world to me.

A few years back, Mike invited me to a monthly lunch with retired homicide investigators from the Los Angeles County Sheriff's Department. I've been going ever since. It is an honor to know Gil Carrillo, Susan Garcia, Don Garcia (who I will always miss), Ike Aguilar, Frank Salerno, Rey Verdugo, Charlie Araujo, and all the others who sit at the table swapping stories. Each of them has a wicked sense of humor and a compassionate heart. Mike also introduced me to Ray Lugo, who investigates Sheriff's cold cases. Ray is a phenomenal detective, and a person for whom I have the utmost respect.

I am grateful to Christina Rice, Tony Mostrom, Amy Inouye, Photo Friends, Margot Gerber, and Celeste Hong, for their expertise on various subjects. It truly isn't what you know. It is who.

It has been over a decade since David Kulczyk and I appeared on the same episode of *Deadly Women*. We bonded over our interest in true crime and have been friends ever since. He read an early draft of this book and I am thankful for his candor and his support.

If I could be anything, I'd be a homicide detective or a librarian. They have more in common than you may think. They are relentless seekers. If not for people like Terri Garst of the Los Angeles Public Library, and Sebastian Nelson of the California State Archive, it would be impossible to find crucial photographs and information.

Jessica Auerbach has helped me stay healthy for years. I count on her to see me to at least 100.

Special thanks to Karie Bible, who started me on my publishing journey. The journey took a surprise turn or two and ended with the fine people at WildBlue Press, I am grateful to Steve Jackson, Michael Cordova, Stephanie Johnson Lawson, and Jazzminn Morecraft for their support. Every writer needs an editor. I won the lottery with Rowe Carenen. Her keen eye is much appreciated, and her sense of humor made the process enjoyable.

Agness Underwood, newspaperwoman extraordinaire, remains my inspiration. I wish we had met, Aggie.

Thank you, one and all.

AUTHOR BIO

Joan Renner is a true crime expert, author, and media commentator. Originally from Chicago, she has lived most of her life in Southern California, where she has pursued her interest in crime since grammar school.

She launched her blog, *Deranged L.A. Crimes*, in December 2012. The blog covers 20th century crimes and scandals. The L.A. Weekly called her book *The First with the latest: Underwood, the Los Angeles Herald, and the Sordid Crimes of a City,* "A great introduction to some long-forgotten L.A. crimes." She has appeared in over sixty TV shows and dozens of podcasts: *City of Angels, City of Death*; *Deadly Women; The Real Murders of Los Angeles; Buried in the Backyard;* and *Hollywood & Crime.*

Joan spends her free time cyberstalking 20th century felons and volunteering at the Los Angeles County Sheriff's Department Museum as an archivist and historian.

BIBLIOGRAPHY

Alessio, Jim. *The Eternal Flapper*. AuthorHouse, 2009.

Anthony, Helen B. *The Search for Lofie Louise*. 1999.

Banham, Reyner. *Los Angeles*. Univ of California Press, 2009.

Belletti, Valeria. *Adventures of a Hollywood Secretary*. University of California Press, 2006.

Biscailuz, Eugene W. and University of Southern California. Living History Program. *Los Angeles County Sheriff's Office*. 1961.

Blanche, Tony, and Brad Schrieber. *Death in Paradise*. Stoddart, 1998.

Bonelli, William G. *Billion Dollar Blackjack*. 1954.

Boyarsky, Bill, et al. *Inventing L.A.* 2009.

Bricklin, Julia. *Blonde Rattlesnake*. Rowman & Littlefield, 2019.

Cairns, Kathleen A. *Front-Page Women Journalists, 1920-1950*. U of Nebraska Press.

---. *The Enigma Woman*. U of Nebraska Press, 2007.

California. *The Penal Code of the State of California, Approved February 14, 1872, with Amendments to and Including the Fifty-Sixth Session of the California Legislature, 1945, Including Legislative History, References, Annotations, Appendix Covering Certain Penal Statutes Not Incorporated in Penal Code*. 1945.

Cantillon, Richard H. *In Defense of the Fox*. 1972.

Caplan, Jerry Saul. *The CIVIC Committee in the Recall of Mayor Frank Shaw*. 1981.

Chandler, Raymond. *The World of Raymond Chandler*. Vintage, 2014.

Clare, Nancie. *The Battle for Beverly Hills*. St. Martin's Press, 2018.

Clinton, Edmond, and Mark A. Vieira. *Clifton's and Clifford Clinton*. 2015.

Clinton, and Al Hirshberg. *88 Men and 2 Women. By Clinton T. Duffy, with Al Hirshberg*. 1962.

Cobb, Sally, and Mark Willems. *The Brown Derby Restaurant*. Rizzoli International Publications, 1996.

Cooper, Courtney Ryley. *Here's to Crime*. 1941.

Crongeyer, Sven, and Lee Baca. *Six Gun Sound*. Linden Pub, 2006.

Dalhart, Vernon. *Little Marian Parker (Recorded March 1928)*. 12 Dec. 2014, https://audio-ssl.itunes.apple.com/itunes-assets/AudioPreview115/v4/b3/79/e8/b379e87d-caba-c90e-fa9f-9dea88a96ec2/mzaf_6286136013632657621.plus.aac.p.m4a.

Davis, Margaret Leslie. *Dark Side of Fortune*. Univ of California Press, 2001.

---. *Rivers in the Desert*. Open Road Media, 2014.

Dawson, Jim. *Los Angeles's Angels Flight*. Arcadia Publishing, 2008.

---. *Los Angeles's Bunker Hill*. History Press (SC), 2012.

Dobkins, J. Dwight, and Robert J. Hendricks. *Winnie Ruth Judd: The Trunk Murders the Classic Edition*. 2014.

Dover, Van. *The Truman Gumshoes*. McFarland, 2022.

Duncan, Dayton, and Ken Burns. *The Dust Bowl*. Chronicle Books, 2012.

Epstein, Daniel Mark. *Sister Aimee*. HMH, 2014.

Eugene Warren Biscailuz, Sheriff, Los Angeles, County. 1957.

Famous Players. Nbm Publishing Company, 2009.

Faragher, John Mack. *Eternity Street: Violence and Justice in Frontier Los Angeles*. W. W. Norton & Company, 2016.

Finney, Guy Woodward. *Angel City in Turmoil*. 1945.

Fitzgerald, F. Scott, and Kirk Curnutt. *Flappers and Philosophers*. Oxford University Press, 2020.

Fitzgerald, Ron, and Rolin Jones. *Perry Mason*. 2020.
Perry Mason is an American period drama television series based on the character of the same name created by Erle Stanley Gardner that premiered on June 21, 2020, on HBO.

Flacco, Anthony, and Jerry Clark. *The Road Out of Hell*. Diversion Books, 2013.

Flowers, R. Barri. *Murderess on the Loose: The 1922 Hammer Wrath of Clara Phillips (A Historical True Crime Short)*. R. Barri Flowers.

Fogelson, Robert M. *The Fragmented Metropolis*. Univ of California Press, 1993.

Fowler, Will. *Reporters*. Roundtable Pub, 1991.

Funderburg, J. Anne. *Bootleggers and Beer Barons of the Prohibition Era*. McFarland, 2014.

Garrigues, Charles Harris. *So They Indicted Fitts!* 1936.

Gary, Keyes, and Lawler, Mike. *Murder & Mayhem in the Crescenta Valley*. The History Press.

Gierucki, Paul E. *The Forgotten Films of Roscoe Fatty Arbuckle*. Directed by Paul E. Gierucki, N/A, 2005, N/A.

Glyn, Elinor. *It*. Paramount, 1927.
Clara Bow

Harris, Nicholas Boilvin. *Famous Crimes*. 1933.

Heimann, Jim. *Los Angeles*. Taschen America LLC, 2013.

---. *Sins of the City*. Chronicle Books, 1999.

Higham, Charles. *Murder in Hollywood*. Terrace Books, 2006.

Hodgson, Barbara. *Opium*. 2000.

Hunt, Thomas. "Informer: DiGiorgio: First Crime Boss of Los Angeles?" *Informer*, 16 July 2010, https://informer-journal.blogspot.com/2010/07/digiorgio-first-crime-boss-of-los.html.

---. "The Writers of Wrongs: Wealthy Los Angeles-Area Mafia Leader Vanishes." *The Writers of Wrongs*, 15 Oct. 2019, http://www.writersofwrongs.com/2019/10/wealthy-los-angeles-area-mafia-leader.html.

(Idwal)), Lindley BYNUM (and JONES, et al. *Biscailuz, Sheriff of the New West, Etc. [With Plates, Including Portraits.]*. 1950.

Jenning, Patrick. *The Long Winding Road of Harry Raymond*. 2021.

Jensen, Ingrid Marie. "RAYMOND CHANDLER: THE PRIVATE EYE AS L.A. POET." *PleaseKillMe*, https://www.facebook.com/pleasekillmebook/, 23 Mar. 2022, https://pleasekillme.com/raymond-chandler/.

Kipen, David. *Dear Los Angeles*. Modern Library, 2018.

Kooistra, AnneMarie. "Previewing 'The Harlot City?: Prostitution in Hollywood, 1920-1940'—CC 4th." *CC 4th*, https://www.facebook.com/WordPresscom, 30 Aug. 2013, https://bethelhistory.wordpress.com/2013/08/29/previewing-the-harlot-city-prostitution-in-hollywood-1920-1940/.

---. "UCS 005 - Hollywood and Los Angeles - Kooistra Reads the Urban Sexual Economy through Films Novels and the Courts - Urban Cultural Studies Podcasts: Benjamin Fraser: Free Download, Borrow, and Streaming: Internet Archive." *Internet Archive*, Urban Cultural Studies, 2013, https://archive.org/details/005-HollywoodAndLosAngeles-KooistraReadsTheUrbanSexualEconomy.
Audio interview with Anne Marie Kooistra.

Ladies Talk About. 1933.

---. 1933.
Barbara Stanwyck

Leff, Leonard J., and Jerold L. Simmons. *The Dame in the Kimono*. University Press of Kentucky, 2013.

Lefler, Timothy Dean. *Mabel Normand*. McFarland, 2016.

Lewis, Tom. *Empire of the Air*. Cornell University Press, 2021.

"Mac and the Winnie Ruth Judd Case, 1933." *Call Him Mac*, University of Arizona Press, pp. 73–82, http://dx.doi.org/10.2307/j.ctv4g1qtb.17.

Mann, William J. *Tinseltown*. Harper Collins, 2014.

Maranian, Matt, and Anthony Lovett. *L. A. Bizzaro!* St. Martin's Griffin, 1997.

Marquez, Ernest. *Noir Afloat*. 2011.

Marsak, Nathan. *Bunker Hill Los Angeles*. Gibbs Smith, 2020.

---. *Bunker Noir!* 2020.

Marx, Samuel, and Joyce Vanderveen. *Deadly Illusions*. Random House Incorporated, 1990.

Mayo, Morrow. *Los Angeles*. 1933.

McQueen, Keven. *Creepy California*. Indiana University Press, 2017.

McWilliams, Carey. *Southern California*. Gibbs Smith, 1973.

Merritt, Greg. *Room 1219*. Chicago Review Press, 2016.

Michael, Newton. *The Encyclopedia of Serial Killers: A Study of the Chilling Criminal Phenomenon from the Angels of Death to the Zodiac Killer (Facts on File Crime Library)*. Facts on File.

Miller, Bettina. *From Flappers to Flivvers--*. Reiman Assoc, 1995.

Monahan, Florence. *Women in Crime*. 1941.

Morris, Gordon Bakken,. *Women Who Kill Men: California Courts, Gender, and the Press (Law in the American West)*. University of Nebraska Press.

Mulholland, Catherine. *William Mulholland and the Rise of Los Angeles*. Univ of California Press, 2002.

Munn, Michael. *Hollywood Connection*. 2013.

Neibaur, James L. *Arbuckle and Keaton*. McFarland, 2015.

---. *Butterfly in the Rain*. Rowman & Littlefield, 2016.

Network, Boxing Podcast. *Ecstasy & Agony | The Story Of Charles "Kid" McCoy*. YouTube, 20 Sept. 2021, https://www.youtube.com/watch?v=uYYrDVCX4Uc.
Story of Kid McCoy

Niotta, J. Michael. *It's a glee: The Men Who Ushered In The Era Of The Floating Casino*. Arcadia Publishing, 2022.

Nuetzel, Charles. *True Stories of Scandal and Hollywood Mysteries*. Wildside Press LLC, 2006.

O'Hara, Sheila, et al. *Legal Executions in California: A Comprehensive Registry, 1851-2005*. McFarland & Co Inc Pub.

Pappas, Charles. *It's a Bitter Little World*. Writer's Digest Books, 2005.

Parmelee, Maurice. *Criminology*. The Macmillan Company, 1918.

Parrish, Michael. *For the People*. 2001.

Patricia, Brooks, and Brooks, Jonathan. *Laid to Rest in California: A Guide to the Cemeteries and Grave Sites of the Rich and Famous*. Globe Pequot.

Paul, James Jeffrey. *Nothing Is Strange with You*. Xlibris Corporation, 2008.

"People v. Blackburn, 214 Cal. 402 | Casetext Search + Citator." *Casetext - CoCounsel*, https://casetext.com/case/people-v-blackburn-7. Accessed 2 July 2023.

"People v. Pantages, 212 Cal. 237 | Casetext Search + Citator." *Casetext - CoCounsel*, https://casetext.com/case/people-v-pantages-2. Accessed 4 July 2023.

"PHOTOS: The Strange Goings-On in Prohibition-Era Los Angeles | Lost L.A. | Food & Discovery | KCET." *KCET*, 30 Oct. 2019, https://www.kcet.org/shows/lost-la/photos-the-strange-goings-on-in-prohibition-era-los-angeles.

Politi, Lea. *Bunker Hill*. 1965.

Rayner, Richard. *A Bright and Guilty Place*. Anchor Books, 2010.

Rebecca. "The History of Booze, Bars, and Prohibition in Los Angeles." *The Best Things to Do in Los Angeles No Matter What Your Age—Booming in L.A.*, https://boominginla.com/drinking-in-los-angeles-history/. Accessed 20 Aug. 2022.

Renner, Joan. *The First with the Latest!* 2016.

Reppetto, Thomas A. *American Detective*. U of Nebraska Press, 2018.

Rice, John R. *Bobbed Hair, Bossy Wives and Women Preachers*. 1941.

Richardson, James H. *For the Life of Me: Memoirs of a City Editor*. G.P. Putnam's Sons, 1954.

Rorabaugh, W. J. *Prohibition*. Oxford University Press, 2018.

Roseman, Curtis C., et al. *The Historic Core of Los Angeles*. Arcadia Publishing, 2004.

Rubio, J'aime. "Preston Castle History - Preston School of Industry: A Murder In The Making—Tuffy Reid's History At Preston." *Preston Castle History - Preston School of Industry*, 29 Mar. 2015, https://prestoncastlehistory.blogspot.com/2015/03/a-murder-in-making-tuffy-reids-history.html. See Rubio's book about the Preston School, Behind the Walls

Schechter, Harold. *The A to Z Encyclopedia of Serial Killers*. Simon and Schuster, 2012.

Schroeder, Barbara, and Clark Fogg. *Beverly Hills Confidential*. 2012.

"Screen Girl's Attack Story To Be Probed." *Cumberland Evening News*, 24 June 1937.
Patricia Douglas

Shuler, Robert. *Fighting Bob Shuler of Los Angeles*. Dog Ear Publishing, 2012.

Sitton, Tom. *The Courthouse Crowd*. 2013.

Slayton, Nicholas. "Downtown's Prohibition History | News | Ladowntownnews.Com." *Los Angeles Downtown News - The Voice of Downtown Los Angeles*, http://www.facebook.com/L.A.DowntownNews, 22 Jan. 2020, http://www.ladowntownnews.com/news/downtowns-prohibition-history/article_73350d22-3c82-11ea-9ecc-37888bcc24a6.html.

Smith, James R., and W. Lane Rogers. *The California Snatch Racket*. Linden Pub, 2010.

Southgatae, Darby. *Encyclopedia of Gangs*. Greenwood Press, 2008.

Spitzzeri, Paul. "The Value of a Girl's Honor: The Remarkable Story of Eunice Pringle -The Homestead Blog." *The Homestead Blog*, 21 Oct. 2019, https://homesteadmuseum.blog/2019/10/20/the-value-of-a-girls-honor-the-remarkable-story-of-eunice-pringle/.

Stans, Lea. "What Happened To Virginia Rappe?–Featuring A Q&A With Tracey Goessel | Silent-Ology." *Silent-Ology*, https://www.facebook.com/WordPresscom, 21 Sept. 2021, https://silentology.wordpress.com/2021/09/21/what-happened-to-virginia-rappe-featuring-a-qa-with-tracey-goessel/.
Roscoe Fatty Arbuckle & Virginia Rappe

Steed, Tobias, and Ben Reed. *Hollywood Cocktails*. 2003.

Stenn, David. *Clara Bow*. Rowman & Littlefield, 2000.

---. *Girl 27*. Directed by David Stenn, N/A, 2007, N/A.

---. "It Happened One Night. . .At MGM." *Vanity Fair*, Apr. 2003.
Patricia Douglas Girl 27

Straczynski, J. Michael. *Changeling*. Directed by Clint Eastwood, N/A, 2008, N/A.
Clint Eastwood, Director Angelina Jolie

"The Bizarre Tale of Murderer Louise Peete In 1944, Her Crime on Hampden Place Led to the Gas Chamber - Palisadian Post." *Palisadian Post*, https://www.facebook.com/palisadian.post, 14 Feb. 2008, http://www.palipost.

com/the-bizarre-tale-of-murderer-louise-peete-in-1944-her-crime-on-hampden-place-led-to-the-gas-chamber/.

"The Harlot City?: Prostitution in Hollywood, 1920–40: Ingenta Connect." *Home: Ingenta Connect*, https://www.ingentaconnect.com/content/intellect/jucs/2014/00000001/00000001/art00004;jsessionid=1yywq2p5owmup.x-ic-live-01#Supp. Accessed 24 Aug. 2022.

The Mammoth Book of Bizarre Crimes. Running Press Adult.

"The Mob Museum in Downtown Las Vegas." *The Mob Museum*, https://www.facebook.com/themobmuseum/, https://themobmuseum.org/. Accessed 15 Sept. 2022.

"The Mysterious Death of Paul Bern (Harlow's Husband)—(Travalanche)." *(Travalanche)*, https://www.facebook.com/WordPresscom, 3 Dec. 2019, https://travsd.wordpress.com/2019/12/03/the-mysterious-death-of-paul-bern/.

"The Roaring 'Twenties | Department of History." *Home | Department of History*, https://history.princeton.edu/centers-programs/center-collaborative-history/special-projects/past-projects/roaring-twenties. Accessed 15 Sept. 2022.

"The Sexual Assault Trial of Alexander Pantages, Los Angeles, October 1929 -The Homestead Blog." *The Homestead Blog*, 11 Oct. 2018, https://homesteadmuseum.blog/2018/10/10/the-sexual-assault-trial-of-alexander-pantages-los-angeles-october-1929/.

Thomas, Lately. *The Vanishing Evangelist*. Pickle Partners Publishing, 2018.

Towne, Charles Hanson. *The Rise and Fall of Prohibition*. DigiCat, 2022.

Towne, Robert, and Roman Polanski. *Chinatown*. Directed by Roman Polanski, N/A, 1974, N/A.

Tygiel, Jules. *The successful Los Angeles Swindle*. Univ of California Press, 1996.

Underwood, Agness. *Newspaperwoman*. New York, Harper, 1949.

Vronsky, Peter. *American Serial Killers*. Penguin, 2021.

Waggoner, Susan. *Nightclub Nights*. Rizzoli International Publications, 2001.

Wagner, Rob Leicester. *Red Ink, White Lies*. 2000.

West, Mae. *Goodness Had Nothing to Do with It*. 1962.

Wilkman, Jon, and Nancy Wilkman. *Picturing Los Angeles*. Gibbs Smith, 2006.

Wilson, David. *Not Just Evil*. Diversion Books, 2016.

"Women Who Kill: Jones, Richard Glyn: Free Download, Borrow, and Streaming: Internet Archive." *Internet Archive*, Edison, NJ: Castle Books, 2004, https://archive.org/details/womenwhokill00rich.

Worel, Janet. *Timeline of Hedvig Samuelson and Winnie Ruth Judd*. Createspace Independent Publishing Platform, 2016.

Worel, Sunny. *Sammy and Sunny*. 2015.

Zeitz, Joshua. *Flapper*. Crown, 2009.

For more news about Joan Renner, subscribe
to our newsletter at ***wbp.bz/newsletter***.

Word-of-mouth is critical to an author's long-term
success. If you appreciated this book, please leave a
review on the Amazon sales page at ***wbp.bz/OMAMS***.

ALSO AVAILABLE FROM WILDBLUE PRESS

https://wbp.bz/tgg

THE GABARDINE GANG: ***Power and Betrayal in Hartford's Mob Scene*** *by Kevin B. DiBacco is a riveting tale of crime, family, and redemption in the gritty underworld of the 1950s and 1960s Hartford, Connecticut.*

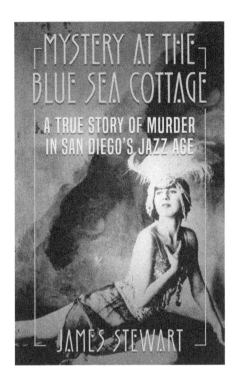

ALSO AVAILABLE FROM WILDBLUE PRESS

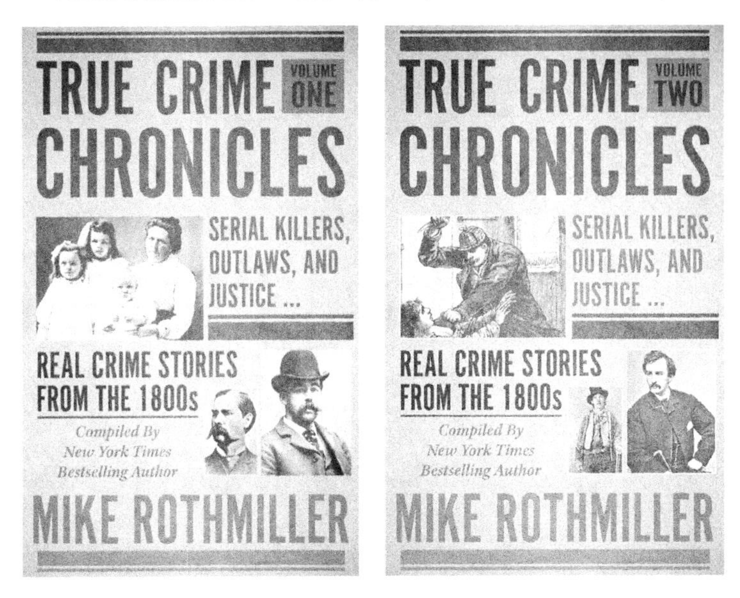

http://wbp.bz/tcc1a

What do Wyatt Earp, Belle Gunness, Big Foot the Renegade, Billy the Kid, and Dr. H.H. Holmes, and The Black Hand have in common?

They were all subjects of true crime newspaper reporting in the 1800s, and now these stories and that of many others are brought together in their original form in a two-volume set: **TRUE CRIME CHRONICLES:** ***Serial Killers, Outlaws, and Justice ... Real Crime Stories From The 1800s.***

ALSO AVAILABLE FROM WILDBLUE PRESS

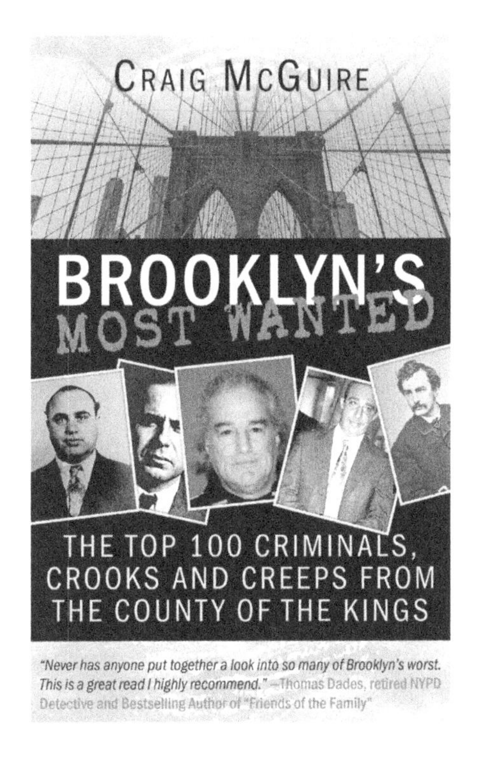

http://wbp.bz/brooklynsmostwanteda

BROOKLYN'S MOST WANTED *parades an impressive perp walk of 100 of the Borough's most notorious, ranking them meticulously from bad to worst. From crime bosses to career criminals to corrupt politicians, pedophile priests to Ponzi scammers, this is not your usual crime chronicle. You want labor racketeering, Ponzi scheming, hijacking, murder, loan sharking, arson, illegal gambling, money laundering? Fugetaboutit!*

Made in the USA
Las Vegas, NV
28 June 2024